The Political Bible

of

Little Known Facts

in

American Politics

* Peculiar Facts
* Unusual Facts
* Bizarre Facts
* Political Firsts

Rich Rubino

Rich Rubino

Library of Congress Control Number: 2011939054
ISBN 978-0-615-52737-6

Printed by The Harvard Book Store
Cambridge, Massachusetts

Cover Photograph by Allen Matheson/Photohome.com

Dedicated to all those political junkies everywhere who can't
stop seeking out political facts, firsts, stories, and trivia:
categorizing it, analyzing it, storing it, indexing it, and
reviewing it.

The quote below from Lyndon Baines Johnson pretty much
captures the essence of the above obsession:

"I seldom think of politics more than eighteen hours a day"

I would also like to thank all of the U.S. politicians, deceased
as well as still living, who did what they did, and/or who do
what they do to make the content of this book possible.

Best Regards

Table of Contents

Introduction   vii

The Federal Government

Part I: The U.S. Presidency

Bizarre Presidential Facts   1
Funny Presidential Facts   11
Presidential Firsts   21
Presidential Onlys   28
Presidential Records   34
Presidential Family Members   36
Presidential First Ladies   43
Vice Presidents   48
Cabinet Members   59
Post Presidencies   66
Peculiar Presidential Facts   69
The Presidential Office   99

Part II: U.S. Presidential Elections

103

Part III: The U.S. Congress

U.S. House of Representatives   153
Speakers of the House   185
U.S. Senate   192
Pertaining to the U.S. Congress   225

Part IV: The U.S. Judiciary

229

Part V: Founding Documents

239

The State and Territorial Government

Part VI: State and Territorial Government

Governorships   245

Governors   246
Gubernatorial Elections   265
Lieutenant Governors   272
Other Constitutional Officers   273
State and Territorial Legislators   274

Part VII: State and Territorial Political Facts   279

Miscellaneous Governmental Facts

Part VIII: Miscellaneous

Other Presidents   289
The White House   290
The Electoral College   291
Budget and Taxes   291
Municipal Officials   294
Odds and Ends   296

Glossary of Political Terminology   313

Index   327

Introduction

I am a voracious collector of political facts, and have been for most of my life. Because I have never found a book that contains the kinds of facts I have cataloged, I decided to write one. While these political facts are known facts, I have grouped them by subject matter for the convenience of the reader.

Some of the facts are funny, some are odd or peculiar, some are downright bizarre, and some are important events and political firsts. The book includes interesting facts pertaining to American Presidents, Vice Presidents, Cabinet Members, First Ladies, Members of Congress, Supreme Court Justices, Governors, and local elected officials. Each political fact is a paragraph in length and is characterized under a section heading. Listed below are a few "summaries" of the examples that appear in my book:

> ➤ **The belief by some that George Washington should not be considered America's First President.**

> ➤ **A President's last words as he ate his soup: "The Nourishment is palatable."**

> ➤ **A Governor once vetoed a bill for "bad spelling, improper punctuation and erasures."**

> ➤ **A political candidate, who after losing an election, complained: "The people have spoken, The Bastards."**

> ➤ **Hillary Clinton was the President of the Young Republicans at Wellesley College.**

> ➤ **A U.S. President who has been forgotten in the U.S., but who is worshiped in Paraguay and has a national holiday named after him in that country.**

> ➤ **After losing re-nomination by his own party, one President deadpanned: "There's nothing left to do but get drunk."**

> ➤ **A First Lady who enjoyed conversing on her CB radio from the White House using the handle "First Mamma."**

> ➤ **A President gave a Pope a bust of "himself" as a gift.**

> ➤ **One state had a 24-year-old Governor.**

> ➤ **A President who in his earlier life worked as a custodian and an auto mechanic.**

- A staph infection that may have altered the course of history.

- A losing Presidential candidate who speculated that his unwillingness to appear on the weekly TV comedy show "Rowan & Martin's Laugh In" may have cost him the election.

- A President whose birth name was Leslie Lynch King.

- A Vice President who regularly presided drunk over the U.S. Senate.

- A state where prisoners make license plates that read: "Live free or die."

- A Vice President who needed additional income took a leave of absence to open a tavern and spa.

- A future President who was the head cheerleader at his High School football games.

- A Congressman who called a colleague on the House floor a "Howdy-Doody-looking nimrod."

- A President that was so large that he got stuck in a White House bathtub and needed assistance in getting out.

- A Congressman who issued a press release deriding the organization known as Americans for Tax Reform as "Lying Sacks of Scum."

- A future President who came in second in the Iowa Caucuses to "None of the above"

- A U.S. Senate candidate who appeared on the ballot as "God Almighty"

- A former 12-year Governor who "subsequently" became a bank teller.

- That one Secretary of State had never left the U.S. before taking office.

- ➢ **A Supreme Court Justice who wrote in the Majority Opinion regarding forced sterilization: "Three Generations of Imbeciles is enough."**

- ➢ **A President's last words as his wife was reading him the newspaper: "Could you please read that again?"**

- ➢ **Two brothers who ran against each other for the Governorship of Tennessee.**

In many of the political passages you will find dates in parenthesis. These are not meant to be birth and death dates, but are most often dates when a particular President, Representative or Senator or state Governor held office.

All of the information in this book I have collected from various sources over the years. As I discover these facts and interesting stories, I verify them as much as reasonably possible. If an information item doesn't seem probable, I discard it.

Finally, the reader might ask, "Why are these particular political facts included and not others?' to which I would reply, "Because these are the facts that I find to be most interesting." That's it. I hope you enjoy my book.

The Federal Government

Part I: U.S. Presidential Elections

Bizarre Presidential Facts

Whole Brained President: James Garfield amused friends by writing with both hands. He could write in Greek with one hand while writing in Latin with the other hand.

James Garfield
Library of Congress

The Jefferson Bible: Not believing in the divinity of Jesus Christ, Thomas Jefferson made his own Bible, crossing out any reference to the supernatural. He called it *"The Life and Times of Jesus of Nazareth."*

Thomas Jefferson
Library of Congress

The People Take Over the White House: Andrew Jackson ran for President in 1828 as a representative of the common people, not of the landed aristocracy. He was the first President elected without a patrician pedigree. Consequently, more than 20,000 common people from all over the nation stormed the White House after his Inauguration to see Jackson and to shake his hand. The President almost suffocated from the unruly mob that surrounded him in an attempt to shake his hand. The President was forced to flee to a nearby hotel, as the revelers exuberantly partook in the Inaugural festivities.

Andrew Jackson being Inaugurated by Chief Justice John Marshall
Library of Congress

Number Please: Not wanting to use "go betweens," Grover Cleveland answered his own telephone at the White House.

Grover Cleveland
Library of Congress

Lincoln's Eerie Dream: A few nights before President Abraham Lincoln's assassination, he had a dream of seeing himself in a coffin surrounded by mourners.

Abraham Lincoln
Library of Congress

The President Meets "The King:" In 1970, Richard M. Nixon met with Singer Elvis Presley and gave him a "Bureau of Narcotics and Dangerous Drugs" Badge, making Pressley a "Federal-Agent-At-Large." The meeting of the two was kept secret until *The Washington Post* uncovered it in 1972. According to the National Archives, the photograph below is their most requested photograph.

Better Late Than Never: Zachary Taylor cast his first vote at age 62. He had been a soldier and traveled so much that he never had the required permanent address needed to register to vote.

Zachary Taylor
Library of Congress

Live Microphone: Before a 1984 weekly radio address, Ronald Reagan joked: "My fellow Americans. I've signed legislation that will outlaw Russia forever. We begin bombing in five minutes." He later found out his microphone was on and that his statement was broadcast worldwide.

Richard M. Nixon with Elvis Presley
National Archives

Ronald Reagan
Ronald Reagan Presidential Library and Museum

Presidential Séances: Abraham Lincoln and his wife Mary Todd Lincoln suffered through the tragedies of losing two sons. Desperate to communicate with their deceased sons, they held séances in the White House.

Abraham and Mary Todd Lincoln with Sons
Library of Congress

Woodrow Wilson's Sheep: Woodrow Wilson kept a herd of grazing sheep on the White House lawn during WW1. The sheep supplanted the White House gardeners, who went off to serve in the war. The wool was auctioned off for the benefit of the Red Cross. It brought in $50,000.

Woodrow Wilson's Sheep
Presidential Pet Museum

If the Animals could Only Talk: Theodore Roosevelt garnered twenty-three pets while President, including a garter snake, a pony, and a one-legged rooster.

Theodore Roosevelt's one-legged rooster
Library of Congress

Monroe's Debt: James Monroe was in so much debt in his later years that he was forced to sell his plantation and move in with his daughter, Maria Hester Monroe Gouverneur, in New York City.

James Monroe
Library of Congress

Little Man, Big Job: James Madison was the smallest President. He was just five feet, four inches tall and weighed just 100 pounds.

James Madison
Library of Congress

3

President's "Good-Luck" Horseshoe: Harry S. Truman hung a horseshoe over his office door believing it would bring him good luck during his Presidency.

Harry S. Truman
Harry S. Truman Library and Museum

Defying your Boss to endorse your Mother: In 2006, Scott McClellan, the Press Secretary for President George W. Bush, endorsed the Independent candidacy of his mother, Carole Keeton Strayhorn, for Governor of Texas, against the Republican nominee, incumbent Governor Rick Perry. Not surprisingly, the White House stalwartly endorsed Governor Rick Perry.

Carole Keeton Strayhorn
U.S. Department of Energy

Presidential Bones: William Howard Taft, George H.W. Bush, and George W. Bush were all members of the elite Skull and Bones Society at Yale University.

Big Shoes to Fill: Warren G. Harding had size 14 feet.

Warren G. Harding
Library of Congress

Lump Sum Van Buren: Martin Van Buren had the government hold his salary and give it to him as a lump sum when he left office.

Martin Van Buren
Library of Congress

Who's Buried in Grants Tomb? No, Not Grant: Despite conventional belief, Ulysses S. Grant and his wife Julia are not buried, but entombed at The General Grant National Memorial a.k.a. Grant's Tomb.

Grant's Tomb
Library of Congress

4

Something Will Eventually Kill You:
George Washington survived smallpox, malaria, and tuberculosis but finally died of a streptococcal throat infection.

George Washington
Library of Congress

Whiskey River Don't Run Dry: James Madison drank a daily pint of whiskey.

James Madison
Library of Congress

Proxies Visited For Him: Though his name will forever be linked to the Watergate Scandal, Richard M. Nixon never visited the complex.

Watergate Complex
Gerald R. Ford Presidential Library and Museum

It seemed like a Good Idea at the Time:
In 1884, Presidential candidate Grover Cleveland endorsed the concept of one four-year term limit for Presidents. However, in 1888 President Cleveland ran for re-election.

Grover Cleveland
Library of Congress

Free Bird: Thomas Jefferson had a pet mocking bird that he hated to coop up in its cage. Accordingly, he allowed the mockingbird to fly around the White House when guests were not visiting him.

Thomas Jefferson
Library of Congress

False Teeth: George Washington only had three teeth left at the beginning of his Presidency. His false teeth were real human teeth inserted into a hippopotamus bone denture. He endured tremendous mouth pain throughout his later life.

George Washington
Library of Congress

Future President Learns English: Martin Van Buren learned English as a second language. He grew up in the Dutch community of Kinderhook, New York, where Dutch was the First language of most residents.

Martin Van Buren
Library of Congress

Young Bill Clinton and the Bible: Bill Clinton's parents did not attend Church. As a young boy, Bill Clinton would walk to Church by himself with Bible in hand.

Bill Clinton as a Boy
William J. Clinton Presidential Museum

Kid Gloves Harrison: Suffering from an unsightly skin condition, President Benjamin Harrison wore gloves. His critics, not cognizant of his medical condition, called him "Kid Gloves Harrison."

Benjamin Harrison
Library of Congress

Lincoln-Kennedy Parallels Abound: Abraham Lincoln was assassinated at Ford's Theater in Washington, D.C. in 1865. President John F. Kennedy was assassinated in a Lincoln automobile manufactured by The Ford Motor Company in 1963.

"S-O-S:" The "S" in Harry S. Truman's name stands for nothing. Truman's two grandfathers, Anderson Shipp Truman and Solomon Young could not agree on a middle name, so they decided to use the letter "S" because one of each of their names begins with the letter "S."

Harry S. Truman
Harry S. Truman Library and Museum

Hiram Grant Becomes President: Ulysses S. Grant's real name was Hiram Ulysses Grant. Somehow his name was incorrectly written when he enrolled in the U.S. Military Academy. The rest is history.

Ulysses S. Grant
Library of Congress

Great Name: High Expectations: John Quincy Adams named one of his sons "George Washington" Adams.

John Quincy Adams
Daguerreotype by Phillip Hass

George W. Bush and Fifty Cent: George W. Bush and gangsta rapper Curtis Jackson, a.k.a. "50 Cent," share the same birthday. Bush was born on July 6, 1946. Cent was born on July 6, 1975. In 2005, Cent told *Gentleman's Quarterly*: "The President is "incredible . . . a gangsta. I wanna meet George [W.] Bush, just shake his hand and tell him how much of *me* I see in him." In 2007, however, the rapper reversed course, telling *New York Magazine* that Bush: "has less compassion than the average human."

The Lincoln-Kennedy Coincidence? It is an urban legend that Abraham Lincoln had a Personal Secretary whose last name was Kennedy. His two secretaries were named John Hay and John G. Nicolay. It is true, however, that John F. Kennedy had a Personal Secretary whose last name was Lincoln (Evelyn Lincoln).

Presidential Duel to the Death: Andrew Jackson is the only President known to have killed a man. In 1806, Jackson killed attorney Charles Dickenson in a duel after Dickinson insulted his wife, Rachel Jackson.

Andrew Jackson Shoots Charles Dickenson
Library of Congress

Some Move Up the Ladder Faster Than Others: In 2005, when he assumed his seat in the U.S. Senate, Barack Obama was ninety-ninth in seniority. Four years later, he was President of the United States.

Barack Obama
White House Photograph by Pete Souza

"Give me a 'W:'" During his senior year at Philips Academy in Andover, Massachusetts, George W. Bush was the "Head Cheerleader."

George W. Bush as head Cheerleader
Philips Andover Academy Yearbook, 1964

First Plot on Assassinate JFK: On December 11, 1960, President-elect John F. Kennedy's life was threatened in Florida by a postal worker who had loaded his car with dynamite and who was planning to crash into Kennedy's car. However, moments before the planned assassination, 73-year old Richard Pavlick backed off when he saw Kennedy saying goodbye to his wife and daughter. Pavlick was arrested just three days later when, after a traffic stop, it was discovered that his car was filled with dynamite. Pavlick was sent to prison for six years.

John F. Kennedy
Executive Office of the President

President Named After Delivery Man:
Chester A. Arthur was named after
Chester Abell, the doctor who delivered
him as a baby.

Chester A. Arthur
Library of Congress

The Irony of it All: In 1957, Dwight D.
Eisenhower made history by ordering the
Arkansas National Guard under federal
control and ordering federal troops to
Little Rock, Arkansas.   He did this to
make   certain   that   African-American
students were allowed to attend Little
Rock Central High School.   Ironically,
Eisenhower never visited the state as
President.

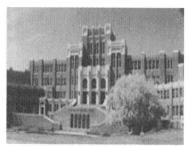

Little Rock Central High School
National Park Service, U.S. Department of the
Interior

There's Nothing Like a Good Cigar:
Ulysses S. Grant smoked about 20 cigars
a day.

Ulysses S. Grant
Library of Congress

**Obama's Peculiar Entry into Elective
Politics**: In 1996, Barack Obama won a
Democratic Primary for a State Senate
seat representing Chicago's South Side.
This was Obama's first foray into elective
politics.   A   campaign   volunteer
successfully challenged the legitimacy of
the other four Democratic candidates,
including the popular incumbent State
Senator Alice Palmer.   Chicago election
officials   ruled   in   favor   of   Obama,
determining   that   he   was   the   only
candidate with enough "valid" signatures
to make the Primary ballot.   Obama
subsequently went on to win the General
Election, garnering 82% of the vote.

Barack Obama
Official Photograph as a State Senator

Speed Reading President: Jimmy Carter can read 2000 words per minute.

Jimmy Carter
Jimmy Carter Library and Museum

Being on the Ballot is a Reason to Vote: Before voting for himself for President in 1868, Ulysses S. Grant had only voted once before.

Ulysses S. Grant
Library of Congress

A Room with a View: In 1949, future President Gerald R. Ford (R-MI) entered the U.S. House of Representatives and ironically was assigned an office directly across the hall from another future President, U.S. House member John F. Kennedy (D-MA).

Destiny? The first known reported break-in at the Watergate Complex in Washington D.C. was not the 1972 break-in at the Democratic Headquarters (which led to the resignation of President Richard M. Nixon). The first break-in was in 1969. Burglars purloined jewelry from an apartment in the building. Ironically, the apartment was rented by Rosemary Woods, the personal secretary to President Nixon. Woods is known in history for admitting to "inadvertently" erasing part of the June 20, 1972 audiotape involving President Richard M. Nixon. The tape was a critical part of the Watergate Investigation.

Rosemary Woods
U.S. National Archives and Records Admin.

A Little Too Late: On April 14, 1865, the day Abraham Lincoln was assassinated, he signed an order establishing the United States Secret Service Agency. The original mission of the Secret Service was not to protect the President, but to combat counterfeit currency.

United States Secret Service Official Seal

Funny Presidential Facts

Nothing Left to do: After losing the Democratic nomination for a second term in office in 1856, Franklin Pierce deadpanned: "There's nothing left to do but get drunk."

Franklin Pierce
Library of Congress

Rutherford B. Hayes, National Hero in Paraguay: Rutherford B. Hayes is a national hero in Paraguay for his role in arbitrating a land dispute between Paraguay and Argentina. Hayes allowed Paraguay to keep a large swath of the cattle-farming Chaco territory. February 16th is a national holiday in Paraguay to honor Hayes.

Rutherford B. Hayes
Rutherford B. Hayes Presidential Center

President Pulls His Weight: William Howard Taft, who while in office weighed 335 pounds, once got stuck in the White House bathtub. It took six White House aids to remove him. A new bathtub was built for the President. The tub they built stands today as the largest bathtub in America.

The White House Bathtub Circa 1911
The White House Museum

Carter's Faux Pas: When President Jimmy Carter delivered his acceptance speech at the Democratic National Convention in 1980, he made a major faux pas. He was paying tribute to the late former Vice President Hubert Horatio Humphrey and mistakenly referred to him as "Hubert Horatio Hornblower Humphrey." Humphrey's full name was Hubert Horatio Humphrey. Horatio Hornblower was a fictional character in novels by author Cecil Scott Forester.

Jimmy Carter and Hubert Humphrey
Library of Congress

Someone Needs to Enroll in World Religions 101: In 1962, John F. Kennedy said: "Moslems, Hindus, Buddhists, as well as Christians, pause from their labors on the 25th day of December to celebrate the birthday of the "Prince of Peace." Kennedy also called Christmas "Universal."

John F. Kennedy
Lyndon Baines Johnson Library and Museum

Luke-Warm Endorsement From Ike: During the 1960 Presidential election, outgoing Republican President Dwight D. Eisenhower was asked by a reporter to name one decision in which his Vice President, Richard M. Nixon (the Republican Presidential nominee), had participated. Eisenhower answered: "If you give me a week, maybe I'll think of one."

Dwight D. Eisenhower and Richard M. Nixon
Eisenhower Presidential Library and Museum

President Gone Wild: John Quincy Adams was known to skinny-dip most mornings in the Potomac River.

John Quincy Adams
Library of Congress

The Wrong Wilson: Richard M. Nixon, an admirer of President Woodrow Wilson, requested "the Wilson desk" to be used in the Oval Office. By mistake, he received the desk used by the obscure Vice President Henry Wilson (1873-1875). Nixon did not find this out until well into his Presidency. He even referenced the desk as belonging to Woodrow Wilson during his famous "Silent Majority" speech in 1969.

Henry Wilson
Library of Congress

The U.S. Presidency

Chester A. Arthur on the Record: Chester A. Author said: "I may be President of the United States, but my private life is nobody's damned business."

Chester A. Arthur
Library of Congress

A "Tin Ear" President: Ulysses S. Grant once said he only knew two songs. "One of them is 'Yankee Doodle' and the other isn't."

Ulysses S. Grant
Library of Congress

Stuff it in your Hat: Abraham Lincoln used his top hat as an extra pocket.

Abraham Lincoln's Top Hat
Smithsonian Institute

Kidnapping the President: In 1882, Chester A. Arthur was aboard a boat off the Massachusetts town of Marblehead with the intention of speaking in neighboring Salem. After landing in Marblehead where the boat was moored, a persistent Marblehead resident, Captain Benjamin Pitman, asked the President to speak in Marblehead. On three occasions the President declined. Finally, it is said that the Marblehead resident jumped into the driver's seat of President Arthur's carriage and brought him the half-mile to Downtown Marblehead, where he gave a brief address. Arthur later said laughingly: "I can never forget the time that I was kidnapped in Marblehead."

Chester A. Arthur
Library of Congress

Cubs Fans Wait Patiently: The last time that the Chicago Cubs won the World Series (1908), Theodore Roosevelt was President.

Theodore Roosevelt
Library of Congress

Harrison's Head: After a long day of campaigning, successful 1888 Republican Presidential nominee Benjamin Harrison would have a family member massage his head.

Benjamin Harrison
Library of Congress

The Pinnacle of Self-Importance: Pope Paul VI was the first Pope to visit America while serving as the Pontiff. He visited New York City and met with President Lyndon B. Johnson at the Waldorf Astoria Hotel, addressed the United Nations, and visited Yankee Stadium. Johnson and the Pontiff exchanged gifts. The Pope gave Johnson a Renaissance era painting of the nativity scene. Johnson gave the Pope a five-inch bust of himself.

Lyndon B. Johnson with Pope Paul VI
Lyndon Baines Johnson Library and Museum

Calvin Coolidge: A Man of Few Words: When Vice President Calvin Coolidge (silent Cal) visited Channing Cox (his successor as Governor of Massachusetts), Cox asked for advice. Cox complained that people talked to him all day and that he could not get out of his office until late at night. Coolidge pointed out Cox's mistake and deadpanned: "You talk back."

Channing Cox
Official Photograph

Deep Thoughts with Calvin Coolidge: Calvin Coolidge refused to use the telephone. He said: "If you don't say anything, you won't be called on to repeat it."

Calvin Coolidge Reluctantly Tries Using the Telephone
Library of Congress

Carter whacks Swimming Rabbit: In 1979, while fishing in his hometown of Plains, Georgia, a swamp rabbit swam toward the President's small boat. Carter swatted at the rabbit with his canoe paddle, scaring it away.

Jimmy Carter with the Swamp Rabbit (Right)
Jimmy Carter Library and Museum

Even a President is not good enough for her daughter: Madge Gates Wallace, the mother-in-law of Harry S. Truman, thought her daughter, Bess Wallace Truman, married beneath her social class. She referred to Harry as Mr. Truman throughout her life, including when he was President.

Madge Gates Wallace
Harry S. Truman Library and Museum

Say that to my Face: because of his heavy weight, John Adams was often called "His Rotundity" behind his back.

John Adams
Library of Congress

Calvin Coolidge Takes a Big Hit: During the contentious police strike of 1919, Boston Mayor Andrew J. Peters was incensed by then Massachusetts Governor Calvin Coolidge. Peters took a swing at Coolidge and hit him in the eye. Coolidge refrained from retaliating.

Andrew J. Peters
Library of Congress

Woodrow Wilson Goes on The Record: Woodrow Wilson was no fan of the U.S. Congress. He called them: "pygmy-minded."

Woodrow Wilson
Library of Congress

Presidential Raccoon: Calvin Coolidge had a pet raccoon named Rebecca. He often walked her on the White House premises.

Rebecca: Calvin Coolidge's Raccoon
Calvin Coolidge Memorial Center

Jackson's Parrot: At the funeral of Andrew Jackson, the late President's pet parrot named "Poll" had to be removed because it was using profane language.

Andrew Jackson
Library of Congress

Be Careful What You Say: James Buchanan earned the unfortunate sobriquet "Ten Cent Jimmy" because he said publicly that the average American could live on just ten cents a day.

James Buchanan
Library of Congress

John Adams Uncensored: John Adams said: "In my many years I have come to a conclusion that one useless man is a shame, two is a law firm, and three or more is a Congress."

John Adams
Library of Congress

Arthur in Fancy Clothes: Chester A. Arthur earned the moniker "Elegant Arthur" for his fancy clothes and sense of fashion.

Chester A. Arthur
Library of Congress

Cognitive Dissonance at the White House: The goodie bags at the White House Easter Egg Roll in 2010 included a booklet on healthy eating as well as Peeps and Hershey candies.

Michelle, Barack, and Malia Obama with Easter Bunny
White House Photograph by Pete Souza

Proper Spelling is Relative: Thomas Jefferson said: "I have nothing but contempt for any man who can spell a word only one way."

Thomas Jefferson
Library of Congress

How Long Did it Take LBJ to think of that? Lyndon B. Johnson named his dogs: "Him" and "Her."

Him and Her
Lyndon Baines Johnson Library and Museum

Can't He Do Better Than That: Millard Fillmore's last words were: "The nourishment is palatable" as he ate soup.

Millard Fillmore
Beinecke Rare Books and Manuscripts Library, Yale University

Unlucky #13: Franklin D. Roosevelt would not travel on the 13th day of the month because he was superstitious about the number 13.

Franklin D. Roosevelt
Franklin D. Roosevelt Presidential Library and Museum

JFK Addicted to Cuban Cigars: In 1961, just before imposing a trade embargo on Cuba, President John F. Kennedy asked his Press Secretary Pierre Salinger to secure at least 1,000 Cuban cigars from a local tobacconist for his personal use. Salinger gave the President 1,200 Cuban cigars before Kennedy signed the document instituting the embargo.

Pierre Salinger
John F. Kennedy Presidential Library and Museum

Obama Not Admitted to Democratic National Convention: In 2000, four years before delivering the keynote address at the 2004 Democratic National Convention, and eight years prior to being the Democratic Party's nominee for Presidents, Illinois State Senator Barack Obama could not get a floor pass entry to the Democratic National Convention in Los Angeles. He instead watched the Convention on a jumbotron (large-screen television set) outside the Staples Center.

Barack Obama
White House Photograph by Pete Souza

Not Exactly Inspiring "Last Words:" Warren G. Harding died as his wife Florence read the newspaper to him. His last words were: "Could you please read that again?"

Warren G. and Florence Harding
Library of Congress

Abe Lincoln Behind the Bar: Abraham Lincoln was a licensed bartender. He once co-owned a bar in his hometown of Springfield, Illinois. During a debate for the U.S. Senate, his opponent, Stephen A. Douglas (D-IL), mentioned that he first met Lincoln as a customer at his bar. Lincoln deadpanned: "I have left my side of the counter. But, Mr. Douglas still sticks as tenaciously as ever, to his."

Abraham Lincoln
Library of Congress

Interesting Take: After the 1923 death of Warren G. Harding, poet Edward Estlin Cummings commented: "The only man, woman, or child who ever wrote a simple declarative sentence with seven grammatical errors is dead."

Edward Estlin Cummings
Library of Congress

Succinct Wins Out Over Bloviation: Abraham Lincoln gave the Gettysburg Address following a two-hour oration delivered by former U.S. Secretary of State and Vice Presidential Candidate Edwin Everett. Lincoln's address lasted just over two minutes.

Edwin Everett
Library of Congress

Words in the Margin don't count: Campaigning for a full term in 1976, Gerald R. Ford read words in the margin of his speech ("with emphasis") as part of the text: "I say to you this is nonsense with emphasis!"

Gerald R. Ford
Gerald R. Ford Presidential Library and Museum

A Man of Two Words: A dinner partner told Calvin Coolidge (a.k.a. Silent Cal) that she made a bet with her friend stating that she could get the President to say at least three words. Coolidge responded: "You Lose."

Calvin Coolidge
Library of Congress

Stupid Criminals: In 1876 grave robbers attempted to steal Abraham Lincoln's carcass from his tomb at Oak Ridge Cemetery in Springfield, Illinois. Their plan was to hold the cadaver for a $200,000 ransom and to convince authorities to free their friend, Benjamin Boyd, from prison. Their ransom plot failed when the police and the media were alerted to the plot. The perpetrators were apprehended before they could remove the body from the sarcophagus. Instead of freeing their friend Benjamin Boyd from jail, the perpetrators were sentenced to one year behind bars.

Abraham Lincoln
Library of Congress

Political Addiction: Lyndon B. Johnson said: "I seldom think of politics more than eighteen hours a day."

Lyndon B. Johnson
Lyndon Baines Johnson Library and Museum

Extreme Micromanager: Within the first six months of his administration, Jimmy Carter made it a policy to personally approve or deny staff members from using the White House Tennis Courts.

White House Tennis Courts
White House Museum

Presidential Verbal Gaff: During a campaign rally in 1988, Republican Presidential nominee George H.W. Bush made the following malapropism: "For seven and a half years I've worked alongside President Reagan. We've had triumphs. Made some mistakes. We've had some sex...uh...setbacks."

George H.W. Bush
George Bush Presidential Library and Museum

Give'em Hell, Harry! Uncensored: While campaigning for 1960 Democratic Presidential nominee John F. Kennedy, former U.S. President Harry S. Truman asserted that anyone who votes for Republican Presidential nominee Richard M. Nixon "Should Go to Hell." Kennedy joked: "I've asked President Truman to please not bring up the religious issue in this campaign . . . "

Richard M. Nixon and Harry S. Truman
Harry S. Truman Library and Museum

TR Unplugged: Theodore Roosevelt once called President Benjamin Harrison: " . . . a cold-blooded, narrow-minded, prejudiced, obstinate, timid old psalm-singing Indianapolis politician."

Theodore Roosevelt
Library of Congress

Fun With Anagrams, Political Style: "He bugs Gore" is an anagram for George Bush.

Presidential Firsts

First Billion-Dollar Congress: During Benjamin Harrison's Administration (1889-1893), spending at the federal level surpassed $1 Billion for the first time.

Benjamin Harrison
Library of Congress

The Origins of the 1st Pitch: At the beginning of a baseball game between the Washington Senators and the Philadelphia Athletics on April 14, 1910 at Griffith Stadium in Washington, D.C., umpire Billy Evans handed a baseball to President William Howard Taft. He asked him to throw it over home plate. The President did, and since then, it has become a tradition for Presidents to throw out the first pitch on Opening Day.

William Howard Taft
White House Web Site

Monroe Takes the Party Outdoors: The 1817 Presidential Inauguration of James Monroe was the first to be held outdoors.

James Monroe
Library of Congress

Once an Eagle, Always an Eagle: Gerald R. Ford was the only U.S. President to have been an Eagle Scout.

Gerald R. Ford on Left as Eagle Scout
Gerald R. Ford Presidential Library & Museum

Oh Christmas Tree: Calvin Coolidge was the first President to light the official White House Christmas Tree. This event occurred in 1923.

The First White House Christmas Tree
Library of Congress

First Use of Presidential Veto Power: In 1792, George Washington issued the first Presidential Veto. He vetoed the *Apportions Bill of 1792*. The legislation would have fixed the size of the United States House of Representatives based on the United States Census of 1790. Washington believed the bill was unconstitutional.

George Washington
Library of Congress

New Digs for Taft: In 1909, William Howard Taft became the first President to work from an Oval Office. This Oval Office burned down in a 1929 fire. Herbert Hoover ordered the Oval Office re-built in 1930.

Postcard of the Original Oval Office in 1909

New States: With Hawaii and Alaska admitted to the Union in 1959, Dwight D. Eisenhower became the first President of all 50 states.

Dwight D. Eisenhower
Library of Congress

The First Attempt to Assassinate a President: In January of 1835, Richard Lawrence, who was mentally ill and believed he was King Richard lll of England, attempted to assassinate President Andrew Jackson at a funeral. Lawrence believed that Jackson was keeping money from him and had killed his father. His shot misfired. This is the first known attempt to assassinate a U.S. President.

Andrew Jackson
Library of Congress

Born West of the Mississippi: Herbert Hoover, born in West Branch, Iowa, in 1874, was the first President to be born west of the Mississippi River.

Herbert Hoover
Library of Congress

New Medium Embraced by Silent Cal: In 1924, Calvin Coolidge delivered the first Presidential Radio Address.

Calvin Coolidge
Library of Congress

Nixon' First: When Richard M. Nixon visited China in 1972, he became the first U.S. President to visit a nation not recognized by the U.S.

Richard M. Nixon with Premier Chou En-Lai in China
Richard M. Nixon Presidential Library and Museum

Say Cheese: In 1848, James K. Polk became the first sitting President to be photographed. Mathew Brady took the picture.

James K. Polk
Photograph by Mathew Brady

Bush Marks New Ground: George W. Bush was the first President to hold a Hanukah party in the White House. This first party was held in 2001.

George W. Bush speaking to guests at a Hanukah celebration at the White House
White House Photograph

Natural Born Citizen: Martin Van Buren was the first President to be born a U.S. Citizen. He assumed office in 1837.

Martin Van Buren
Library of Congress

Old Hickory Departs from a Tedious Precedent: Andrew Jackson was the first President who did not personally sign all land grants. He had his personal secretary sign for him. Prior to Jackson, Presidents personally signed each one.

Andrew Jackson
Library of Congress

Carter Kicks off Hanukah: In 1979, Jimmy Carter became the first President to publicly acknowledge the celebration of Hanukah. He lit the National Menorah.

Jimmy Carter
Jimmy Carter Library and Museum

Reagan's Vision: Ronald Reagan was the first President to admit to wearing contact lenses.

Ronald Reagan
Ronald Reagan Presidential Foundation and Library

Finally, a Keeper: In 1888, Grover Cleveland became the first incumbent Democratic President re-nominated by his party since 1840.

Grover Cleveland
Library of Congress

Hayes Rings Bell: When Rutherford B. Hayes had the first telephone installed in the White House, the inventor, Alexander Graham Bell, offered the 4-1-1 on how to operate the device safely.

Alexander Graham Bell
Library of Congress

Nixon in a Communist Land: In 1969, Richard M. Nixon became the first U.S. President to visit a Communist Nation, Romania.

Richard M. Nixon
Richard M. Nixon Library and Museum

The U.S. Presidency

JFK Live: On January 25, 1961, just five days after being sworn into office, t John F. Kennedy held the first live television Presidential press conference.

John F. Kennedy
Harry S. Truman Library and Museum

Switching Branches: James Madison, elected President in 1812, was the first President who had served in the U.S. Congress. He was a member of the U.S. House of Representatives from Virginia from 1789-1797.

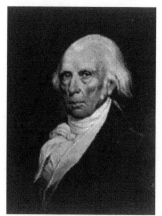

James Madison
Library of Congress

Canada First: By tradition, the first nation that a new U.S. President visits is Canada.

Left-handed President: James Garfield (1881) was the nation's first left-handed President.

James Garfield
Library of Congress

Booked at The White House: In 1901, Booker T. Washington, the author of *Up From Slavery*, became the first African-American invited to the White House. President Theodore Roosevelt invited him.

Booker T Washington
Library of Congress

Hayes on the Line: In 1879, Rutherford B. Hayes became the first U.S. President to have a telephone installed in the White House.

Rutherford B. Hayes
Library of Congress

Biblical Precedent: In 1853, Franklin Pierce became the first President not to kiss the Holy Bible after being inaugurated.

Franklin Pierce
Library of Congress

Electrophobia: Benjamin Harrison was the first President to have electricity installed in the White House. But fearing his own electrocution, he was unwilling to touch any of the White House light switches.

Benjamin Harrison
Library of Congress

Back-to-Back Two-Termers and Rare: Bill Clinton (1993-2001) and George W. Bush (2001-2009) had the first "consecutive" two-term Presidencies since James Madison (1809-1817) and James Monroe (1817-1825).

Historic Birth: Millard Fillmore was the first President born after the death of another President. Fillmore was born on January 7, 1800. George Washington died on December 14, 1799.

Millard Fillmore
Library of Congress

On the Road Again: Richard M. Nixon was the first President to visit all fifty states as President.

Richard M. Nixon
Library of Congress

Winning without Golden State: In 2000, Republican George W. Bush became the first Presidential nominee to win the Presidency without carrying California since Democrat Woodrow Wilson in 1912.

George W. Bush
White House Photograph by Eric Draper

Let the Games Begin: Ronald Reagan was the first President to open the Olympic Games. He did this in 1984.

Ronald Reagan
Official portrait

Millard Fillmore the Comptroller: Future President Millard Fillmore was the first Comptroller of New York.

Millard Fillmore
Library of Congress

Clinton and the Flag: The official Presidential portrait of Bill Clinton is the first in history to include an American flag.

Bill Clinton
Official Portrait

"W" and "Ike:" George W. Bush was the first President not to appoint any incumbent members of the U.S. Congress to his Cabinet in his first term since Dwight D. Eisenhower.

George W. Bush
White House Photograph by Eric Draper

FDR and WJC: Bill Clinton was the first Democratic President to be re-elected since Franklin D. Roosevelt in 1936.

Bill Clinton
William Jefferson Clinton Library Museum

Odd Situation for President: In 1969, Republican President Richard M. Nixon assumed office as the first President since Whig Zachary Taylor (in 1849) with both Houses of the U.S. Congress controlled by the opposition party.

Richard M. Nixon
Official Portrait by J. Anthony Wills

Clinton attends a game of Hoops: In 1994 President Bill Clinton became the first sitting President to attend a college basketball game. He attended a game between the University of Arkansas Razorbacks and the Texas Southern Tigers in Fayetteville, Arkansas.

Bill Clinton wearing an Arkansas Razorbacks Jacket
William J. Clinton Presidential Library and Museum

One Giant Leap for Bloggers: Barack Obama was the first President to call on a blogger during a Presidential News Conference. He called on Sam Stein from the *Huffington Post* during his first Primetime Press Conference.

Barack Obama
White House Photograph by Pete Souza

The Johnson Stones: The only Presidents who suffered from urethral stones were Andrew Johnson and Lyndon B. Johnson (James K. Polk had a urinary stone but it was dislodged at age 17).

Presidential Onlys

Future President Wounded Four Times: Rutherford B. Hayes was the only U.S. President who was wounded during the Civil War. Major General Hayes was wounded four times.

Major General Rutherford B. Hayes
The Rutherford B. Hayes Presidential Center

Birthday Boys: The only Presidents who share a birthday are James K. Polk and Warren G. Harding. Polk was born on November 2, 1795. Harding was born on November 2, 1865.

The Presidential First Pitch: There have been only four U.S. Presidents to have thrown out the ceremonial first pitch at the Major League Baseball All-Star Game. They were: John F. Kennedy in 1962, Richard M. Nixon in 1970, Gerald R. Ford in 1976, and Barack Obama in 2009.

Military Men First and Foremost: George Washington and Dwight D. Eisenhower were the only two Presidents to have their military commission reactivated after leaving the Presidency.

The U.S. Presidency

No Slaves in the Adams House: John Adams was the only President of the first five Presidents not to own slaves.

John Adams
Library of Congress

Comeback Grover: Grover Cleveland is the only President to serve two non-consecutive terms (1885-1889 and 1893-1897).

Grover Cleveland
Library of Congress

No Pets: Franklin Pierce (1853-1857) and Chester A. Arthur (1881-1885) were the only U.S. Presidents who did not have any pets while in the White House.

Debt-Free Nation: Andrew Jackson was the only President to lead a debt-free United States.

Andrew Jackson
Library of Congress

John Tyler's Distinction: The Only former President pro tempore of the U.S. Senate to become President of the United States was John Tyler.

John Tyler
Library of Congress

"W" in Mongolia: George W. Bush is the only U.S. President to visit Mongolia while in office.

George W. Bush
Official Portrait

The U.S. Presidency

President "Brings In" the Artillery: Harry S. Truman was the only U.S. President to see combat during World War I. Truman was an artillery officer.

Harry S. Truman as an Artillery Officer
Harry S. Truman Library and Museum

Ike Goes to War: Dwight D. Eisenhower was the only U.S. President to serve in both WWI and WWII.

Dwight D. Eisenhower as a Young Military Officer
Dwight D. Eisenhower Presidential Library and Museum

Quaker Presidents: Herbert Hoover and Richard M. Nixon were the only Presidents who were Quakers.

Presidential Alliteration: The only Presidents with double initials were: Woodrow Wilson, Calvin Coolidge, Herbert Hoover, and Ronald Reagan.

Former Chief Swears in New Chief: The only two Presidents to be sworn in by a former President were Calvin Coolidge in 1925 and Herbert Hoover in 1929. Former President and at the time, Chief Justice of the United States William Howard Taft swore in both men.

Calvin Coolidge and Herbert Hoover
Library of Congress

LBJ in Malaysia: Lyndon B. Johnson was the only U.S. President to visit Malaysia while in office.

Lyndon B. Johnson Catches a Nap on his Trip to Malaysia
Lyndon Baines Johnson Library and Museum

No Justices: William Henry Harrison, Zachary Taylor, Andrew Johnson, and Jimmy Carter are the only Presidents who never nominated a U.S. Supreme Court Justice.

The U.S. Presidency

Only President Sworn In by a Woman: Lyndon B. Johnson was the only President to be sworn in by a woman. Judge Sarah T. Hughes swore him in after the assassination of President John F. Kennedy in Dallas, Texas.

Lyndon B. Johnson being Sworn in as President by Sarah T. Hughes
John F. Kennedy Presidential Library and Museum

The Nixon Distinction: Richard M. Nixon is the only person to be elected twice as both Vice President and President.

Richard M. Nixon
Richard M. Nixon Presidential Library and Museum

M.B.A. President: George W. Bush is the only President to have an MBA Degree. He earned it from the Harvard University Business School in 1975.

Harvard University Business School Official Logo

Hoosier President: Benjamin Harrison is the only President to be an Indiana citizen when elected President. He was elected in 1888.

Benjamin Harrison
Official Portrait

Coolidge in Cuba: Calvin Coolidge was the only President to visit Cuba while in office.

Calvin Coolidge
Library of Congress

Bush in the Balkans: George W. Bush is the only President to visit Albania while in office.

George W. Bush
White House Photograph by Eric Draper

From U.S. House to White House: The only member of the U.S. House of Representatives to advance directly to the Presidency was James Garfield (R-OH) in 1881.

James Garfield
Library of Congress

Divorced President: Ronald Reagan is the only President to have been divorced. In 1948, Reagan and actress Jane Wyman divorced. This was Wyman's third divorce. Four years later, Mr. Reagan married actress Nancy Davis.

Jane Wyman and Ronald Reagan
Los Angeles Times

Two Future Presidents Sign On: The only future Presidents who signed the *U.S. Constitution* were James Madison and George Washington.

President Did Not Swear: Article 11, Section 1 of the *U.S. Constitution* requires upon taking office that the presidents " . . . solemnly swear (or affirm) that I will faithfully execute the Office of President of the United States, and will to the best of my Ability, preserve, protect and defend the Constitution of the United States." The only President who chose to affirm rather than swear was Franklin Pierce. He did this because he believed God had punished him when his only son, Benjamin, was killed in a train collision just two months before his inauguration. Because of this incident, he began to question his Christianity, and accordingly, he decided not to swear on the Holy Bible.

Franklin Pierce
Library of Congress

Sad Distinction: John F. Kennedy was the only President who was outlived by a grandparent. Kennedy's grandmother, Mary Josephine "Josie" Hannon died in 1964, less than a year after the President was assassinated.

West Virginia State Archives
Emil Varrney Collection

32

It takes One to Know One: Herbert Hoover is the only former president to author a book about a predecessor. The title of this book is: *The Ordeal of Woodrow Wilson.*

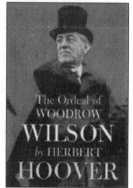

The Ordeal of Woodrow Wilson
By Herbert Hoover

Thomas and Martin at the Pinnacle of Power: The only two men to serve as U.S. Secretary of State, Vice President and President were Thomas Jefferson and Martin Van Buren.

Unfortunate Parents: John F. Kennedy is the only President to be outlived by both of his parents.

John F. Kennedy
John F. Kennedy Presidential Library and Museum

Republican Surrounded by a Sea of Democratic Presidencies: The only Republican President between 1933 and 1969 was Dwight D. Eisenhower who served from 1953-1961.

Dwight D. Eisenhower
The Eisenhower Presidential Library and Museum

Buried in Hallowed Ground: The only two Presidents buried at Arlington National Cemetery are William Howard Taft and John F. Kennedy.

Arlington National Cemetery
Library of Congress

Minority Presidents: The only Presidents to be elected twice without winning a majority of the popular vote either time were Democrats Grover Cleveland, Woodrow Wilson, and Bill Clinton. Cleveland garnered 48.5% of the vote in 1884 and 46.0% in 1892 (Cleveland served two non-consecutive terms). Wilson mustered 41.8% of the vote in 1912 and 49.2% in 1916. Clinton collected 43.0% of the vote in 1992 and 49.2% of the vote in 1996.

From Commander-in-Chief to Chief Justice: William Howard Taft was the only former President to serve on the U.S. Supreme Court. President Warren G. Harding nominated Taft and the U.S. Senate confirmed him in 1921 to the position of Chief Justice of the United States. He served until his death in 1930.

Chief Justice William Howard Taft
Library of Congress

Carter's Prize: Jimmy Carter is the only former President to win a Nobel Peace Prize. He won the award "for his decades of untiring effort to find peaceful solutions to international conflicts, to advance democracy and human rights, and to promote economic and social development."

Jimmy Carter
The Noble Foundation

Obama in China: Barack Obama is the only President to visit China during his first year in office.

Barack Obama in China
White House Photograph by Pete Souza

Not Elected: The only Presidents who were never elected to the office were John Tyler, Millard Fillmore, Andrew Johnson, Chester A. Arthur, and Gerald R. Ford. All were Vice Presidents who succeeded to the Presidency upon the death or resignation of the previous President.

Presidential Records

He Was Not a Happy Man: Andrew Johnson's veto was overridden 15 times. That is more than any other American President.

Andrew Johnson
Library of Congress

Media Friendly: Franklin D. Roosevelt held a record 998 press conferences during his twelve years as President.

Franklin D. Roosevelt
Harry S. Truman Library and Museum

A Man of Very Few Words: George Washington's 1793 Inauguration Address was just 135 words, the shortest in history.

George Washington
Library of Congress

President for a Month: William Henry Harrison served the shortest tenure of any President. He died from pneumonia just 32 days into his term.

William Henry Harrison
Library of Congress

Young Man with a Big Job: Theodore Roosevelt was the youngest person ever to assume the Presidency. He took the office after the death of President William McKinley in 1901. Roosevelt was just 41 years old.

Theodore Roosevelt
Library of Congress

George Washington Shapes the Court: George Washington holds the record for nominating U.S. Supreme Court Justices. He nominated ten Supreme Court justices during his eight years in office.

George Washington
Library of Congress

How Low Can Truman Go: At the end of his Presidency in 1953, Harry S. Truman suffered a 22% job approval rating, the lowest in the history of polling.

Harry S. Truman
Harry S. Truman Library and Museum

Warm and Cold Days for Reagan: The warmest day for a Presidential inauguration was when Ronald Reagan was sworn into office on January 20, 1981. The temperature in Washington, DC reached 56 degrees. The coldest day was four years later, in 1985, when the temperature in the District of Columbia reached just 9 degrees. Reagan's' Inauguration was taken inside to the Capitol Rotunda because of the extreme cold.

**Ronald Reagan Delivering 1981 (top)
and 1985 (bottom) Inaugural Address**
Ronald Reagan Presidential Library and Museum

Presidential Family Members

Presidential Bigamy: Andrew Jackson married his wife Rachel before her divorce was finalized, making her a bigamist. Jackson's political opponents exploited this issue.

Rachel Jackson
Library of Congress

The Polk Death Dichotomy: James K. Polk had the shortest ex-presidency in American history, dying of Cholera in 1849, just 103 days after leaving the presidency. His wife, Sarah Polk, had the longest tenure as an ex-first lady. She died in 1891, more than forty-two years after her husband. James K. Polk left the White House in 1849.

James K. and Sarah Polk
Photograph by Unknown Photographer

Benjamin Harrison's New Girl: After leaving office, President Benjamin Harrison, a widower, got re-married to Mary Scott Lord Dimmick, who was the niece of Harrison's first wife and 25 years Harrison's junior. Harrison's children did not approve of the marriage and boycotted the wedding.

Mary Scott Lord Dimmick
Library of Congress

Dad Swears-in Son as President: While visiting his father in Plymouth Notch, Vermont, Vice President Calvin Coolidge received word that President Warren G. Harding had died. The Vice President's father, John Calvin Coolidge Sr., who was a Notary Public, swore him in as President. Later that day, Coolidge went back to Washington and was sworn in by Federal Judge Adolph A. Holing Jr. U.S. Attorney General Harry M. Daugherty feared that the legitimacy of the first oath could be questioned because Coolidge's father was not a federal official.

Calvin Coolidge being Sworn in by his Father, John Calvin Coolidge Sr.
Artist's Rendering by Arthur I. Keller

John Tyler's Offspring: John Tyler (1841-1845) had 44 grand children.

John Tyler
Library of Congress

But They're Cousins: Franklin Roosevelt and his wife Eleanor Roosevelt were fifth cousins, once removed.

Franklin and Eleanor Roosevelt
Franklin D. Roosevelt Presidential Library and Museum

Oops: In 2008, the Bush family sent out invitations to a number of prominent Jewish Americans, inviting them to the White House Hanukkah Party. Inadvertently, the invitations had a photograph of a Christmas tree on the front side. The White House staff had used the same photograph it had commissioned to invite guests to the official White House Christmas Party. When the staff realized their mistake, they apologized and sent out invitations with a picture of a menorah on the front.

37

The Taft Tradition of Public Service: Alphonso Taft, the father of William Howard Taft, served as the U.S. Secretary of War in 1876 and as the U.S. Attorney General from 1876-1877 under President Ulysses S. Grant.

Alphonso Taft
Library of Congress

Adams and England: Both John Adams and John Quincy Adams once served as the Ambassador to the Court of St. James (England).

Small World: In 1835, Sarah Knox Taylor (the daughter of President Zachary Taylor), married Jefferson Davis; then a former Lieutenant in the United States Army and a future President of the Confederate States of America. Sarah Knox Taylor died three months into the marriage.

Sarah Knox Taylor
Vicksburg, Mississippi Court House

Perennial Bushes: George W. Bush is the only President who left office with both parents still living.

George H.W. Bush and Barbara Bush
George Bush Presidential Library and Museum

Kissing Cousins: John F. Kennedy's maternal grandparents, Mary Josephine "Josie" Hannon and John Fitzgerald (married in 1889), were in-fact second cousins.

Twenty-Five Year Old Bank President: In 1913, Kennedy family patriarch Joseph Kennedy Sr. became the President of Columbia Trust Bank. The Senior Kennedy was just 25 years of age and was the youngest bank President in America.

Joseph Kennedy Sr.
John F. Kennedy Presidential Library and Museum

First Daughter named After a Song:
Chelsea Clinton is named after the song
Chelsea Morning written by songwriter
Joni Mitchell and sung by Judy Collins.

Chelsea Clinton with Parents
William J. Clinton Presidential Library

Must be "Fun" Family Reunions:
Barack Obama is an eighth cousin of
Republican Vice President Dick Cheney
(2001-2009) and tenth cousin of Governor
Sarah Palin (R-AK 2007-2009).

Killed in the Line of Duty: Quentin
Roosevelt, the fourth son of Theodore
Roosevelt, was killed while serving as a
fighter pilot during WW1.

Lt. Quentin Roosevelt
Quentin Roosevelt
USAF Air Force Museum at Wright-Patterson Air
Force Base

Washington and Lee: General Robert E.
Lee, who commanded the Confederate
Army of Northern Virginia during the
Civil War, was married to Marry Anna
Randolph Custis Lee, the step great
granddaughter of George Washington.

Mary Anna Randolph Custis Lee
National Park Service

First Cousins Marry in White House: In
1820, the daughter of James Monroe,
Maria Hester Monroe, married her first
cousin, Samuel L. Gouverneur, a former
secretary to President Monroe. This was
the first time a Presidential offspring was
married in the White House.

James Monroe
Library of Congress

Baby Ruth Candy Bar not Named for "The Babe:" The candy bar: "Baby Ruth" is named in memory of Ruth Cleveland, who was the daughter of former President Grover Cleveland. Ruth Cleveland died at age 13 of diphtheria.

Grover and Frances Cleveland with "Baby Ruth"
Library of Congress

Political Family: Alice Roosevelt, the daughter of former President Theodore Roosevelt, married Nicholas Longworth, who served as a Republican member of the U.S. House of Representatives from Ohio, and who later became Speaker of the House from 1925-1931.

Nicholas Longworth, Alice Longworth Roosevelt pose at their wedding with Theodore Roosevelt
Library of Congress

Bill and Rodger: Bill Clinton was born on the birthday of his grandfather Eldridge Cassidy. Clinton's half-brother, Roger, was born on the birthday of his father, Roger Clinton Sr.

Roger Clinton Right and Bill Clinton left with mother Virginia Kelley
William J. Clinton Presidential Library

President Does his Part in Helping County to Grow: President John Tyler had 15 children.

John Tyler
Library of Congress

Oldest and Youngest Child: Eleven Presidents were the oldest child in their families. Six Presidents were the youngest child in their families.

The Johnson's of Johnson City: Lyndon B. Johnson grew up outside of Johnson City, Texas, a small community of about 600 people. The town was named after Johnson's great grandfather, cattle-rancher, Sam E. Johnson Sr.

The Home of Sam E. Johnson Sr., Circa 1915
Lyndon Baines Johnson Library and Museum

Tyler Dynasty: The father of John Tyler, John Tyler Sr., served as Governor of Virginia from 1808-1811. John Tyler Jr. served as Governor of Virginia from 1825-1827.

John Tyler
Library of Congress

Same Family, Same Path to the Presidency: Both Theodore and Franklin D. Roosevelt served in the New York State Legislature, served as Assistant Secretary of the U.S. Navy, and served as Governor of New York before ascending to the Presidency.

Love and Marriage: The only time in history that a President has had a wife serving in the U.S. Senate was in 2001, during the last 17 days that Bill Clinton was President. At that time, Hillary Clinton was representing New York in the U.S. Senate.

Hillary Clinton being sworn into the U.S. Senate as Husband Bill and Daughter Chelsea look on
William J. Clinton Presidential Library

Mom Gets to Vote for Son: Franklin D. Roosevelt was the first President whose mother was eligible to vote for him. The Eighteenth Amendment to the *U.S. Constitution* granting women the right to vote took effect in 1920. Roosevelt first ran for President in 1932.

A Young Franklin D. Roosevelt with his mother, Sarah Ann Delano Roosevelt
Franklin D. Roosevelt Presidential Library and Museum

Role Model in Kennedy Family: John F. Kennedy was both the older brother and the godfather of his younger brother Edward M. Kennedy.

John and Edward M. Kennedy set Sail
John F. Kennedy Presidential Library and Museum

First Couple Breaks the Language Barrier: Herbert Hoover and his wife Lou Hoover were fluent in Mandarin Chinese and Latin.

Herbert and Lou Hoover
Library of Congress

Former President's Son goes Local, Real Local: Francis Grover Cleveland, the son of Grover Cleveland, was a Selectman in Tansworth, New Hampshire. President Cleveland built a summer home in Tansworth for his retirement. Tansworth has a population of about 2,500 people. When he was only five-years-old, Francis was staying at the summer home with his mother and siblings, when he learned of his father's death. Francis lived in Tansworth until his death in 1995.

Millard Fillmore is "Hot for Teacher:" At age 19, future President Millard Fillmore was a student at the New Academy in New Hope, New York. His teacher was Abigail Powers, just two years his senior. The two got married.

Abigail Powers Fillmore
Library of Congress

A President in Mourning: Chester A. Arthur's wife, Ellen Lewis Arthur, died more than a year and a half before Arthur assumed the Presidency. In mourning throughout his Presidency, the President performed the daily ritual of ordering new flowers to put in front of her portrait, which hung in the White House.

Ellen Lewis Arthur
Library of Congress

Twilight Zone: Robert Todd Lincoln, son of Abraham Lincoln, was slated to attend the play *My American Cousin* with his father in 1865. Feeling fatigued, he canceled. He would have been seated behind his father, making it hard for actor John Wilkes Booth to assassinate his father. In 1881, Todd Lincoln, now Secretary of War, was with President James Garfield when the President was shot in Washington, D.C. In 1901, Lincoln was on his way to visit President William McKinley when McKinley was shot. Quite ironically, in 1864, Todd Lincoln fell off a train platform and onto the tracks as a train was approaching. In a twist of fate, Lincoln was saved by Edwin Booth, the brother of John Wilkes Booth.

Robert Todd Lincoln
Library of Congress

Watching election returns with Mom: Franklin D. Roosevelt spent election days with his mother, Sarah Ann Delano Roosevelt, at her residence in Hyde Park, New York.

Franklin D. Roosevelt with his mother Sarah Ann Delano Roosevelt
Franklin D. Roosevelt Presidential Library and Museum

Presidential First Ladies

First Lady: Zachary Taylor coined the term "First Lady" at the funeral of Dolly Madison in 1849. Taylor eulogized her by saying: "She will never be forgotten, because she was truly our First Lady for a half-century."

Zachary Taylor
Library of Congress

21-year-old First Lady: The youngest First Lady in American history was Frances Folsom Cleveland. In 1885, when she was just 21 years old, she married President Grover Cleveland in the White House. President Cleveland was 49 at the time. Cleveland remains the only President to be married in the White House. Folsom was the daughter of Cleveland's former law partner, Oscar Folsom. Cleveland knew her since she was born. In fact, he was her guardian.

Grover Cleveland and Frances Folsom
Library of Congress

Hillary Leads the Young Republicans: As a student at Wellesley College in Wellesley, Massachusetts, Hillary (Rodham) Clinton was President of the College's chapter of The Young Republicans.

Hillary Clinton
William J. Clinton Presidential Library

Van Buren's Obscure Wife: Martin Van Buren never mentioned his late wife Hannah in his autobiography. She died about eighteen years before Van Buren assumed the Presidency in 1837.

Hannah Van Buren
Library of Congress

First Lady born Abroad: The only First Lady born outside of the United States was Louisa Catherine Johnson Adams, the wife of President John Quincy Adams. She was born in London, England.

Louisa Catherine Johnson Adams
Library of Congress

The First Lady Unplugged: Eleanor Roosevelt was the first "First Lady" to hold press conferences. They were open only to women. Consequently, many news outlets had to hire their first female reporters to cover the press conferences.

Eleanor Roosevelt
Franklin D. Roosevelt Presidential Library and Museum

Lady Bird: Lady Bird Johnson's real name was Claudia. The nickname Lady Bird was coined by a nurse who said she was as pretty as a "Lady Bird."

Lady Bird Johnson
Lyndon Baines Johnson Library and Museum

Birthplaces of Historic Women: The only two First Ladies whose birthplaces are official historic sites are Abigail Adams (birthplace is Weymouth, Massachusetts), and Mamie Eisenhower (birthplace is Boone, Iowa).

Long Live Bess Truman: Bess Truman was the longest living former First Lady. She died in 1982 at age 97.

Bess Truman
Harry S. Truman Library and Museum

A Nation Mourns: Jacquelyn Bouvier Kennedy received over one and a half million condolence letters after the assassination of her husband, John F. Kennedy in 1963.

Jacquelyn Kennedy at her husband's Funeral
John F. Kennedy Presidential Library and Museum

Betty Ford Makes it On Her Own: First Lady Betty Ford played a cameo role as herself in a 1975 episode of *The Mary Tyler Moore Show*.

Betty Ford with Mary Tyler Moore and co-producer Ed Weinberger
Gerald R. Ford Library & Museum

Relentless Rosalynn goes on Hustings; Rosalynn Carter campaigned in 41 states on behalf of her husband Jimmy in his successful 1976 Presidential campaign.

Rosalynn Carter
Jimmy Carter Library & Museum

Historic Women: The only First Ladies inducted into the National Woman's Hall of Fame in Seneca Falls, New York are: Abigail Adams, Eleanor Roosevelt, and Rosalynn Carter.

First Lady Dolly Madison Saves George Washington: Before the British burned down the original White House in 1812, First Lady Dolly Madison made certain that a large portrait of George Washington was saved. In fact, she refused to leave until it was secure. It hangs in the White House today.

Saved Portrait of George Washington

First Lady Bears a Child: Frances Folsom Cleveland was the only First Lady to give birth in the White House. She gave birth to Ruth Cleveland in 1891.

Frances Folsom Cleveland
Library of Congress

The Changing names of Nancy Reagan: Nancy Reagan's birth name was Anne Frances Robbins. Her father, Kenneth Seymour Robbins, divorced her mother, Edith Luckett, while Nancy was an infant. Edith subsequently married Loyal Davis and Nancy legally changed her surname to Davis. Her last name became Reagan when she married Ronald Reagan.

Nancy Reagan
Ronald Reagan Presidential Foundation and Library

First Lady Tradition: It is a tradition that every First Lady serves as the Honorary Chairwoman of the Girl Scouts of America. This tradition began in 1917 with First Lady Edith B. Wilson.

Girl Scouts meet First Lady Bess Truman
Harry S. Truman Library and Museum

The Bush-Pierce Connection: First Lady Barbara Pierce Bush (1989-1993) and President Franklin Pierce (1853-1857) are distant cousins.

Barbara Pierce Bush
George Bush Presidential Library and Museum

Widows of Adversaries Become Close Friends: While living in New York City, Julia Dent Grant (the widow of Northern General and President Ulysses S. Grant), and Varina Davis (the widow of Jefferson Davis, the former President of the Confederate States of America), became close personal friends.

She was Right, Bold, But Right: In 1889, after Grover Cleveland had been defeated for the Presidency, First Lady Francis Cleveland told the White House Staff that the family would be back in the White House in four years. Sure enough, after beating Harrison in 1893, the Cleveland's were back in the White House for a non-consecutive four-year term.

Frances Folsom Cleveland
Library of Congress

Still "Doing a Good Turn Dailey:" The oldest Girl Scout House still in use is located in Palo Alto, California. The construction effort was led by future First Lady Lou Hoover in 1922. At that time, Mrs. Hoover was the National President of the Girl Scouts of America.

Lou Hoover
Library of Congress

Former First Lady Pitches Margarine In 1959, former First Lady Eleanor Roosevelt (1933-1945) starred in a commercial for "Good Luck Margarine." In the commercial, Roosevelt asserts: "Years ago, most people never dreamed of eating margarine, but times have changed. Nowadays, you can get margarine like the new Good Luck, which really tastes delicious. That's what I've spread on my toast, Good Luck. I thoroughly enjoy it." Eleanor Roosevelt donated the Money earned from her appearance to UNICEF.

Eleanor Roosevelt
Franklin D. Roosevelt Presidential Library and Museum

Breaker Breaker, Do You Copy? As First Lady, Betty Ford enjoyed conversing with Americans via her CB radio. Her handle was: "First Mama."

Betty Ford
Gerald R. Ford Presidential Library and Museum

47

Laura Bush was Not Always a Republican: First Lady Laura Bush (2001-2009) was a liberal Democrat before marrying George W. Bush. In fact, she was a supporter of anti-Vietnam War crusader U.S. Senator Eugene McCarthy (D-MN) in his unsuccessful bid to win the Democratic Presidential nomination in 1968.

Laura and George W. Bush
White House Photograph by Eric Draper

Lemonade Lucy: Rutherford B. Hayes, with the support of his wife "Lemonade" Lucy Hayes, disallowed tobacco, alcohol, and profanity from the White House.

Rutherford and Lucy B. Hayes on their Wedding Day
The Rutherford B. Hayes Presidential Center

Vice Presidents

Drunk Man Presides Over Senate: During his second term as Vice President, Daniel D. Tompkins (1821-1825) became an alcoholic and would preside over the U.S. Senate drunk.

Daniel D. Tompkins
Official Portrait

VP Reelected: Not as Frequent as one might Think: In 1916, Vice President Thomas Riley Marshall became the first Vice President to be re-elected since John C. Calhoun in 1832.

Thomas Riley Marshall
Library of Congress

War Monger: Vice President Elbridge Gerry, a supporter of the War of 1812, opined: "We have been at peace too long. A good war will help us."

Elbridge Gerry
Library of Congress

It's All In a Day's Work: John Nance Garner is the only man to serve as both Speaker of the U.S. House of Representatives and Vice President on the same day. On March 4, 1933, Garner resigned his position as Speaker of the House and assumed the office he was elected to in 1932, the Vice Presidency.

John Nance Garner
Library of Congress

Dying on His Birthday: Vice President Levi Morton is the only U.S. President or Vice President to have died on his birthday. He was born on May 16, 1824 and died on May 16, 1920.

Levi Morton
Library of Congress

Marrying the Veep: The only Vice President to marry while in office was Alben Barkley (a widower). He married Elizabeth Jane Rucker Hadley on November 18, 1949.

Alben and Jane Rucker Hadley Barkley with President Harry S. Truman
Harry S. Truman Library and Museum

From Number 3 to Number 2: Schuyler Colfax, Jr. (1869-1873) and John Nance Garner (1933-1941) are the only Vice Presidents to have previously served as Speaker of the U.S. House of Representatives.

36-year-old VP: The youngest Vice President was John C. Breckinridge who served with President James Buchanan (1857-1861). Breckinridge was just 36 years old when he was sworn in.

John C. Breckinridge
Library of Congress

The Vice President Ain't a drunkard
Vice President Andrew Johnson was drunk at the 1865 Presidential Inauguration. Johnson had taken "medicinal" whiskey to cure a bout of Malaria. He slurred his Inaugural Address. President Abraham Lincoln later defended Johnson, saying "I have known Andrew Johnson for many years. He made a slip the other day, but you need not be scared; Andy ain't a drunkard."

Andrew Johnson
Library of Congress

Church, State, and the Post Office: Vice President Richard M. Johnson (1837-1841) believed that the postal service not delivering mail on Sundays was a violation of church and state.

Richard M. Johnson
Library of Congress

Oldest Vice President: Vice President Alben Barkley (1949-1953) was the oldest Vice President. He was 74 years old at the end of his term. In 1952 he unsuccessfully sought the Democratic Party's nomination for the Presidency.

Alben Barkley
Library of Congress

Number of Veeps: Forty-Seven Men have served as Vice President of the United States.

You Snooze, You Lose: In 1925 the U.S. Senate was debating the confirmation of U.S. Attorney General nominee Charles B. Warren. Vice President Charles Gates Dawes, a steadfast supporter of Warren, customarily took a nap every afternoon. Opponents of Mr. Warren brought the vote up while Dawes was on his way back from his nap to the Capital. The U.S. Senate voted by one vote not to confirm Warren. Had the Vice President been in the Senate chamber rather than napping, he would have cast the tie-breaking vote and Warren would have been confirmed.

Charles G. Dawes
Library of Congress

Three against Ford: In 1974, Gerald R. Ford was confirmed by the U.S. Senate as Vice President by a vote of 97-3. The three senators who voted against the confirmation were Democrats Gaylord Nelson of Wisconsin, Thomas Eagleton of Missouri, and William Hathaway of Maine.

Gerald R. Ford
Gerald R. Ford Presidential Library & Museum

Short Retirement: Daniel D. Tompkins had the shortest retirement of any former Vice President. He died just 99 days after leaving office in 1825.

Daniel D. Tompkins
Marble Bust by Henry Niehaus

No Love for John Connally: When Vice President Spiro Agnew resigned his post after pleading *nolo contender* (no contest) to charges of not reporting income, President Richard M. Nixon's first choice to succeed Agnew was Treasury Secretary John Connally. Congressional leaders told Nixon that Connally would have problems being confirmed, so Nixon went with his second choice, U.S. House Minority Leader Gerald R. Ford (R-MI). A year later, Nixon was forced to resign from office, and Ford became President.

John Connally
Official Portrait

Al Gore and Vietnam: Vice President Al Gore (1993-2001) was one of just twelve members of the 1,115 alumni of the Harvard Class of 1969, who served in the Vietnam War. He served as an Army journalist with the *Castle Courier.*

Al Gore in Vietnam
National Archives and Records Administration

Humphrey's Hernia: Vice President Hubert Humphrey was rejected twice when he tried to join the military during World War I because he suffered from a hernia.

Hubert Humphrey
West Virginia State Archives
Harry Brawley Collection

Veeps Quit: Two Vice Presidents resigned during their terms. John C. Calhoun resigned in 1832 in protest over President Andrew Jackson's support of the Tariff Act of 1832 and to seek a seat in the U.S. Senate representing South Carolina (He won that seat). Spiro Agnew resigned in 1973 after pleading *nolo contender* (no contest) to charges of not reporting income to the government.

The First VP Who Never Ran for President: Elbridge Gerry, elected in 1812, was the first Vice President not to run for President.

Elbridge Gerry
Independence National Historical Park

A Teething Tradition: Vice President Dan Quayle habitually got his teeth cleaned on election days.

Dan Quayle
Official Photograph

Pension for the Veep: Since the Vice President is President of the U.S. Senate, his pension is awarded not as a member of the executive, but as a member of the legislative branch. However, the Vice President only receives a Vice Presidential pension after serving at least five years as President of the U.S. Senate.

Veep First: Alben Barkley, who served under President Harry S. Truman, was the first Vice President to attend Cabinet Meetings.

Alben Barkley
Library of Congress

Native American VEEP: Vice President Charles Curtis (1929-1933) has the distinction of being the only Vice President with Native American ancestry. He was one-eighths Kaw Indian.

Charles Curtis
Library of Congress

From Harvard to Hollywood: At Harvard University, future Vice President Al Gore and future actor and director Tommy Lee Jones were roommates, and both inspired, in part, the book *Love Story* by author Erich Segal, who was on sabbatical at Harvard at the time.

Tell Us How You Really Feel, John: Vice President John Adams (1789-1797) called the Vice Presidency " . . . the most insignificant office that ever the invention of man contrived or his imagination conceived."

John Adams
Library of Congress

Tar Heel Veep Hiatus: In 1852, both of the major party Vice Presidential nominees were native North Carolinians. The Democrats nominated William Rufus King (at the time a U.S. Senator from Alabama). The Whigs nominated North Carolina's William Alexander Graham (a former Governor and U.S. Senator from that state). The Democratic ticket of Franklin Pierce and William Rufus King defeated the Whig ticket of Winfield Scott and William Alexander Graham. The only other Native North Carolinian to garner the nomination of a major Party for the Vice Presidency was U.S. Senator John Edwards in 2004.

Interesting Loophole: While the President is disallowed under the Twenty-second Amendment to the *U.S. Constitution* from serving amore than two terms, there is no such provision for a Vice President to serve more than two terms. However, no Vice President has run for a third term.

No Safety Schools for Gore: As a High School senior at St. Albans School in Washington, D.C., Al Gore applied to just one college, Harvard University. He was accepted.

Al Gore
Official Photograph

Ideological Feud Between President and Vice President: Theodore Roosevelt had a contentious relationship with his Vice President Charles Fairbanks. Fairbanks was from the conservative wing of the Republican Party, while Roosevelt was from the progressive wing. Fairbanks opposed much of Roosevelt's domestic agenda, which was known as "The Square Deal." When Fairbanks sought the Republican Presidential nomination to succeed Roosevelt in 1908, Roosevelt gave his coveted endorsement to Secretary of War William Howard Taft, the eventual winner of the nomination.

Theodore Roosevelt & Charles Fairbanks
Library of Congress

Sticking to his Guns: Vice President John C. Calhoun (1829-1832) was called "The Cast Iron Man" for his intransigence in defending the principle of States' Rights.

John C. Calhoun
Library of Congress

Former Veep Moves Down the Political Ladder, Way Down: In 1850, former Vice President Richard M. Johnson was elected to a seat in the Kentucky State Legislature.

Richard M. Johnson
Library of Congress

The U.S. Presidency

Lincoln's GOP Vice President: The first Republican Vice President was Hannibal Hamlin Jr., who served as Vice President under President Abraham Lincoln from 1861-1865.

Hannibal Hamlin Jr.
Library of Congress

Veep's Crib: The Vice President resides in a mansion located at One Observatory Circle at the United States Naval Observatory in Washington D.C. The mansion was originally built to house the Superintendent of the Observatory. In 1974, Congress declared it the official residence of the Vice President. The first Vice President to live there full-time was Walter Mondale, who took office in 1977.

The Vice Presidents Residence
White House Museum

Bad Omen: Both Vice Presidents under James Madison died while in office. Both George Clinton and Elbridge Gerry died of heart failure.

James Madison
library of Congress

Volunteer State Turns on a Native Son: In 1990, U.S. Senator Al Gore (D-TN) was re-elected with 67.72% of the vote. He won all 95 of Tennessee counties. Ten years later as a Presidential candidate, Gore lost the state to Republican Nominee George W. Bush. Ironically, had Gore won his home state he would have been elected as President.

Al Gore
Executive Office of the President

Long Live the Veep: Vice President John Nance Garner (1933-1941) lived longer than any President or Vice President. He died in 1967, 15 days short of turning 99 years of age.

John Nance Garner
Harry S. Truman Library and Museum

Veep: The term "Veep" stands for Vice-President. This was a nickname given to Vice President Alben Barkley (1949-1953) by his grandson.

Alben Barkley
Harry S. Truman Library and Museum

Cheney Not Down with Rap: Vice President Dick Cheney (2001-2009) told the *Washington Times* in December 2008 that he is not a rap fan: "I have trouble even following it."

Dick Cheney
White House Photograph by David Bohrer

Nixon Pinch Hits for Ike: Richard M. Nixon was the first Vice President to preside over a cabinet meeting. He did this in 1955 when President Dwight D. Eisenhower was recovering from a heart attack.

Dwight D. Eisenhower with Richard M. Nixon
The Eisenhower Presidential Library and Museum

Truman Left in the Dark by FDR: During his 82-day stint as Vice President, Harry S. Truman was given little influence or authority. He rarely met with President Franklin D. Roosevelt, and was not even told that Roosevelt had approved the secret Manhattan Project which employed more than 130,000 people, and cost more than $2 billion, leading to the creation of the Atomic Bomb. When Roosevelt died, and Truman assumed the Presidency, he was told of the Project and was forced to make the decision to order the bomb dropped on the Japanese cities of Hiroshima and Nagasaki, which resulted in the surrender by the Japanese and the end of WW11.

Harry S. Truman (left) with Franklin D. Roosevelt, right
Harry S. Truman Library and Museum

56

The "Headsman:" Vice President Adlai E. Stevenson I (1893-1897) received the unfortunate moniker of "Headsman," because during his stint as Postmaster General, he fired 40,000 postmasters.

Adlai E. Stevenson I
Library of Congress

Veep Gives Constituent the Bird: in 1976 Vice President Nelson Rockefeller was delivering a speech in Binghamton, New York when a spectator heckled him. In public view, Rockefeller leaned over the lectern and gave him the middle finger.

Nelson Rockefeller
Library of Congress

Veep Given Prime Real Estate: Vice President Walter Mondale (1977-1981) was the first Vice President to receive an office in the West Wing.

Walter Mondale
Official Photograph

Inharmonious Cohabitation Between President and Vice President: President Calvin Coolidge and Vice President Charles G. Dawes had an antagonistic relationship. It began in 1925 on the day Coolidge gave his Inauguration Address. Dawes, in his role as President of the U.S. Senate, lectured members on the fecklessness of the Senate rules. The press gave Dawes' speech almost as much coverage as Coolidge's Inaugural Address. Dawes added to the tension by sending the President a letter, refusing his request to sit in on Cabinet meetings.

Calvin Coolidge and Charles E. Dawes
Library of Congress

By George, I think he's Dead: In 1812, George Clinton became the first incumbent Vice President to die while in office. Clinton served during the administration of James Madison.

George Clinton
Library of Congress

Cheney gets Shown the Money: In 2000, when Dick Cheney left his job as CEO of Halliburton to become the Republican Vice Presidential Nominee, he was awarded a $34 million retirement package.

Dick Cheney
White House Photograph by David Bohrer

Veeps Re-elected: Ten Vice Presidents have been re-elected. These Vice Presidents were John Adams in 1796 (with George Washington), George Clinton in 1808 (He had been elected in 1804 with President Thomas Jefferson. Clinton was re-elected in 1808 with President James Madison), Daniel D. Tompkins in 1820 (with President James Madison), John C. Calhoun in 1828 (he had been elected with John Quincy Adams in 1828, and was re-elected with Andrew Jackson), Thomas Riley Marshall in 1916 (with President Woodrow Wilson), John Nance Garner in 1936 (with President Franklin D. Roosevelt), Richard M. Nixon (with President Dwight D. Eisenhower), Spiro Agnew in 1972 (with President Richard M. Nixon), George H.W. Bush in 1984 (with President Ronald Reagan), Al Gore in 1996 (with President Bill Clinton), and Dick Cheney in 2004 (with President Bill Clinton).

Short Tenure: The shortest tenure for any Vice President was 31 days. That was the time John Tyler served in 1841, until succeeding to the Presidency upon the death of William Henry Harrison.

John Tyler
Library of Congress

Burr's Alleged Excellent Adventure: Former Vice President Aaron Burr (1801-1805) was arrested in 1807 on charges of Treason by U.S. officials. It was alleged that Burr had organized an unauthorized military adventure to overthrow Spanish power in Mexico. However, the U.S. Court of Appeals for the Fourth Circuit acquitted Burr, despite intense pressure by President Thomas Jefferson and his Administration to convict him.

Aaron Burr
Library of Congress

Short Tenure for a King as Vice President: William Rufus King, who served as Vice President under Franklin Pierce, served the shortest tenure of any Vice President who did not succeed to the Presidency. He died in 1853 of tuberculosis, just 45 days into his term in office as Vice President.

William Rufus King
Library of Congress

Vice President Takes a Leave of Absence: Faced with personal financial turmoil, Vice President Richard M. Johnson (1837-1841) took a nine-month leave of office to open up a tavern and spa.

Richard M. Johnson
Library of Congress

Paying the Veep: The Vice President of the United States of America is paid not as a member of the Executive branch, but as a member of the Legislative branch because he serves as President of the U.S. Senate.

Cabinet Members

Original Cabinet: The original federal Cabinet Departments were the Departments of Justice, State, Treasury, and War (now called the Department of Defense).

Present Cabinet: There are 15 federal cabinet departments.

Twelve-Year AG: The longest serving U.S. Attorney General was William Wirt, who served in that post from November 3, 1817 - March 4, 1829. He served under Presidents James Monroe and John Quincy Adams.

William Wirt
Library of Congress

Breaking Another Glass Ceiling: In 1993, Janet Reno became the first female U.S. Attorney General.

Janet Reno
Official Photograph

Mending Fences: The phrase "Mend fences" was coined by U.S. Treasury Secretary John Sherman in 1879. He told an audience in his native Ohio: "I have come home to look after my fences." While Sherman likely meant that he was coming home to look after the fences on his farm, the line came to mean that he was trying to consolidate political support in his home state.

John Sherman
Library of Congress

Webster the Whig: Daniel Webster served as U.S. Secretary of State under three Whig Presidents. He served under Presidents William Henry Harrison, John Tyler, and Millard Fillmore. The only Whig President he did not serve under was Zachary Taylor.

Daniel Webster
Library of Congress

George W. Ball's Portentous Advice: In 1961, George W. Ball, Undersecretary of State for Economic and Agricultural Affairs, advised President John F. Kennedy that a continued commitment in Vietnam could rise to 300,000 U.S. troops. Kennedy said Ball was: "Crazier than Hell." U.S. troop levels reached 543,00 by 1969.

George W. Ball
Official Photograph

Jewish Milestone: In 1906, President Theodore Roosevelt nominated and the U.S. Senate confirmed former diplomat and lawyer Oscar Solomon Strauss as Secretary of what was then known as the Department of Commerce and Labor. He became the first Jewish American to serve in a Presidential Cabinet. He served until Roosevelt left office in 1909.

Oscar Solomon Strauss
Library of Congress

Government Advises Farmers: "Kill Your Pigs: U.S. Agricultural Secretary Henry A. Wallace (1933-1940) told farmers to kill 6,000,000 baby pigs as a way of raising prices during the Great Depression.

Henry A. Wallace
Library of Congress

No Hard Feelings: In 1936, Franklin Knox ran for Vice President on the Republican ticket with Presidential Nominee Alfred Landon against Democratic President Franklin D. Roosevelt and Vice President John Nance Garner. Although the Landon-Knox ticket lost the election, Knox was nominated by Roosevelt for the post of U.S. Navy Secretary in 1940. A Democratic U.S. Senate subsequently confirmed him.

Franklin Knox
Library of Congress

Successful Tenure for Brown: In 1989, Democratic operative Ron Brown became the first African-American elected as Chairman of a major political party: the Democratic National Committee. He served in that post for four years, and was the Chairman during the time of Bill Clinton's 1992 Presidential election victory. As President, Clinton rewarded Brown by nominating him to the post of U.S. Secretary of Commerce. The U.S. Senate confirmed him.

Ron Brown
Official Photograph as U.S. Secretary of Commerce

Easy for "You" to Say: In 1826, Former U.S. Secretary of State Daniel Webster delivered a eulogy for former President John Adams that lasted for over two hours.

Daniel Webster
Library of Congress

61

Hillary's Roommate: Eleanor "Eldie" Acheson, Hillary Clinton's roommate at Wellesley College in Wellesley, Massachusetts, was the granddaughter of former Secretary of State, Dean Acheson.

Dean Acheson
Lyndon Baines Johnson Library and Museum

End of an Era: Christian Herter was the last U.S. Secretary of State born in the eighteenth century. He was born in 1895. He served under President Dwight D. Eisenhower from 1959-1961.

Christian Herter
Library of Congress

Playing Well in Peoria: New York Yankees Manager Joe Giradi and U.S. Transportation Secretary Ray LaHood are both alumni of Peoria Notre Dame High School, located in Peoria, Illinois.

Not a "Worldly" Choice for a Secretary off State: When William Jennings Bryan was confirmed by the U.S. Senate as U.S. Secretary of State in 1913, he had never left the United States.

William Jennings Bryan
Library of Congress

Jefferson Davis Prepares for War: Jefferson Davis, President of the Confederate States of America, was Secretary of War (Now called the Secretary of Defense) under President Franklin Pierce from 1853-1857.

Jefferson Davis
Library of Congress

Wellesley and Secretaries of State: Two of the three female U.S. Secretaries of State, Madeline Albright (1997-2001) and Hillary Clinton (2009-Present), are graduates of Wellesley College in Wellesley, Massachusetts.

Four Democrats Against Geithner: Three Democratic Senators voted against the confirmation of Treasury Secretary Timothy Geithner. They were: Robert C. Byrd (D-WV), Tom Harkin (D-IA) and Russell Feingold (D-WI). Independent Bernie Sanders (who caucuses with the Democrats) also voted against the Geithner confirmation.

Timothy Geithner
Official Photograph

Wonder Woman: U.S. Secretary of State Condoleezza Rice (2005-2009) graduated from the University of Denver at age 19.

Condoleezza Rice
Official Photograph

Dubious Distinction: John Mitchell, the U.S. Attorney General in the Nixon Administration, was the only former U.S. Attorney General ever to be convicted of a crime. He was sent to prison for the role he played as the head of the Committee to re-elect the President in the cover-up of the Watergate affair.

Teaching the "Say Hay Kid:" As a pupil at Fairfield Industrial High School in Birmingham, Alabama, future major league baseball Hall of Famer Willie Mays was a student of Angelina Rice, the mother of future U.S. Secretary of State Condoleezza Rice.

Willie Mays
Library of Congress

Remembering the Warriors: The motto for the United States Department of Veterans Affairs comes from Abraham Lincoln's 1865 Inaugural Address. Veterans Administration Director Sumner G. Whittier made it official in 1959: "To care for him who shall have borne the battle and his widow and his orphan."

Department of Veterans Affairs Official Logo

Seven Degrees of Political Separation: As a student at the University of Denver, future Bush administration Secretary of State Condoleezza Rice took a course in international politics taught by Joseg Korbel, the father of future Clinton administration Secretary of State Madeline Albright.

From Number Three to Number One: James Buchanan is the last former U.S. Secretary of State to become President. He served in that post under President James K. Polk from 1845-1849.

James Buchanan
Library of Congress

Father and Son Collide over War: While U.S. Defense Secretary Robert McNamara prosecuted America's role in the Vietnam War, his son Craig was protesting the U.S. involvement in the war.

Robert McNamara
Lyndon Baines Johnson Library and Museum

The First African-American Cabinet Member: U.S. Housing and Urban Development Secretary Robert C. Weaver was the first African-American Cabinet Secretary in U.S. History. President Lyndon B. Johnson nominated Weaver, and the U.S. Senate confirmed him in 1966 to that post.

Lyndon B. Johnson with Robert C. Weaver
Lyndon Baines Johnson Library & Museum

Charismatically Challenged: John Sherman, who served as U.S. Treasury Secretary under President Rutherford B. Hayes, and as U.S. Secretary of State under President William McKinley received the unfortunate moniker of "The Ohio Icicle" for his lack of charisma.

John Sherman
Library of Congress

Early Television History: The first public demonstration of long distance television transmission used Herbert Hoover, U.S. Secretary of Commerce at that time (1927), to demonstrate the process. The transmission was sent from Washington D.C. to an auditorium in Manhattan.

Herbert Hoover
Library of Congress

Rumsfeld Makes His Mark at Defense: Donald Rumsfeld was both the youngest and oldest U.S. Secretary of Defense. He served under President Gerald R. Ford from 1975-1977, being sworn in at age 43. He also served under President George W. Bush from 2001-2006. He left office at age 74.

Donald Rumsfeld
Library of Congress

Stuck in the Twenties: In 1914, Treasury Secretary William Gibbs McAdoo Jr., age 50, married President Woodrow Wilson's daughter, Eleanor, who was just 24 years of age. The couple divorced in 1934. The next year McAdoo, then a 71-year old U.S. Senator from California, married his 26-year old nurse, Doris Cross. McAdoo was 16 years older than his new father-in-law.

William Gibbs McAdoo
Library of Congress

He Was Busy: Elliot Richardson served in more Presidential cabinet positions than any other American. During the administration of President Richard M. Nixon, Richardson served as U.S. Secretary of Health, Education, and Welfare (1970-1973), U.S. Secretary of Defense (January–May of 1973), U.S. Attorney General (May-October of 1973), and as U.S. Commerce Secretary under the administration of President Gerald R. Ford (1976-1977).

Elliot Richardson
Official Photograph as U.S. Secretary of Commerce

CIA Distinction: William Casey (1981-1987) was the first person to direct the CIA as a cabinet-level position.

William Casey
CIA Photograph

Standing for a Principle: Three U.S. Secretaries of State resigned their post in protest of Administration policy. The first was Lewis Cass; a steadfast supporter of the Union who resigned in 1860 because he thought President James Buchanan should take a harder line against secessionists. The second was William Jennings Bryan who opposed President Woodrow Wilson's desire to enter World War I. The third was Cyrus Vance, who resigned his post as a protest of President Jimmy Carter's military plan to rescue American hostages held in Iran.

Precautionary Measure: During the State of the Union Address, or during any event where the President, Vice President, and President's Cabinet are in one room, one member of the President's cabinet is declared the "designated survivor." He/she is brought to an undisclosed location so that if a cataclysmic event occurs, there would be someone to take the reigns of power and become the President.

Post Presidencies

LBJ Takes Up Smoking Again: After suffering a heart attack in 1955, U.S. Senate Majority Leader Lyndon B. Johnson (D-TX) quit smoking. He did not smoke again until the day he left the Presidency in 1969. As an Ex-President, Johnson was an habitual smoker.

Lyndon B. Johnson as an Ex-President
Lyndon Baines Johnson Library and Museum

Grant Hits the Hustings: In 1880, Ulysses S. Grant became the first former President to barnstorm the country campaigning for his party's Presidential nominee. The popular former President campaigned for Republican James Garfield.

Ulysses S. Grant
Library of Congress

Former President Actively Supported the Confederacy: Former President John Tyler, a steadfast Confederate supporter, was elected to the House of Representatives of the Confederate Congress during the Civil War, but died before he could assume the office. Because of his fidelity to the Confederacy, he was the only President not mourned in Washington, D.C.

John Tyler
Library of Congress

Long Ex-Presidency: Herbert Hoover had the longest ex-presidency. He left office on March 20, 1933 and died on October 20, 1964, at the age of 90.

Herbert Hoover
Library of Congress

Talk About Humiliation: In 1872, four years after leaving the Presidency, Andrew Johnson lost a race for a seat in the U.S. House of Representatives in his home state of Tennessee.

Andrew Johnson
Library of Congress

He Gave Them Hell: Harry S. Truman was the first former U.S. President to address the U.S. Senate. He did this in 1965 on his eightieth birthday.

Harry S. Truman
Harry S. Truman Library and Museum

Looking Out For Former Presidents: Under the *Former Presidents Act of 1958*, former Presidents are entitled to a pension, staff, and a Secret Service Detail.

Popular Spokesperson: In 1883, six years after leaving the Presidency, Ulysses S. Grant became the eighth President of the National Rifle Association (NRA).

Ulysses S. Grant
Library of Congress

No Job is too Small for this Former President: John Quincy Adams was the only former President to win a seat in the U.S. House of Representatives. He served the Twelfth Congressional District of Massachusetts from 1831-1848. Unfortunately, Adams suffered a cerebral hemorrhage on the House floor during a debate honoring veterans of the Mexican-American War. He died two days later.

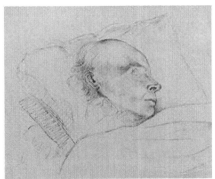

John Quincy Adams on his Death Bed
Library of Congress

The Presidential Pension: The annual pension for former Presidents is $191,300.

Former President Goes back to the Senate: Andrew Johnson was the only former President to serve in the U.S. Senate after leaving office. He represented his native state of Tennessee in 1875. He died less than five months into his term.

Andrew Johnson
Library of Congress

Bid to Get Former President Back in Office: Ulysses S. Grant was the first former two-term President who sought to serve a third term. Though he never declared himself a candidate, he pushed his surrogates to advance his name as a candidate in 1880 for the Republican Presidential nomination. Grant lost the nomination to U.S. Representative James Garfield (R-OH).

Ulysses S, Grant
Library of Congress

Burying the Hatchet, Big Time: As an Ex-President, Bill Clinton has struck up an unlikely friendship with Christopher S. Ruddy, a former vociferous critic of Mr. Clinton. Ruddy is now CEO of conservative *Newmax Media*. In 1994, Ruddy published *The Strange Death of Vincent Foster: An Investigation* where he linked Mr. Clinton to the death of Deputy White House Council and lifetime Clinton friend, Vincent Foster. Clinton and Ruddy became allies in the fight against poverty. Mr. Ruddy now says: "I am a great admirer of President Clinton. He has not only redefined the post-presidency, but has served as an exemplary goodwill ambassador for our country throughout the whole world. His efforts transcend politics and deserve support."

Bill Clinton
William J. Clinton Presidential Library and Museum

Don't Forget the Fact that he was President Too: Thomas Jefferson's grave at Monticello, in Charlottesville, Virginia says nothing of his Presidency. It reads: "Here was Buried Thomas Jefferson Author of the Declaration of American Independence of the Statute of Virginia for Religious Freedom and Father of the University of Virginia."

Thomas Jefferson's Grave
Library of Congress

Peculiar Presidential Facts

That's OK with Me: Martin Van Buren was nicknamed "Old Kinderhook" simply because he hailed from Kinderhook, New York. Van Buren became known as "OK" for short. During his 1840 re-election campaign, his supporters created OK clubs. Although the expression OK had been around for some time, Van Buren's Campaign popularized the expression. Van Buren's political adversaries mendaciously claimed that OK originated from his predecessor and ally Andrew Jackson. They alleged that Jackson was a poor speller, and that Jackson believed that OK was the abbreviation for "all correct."

Martin Van Buren
Library of Congress

Renaissance Man: Samuel Morse, the inventor of Morse Code and the Single-Wire Telegraph, painted the White House Portrait of James Monroe.

James Monroe
Official Portrait by Samuel Morse

Democratic Icon Opposed Public Sector Unions: Franklin D. Roosevelt was a staunch opponent of public sector unions. He feared they would strike, resulting in the "paralysis of government by those who have sworn to support it."

Franklin D. Roosevelt
Franklin D. Roosevelt Presidential Library and Museum

Reagan Says Yes to Collective Bargaining: In 1979, Republican Presidential Candidate Ronald Reagan endorsed the concept of collective bargaining, saying: "When Collective Bargaining is forbidden, Freedom is lost."

Ronald Reagan
National Archives

Courting the Irish: The University of Notre Dame has awarded 10 U.S. Presidents an honorary degree. Presidents Franklin D. Roosevelt, Dwight Eisenhower, John F. Kennedy, Gerald R. Ford, Jimmy Carter, Ronald Reagan, George H.W. Bush and George W. Bush, and Barack Obama respectively received honorary degrees.

One And Done: There have been seventeen one-term Presidencies.

Calvin's Commute to Work: When Calvin Coolidge was serving in the Massachusetts General Court (State Legislature) as Lieutenant Governor, and then as Governor of Massachusetts, he rented an apartment in the state's capital, Boston. His wife Grace and their children stayed at the family home in North Hampton, Massachusetts, 56 miles west of Boston.

Calvin Coolidge
Official Photograph as
Governor of Massachusetts

Home Schooling: President Andrew Johnson had no formal education. His wife Martha taught him reading, writing and arithmetic.

Andrew Johnson
Library of Congress

No Lawyer Jokes Please: Twenty-Six of the forty-four U.S. Presidents were lawyers.

1942 Model Ford: In 1942, while working part-time as a model, Gerald R. Ford and his girlfriend Phyllis Brown were featured on the cover of *Cosmopolitan Magazine.*

Gerald R. Ford as a Young Man
Gerald R. Ford Presidential Library & Museum

Humble Millard Fillmore: Millard Fillmore was contacted by the University of Oxford in England to discuss giving him an honorary degree. Fillmore humbly declined. Feeling unworthy of the honor, Fillmore wrote: "I have neither literary nor scientific attainment."

Millard Fillmore
Library of Congress

Presidents Have Siblings: No U.S. Presidents have been "only children."

Fatal Trolley Car Accident: In 1902 in Pittsfield, Massachusetts, a trolley car rammed into a horse-carriage carrying President Theodore Roosevelt and Massachusetts Governor Winthrop Crane. While Roosevelt and Crane escaped with minor injuries, Secret Service agent William Craig died from his injuries. Craig was the first Secret Service Agent to die in the line of duty.

William Craig
Official Secret Service Photograph

Substitute Officer: Grover Cleveland hired a substitute to serve for him after being drafted for the Civil War. This practice was legal at the time.

Grover Cleveland
Library of Congress

Presidents Who Never Received College Sheepskins: Presidents George Washington, Andrew Jackson, Martin Van Buren, Zachary Taylor, Millard Fillmore, Abraham Lincoln, Andrew Johnson, Grover Cleveland, and Harry S. Truman did not have college degrees.

Lincoln Supports the Farmers: In 1862, Abraham Lincoln signed legislation establishing the U.S. Department of Agriculture.

Abraham Lincoln
Library of Congress

Benjamin Harrison Signs Legislation: In 1889, Benjamin Harrison signed 531 bills into law.

Benjamin Harrison
Library of Congress

Cleveland's Deception: When Grover Cleveland was hospitalized for cancer surgery on his upper jaw, the press was told that the President was having a few teeth extracted.

Grover Cleveland
Library of Congress

There's No "W" in Vermont: Vermont is the only state that George W. Bush did not visit as President.

George W. Bush
White House Photograph by Eric Draper

Clinton Finally Greets Cornhuskers: Bill Clinton visited all 50 states as President. The last state that he visited was Nebraska.

Bill Clinton
William Jefferson Clinton Library

Obama's Boyhood Name: As a boy growing up in Indonesia, Barack Obama went by the name Barry Sorento, his stepfather's last name.

Barack Obama
White House Photograph by Pete Souza

A Matter of Self-Defense: The Boston Massacre took place in 1770. British soldiers killed five Bostonians. This was an important event leading up to the American Revolution. Ironically, John Adams, a future advocate of Colonial Revolution, was the defense counsel for the British soldiers. He got most of them off by arguing self-defense to the jury.

John Adams
Library of Congress

The Buck Stops with the Man from Missouri: Harry S. Truman brandished a sign on his desk that read: "The Buck Stops Here." On the back of the sign was written: "I'm from Missouri." The sign was a gift to Mr. Truman from a prison warden.

Front & Back of President Harry S. Truman's Desktop Sign
Harry S. Truman Library and Museum

Crimson Pride: John Adams, John Quincy Adams, Theodore Roosevelt, Franklin D. Roosevelt, and John F. Kennedy all earned undergraduate degrees from Harvard University.

Be Careful What You Wish For: New York Republican Party boss and U.S. Senator Thomas C. Platt, a rival of New York Governor Theodore Roosevelt, successfully urged the Republican Party to select Roosevelt as the running mate to President William McKinley in 1900. Platt did this to get Roosevelt out of the Governorship because Roosevelt was challenging the Platt political machine in New York. Platt thought that with Roosevelt gone that Lieutenant Governor Benjamin Barker Odell Jr. would become the Governor and would be more compliant to Platt's political machine. As luck would have it, President McKinley was assassinated in 1901 during the first year of his second term in office, and Roosevelt became President. And to add insult to injury, Governor Odell, similar to Roosevelt, became a crusader for reform, shunning the Thomas C. Platt political machine.

Thomas C. Platt
Library of Congress

Jefferson's Capitol: Thomas Jefferson designed the Virginia State Capitol Building in Richmond.

Thomas Jefferson
Library of Congress

All the Way with LBJ for Free: The Lyndon Baines Johnson Library and Museum is the only Presidential Library that does not charge admission.

Lyndon Baines Johnson Library and Museum
Lyndon Baines Johnson Library and Museum

Rebel Rebel: Although many think of Gerald R. Ford as a Republican establishmentarian, he thought of himself as a rebel. Ford won a Michigan Congressional seat in 1948 by defeating incumbent U.S. Representative Bartel J. Jonkman in the Republican Primary. Then in 1964, Ford Challenged incumbent House Minority Leader Charles A. Halleck (R-IN) and beat him as well.

Gerald R. Ford
Library of Congress

Presidents Born British Subjects: The first Eight Presidents were born British subjects. They were: George Washington, John Adams, Thomas Jefferson, James Madison, James Monroe, John Quincy Adams, Andrew Jackson, and William Henry Harrison. Martin Van Buren was the first U.S. President to be born as an American Citizen.

JFK and Vietnam: When John F. Kennedy assumed the Presidency in 1961, there were 600 military advisors in Vietnam. At the time he was assassinated in 1963, there were 16,000 military advisors in Vietnam.

John F. Kennedy
Harry S. Truman Library and Museum

No Chief of Staff for LBJ: Lyndon B. Johnson was the last President who chose not to hire a Chief of Staff.

Lyndon B. Johnson
Library of Congress

The "Honest Abe" Collection: There have been more than 1,500 biographies on Abraham Lincoln.

Abraham Lincoln
Library of Congress

From College Founder to President: In 1846, four years before becoming President, Millard Fillmore founded what is today the State University of Buffalo (SUNY).

Millard Fillmore
Library of Congress

Buckeye Rutherford B, Hayes: As Governor of Ohio from 1868-1872, future President Rutherford B. Hayes helped to found Ohio State University. After leaving the Presidency, he served as a member of the University's Board of Trustees.

Rutherford B. Hayes
Library of Congress

Keeping Power: Fifteen Presidents have been re-elected to office at least once.

His Excellency's Famous Unspoken Address: George Washington's Farewell Address was never given orally by the President. It was published in 1796 in *The Dailey American Advertiser* and other newspapers.

George Washington
Library of Congress

Young Biblical Scholar from Missouri: President Harry S. Truman had read the Holy Bible twice by the age of 12.

A Young Harry S. Truman
Harry S. Truman Library and Museum

State of the Union Tradition: It is a tradition that on the Day the President delivers the State of the Union Address, he has lunch with network news anchors.

The Gipper Salutes: Ronald Reagan made it a custom for U.S. Presidents to salute the Marine standing outside of "Marine 1" when boarding or egressing from the helicopter.

Ronald Reagan Saluting
Ronald Reagan Presidential Foundation and Library

Hail to The Victors: Instead of playing the traditional *Hail To the Chief*, President Gerald R. Ford often ordered the U.S. Navy band to play the University of Michigan victory song called: *The Victors.*

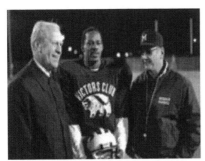

Gerald R. Ford with Michigan Receiver Anthony Carter and Head Coach Bo Schembechler
Gerald R. Ford Presidential Library and Museum

Republican Era: Between 1869 and 1933, only two Democrats served as President: Grover Cleveland (1885-1889 and 1893-1897) and Woodrow Wilson (1913-1921), respectively. During that same time period, ten Republicans were elected President.

Coolidge Court: In 1925, President Calvin Coolidge spent a three-month summer vacation at a mansion known as "White Court" in Swampscott, Massachusetts. Today, the mansion is owned by Marion Court College (a two-year junior College).

Calvin Coolidge
Library of Congress

Rawhide Ronny: Ronald Reagan's Secret Service codename was: "Rawhide."

Ronald Reagan at his Ranch
Ronald Reagan Presidential Foundation and Library

Secretary to JFK Gossips: Evelyn Lincoln, President John F. Kennedy's personal secretary, claimed that the President told her that he would not select Vice President Lyndon B. Johnson to be his running mate when he sought re-election in 1964. Evelyn Lincoln said that Kennedy was leaning toward choosing North Carolina Governor Terry Sanford instead. This never came to fruition as the President was assassinated in 1963.

Patriotic Burial: Andrew Johnson is buried wrapped in an American flag with a copy of the *U.S. Constitution* under his head.

Andrew Johnson
Library of Congress

Speechless Tom: Thomas Jefferson only gave two public speeches during his eight year Presidency.

Thomas Jefferson
Library of Congress

Speaking at Inauguration Without Notes: Franklin Pierce delivered his Inaugural Address without any notes.

Franklin Pierce
Library of Congress

No One Could Have Known That We'd Be Living That Much Longer: When Franklin D. Roosevelt signed the Social Security Act in 1935, the average life expectancy for Americans was 61. Today it is 78.

Franklin D. Roosevelt Signing the Social Security Act into Law
Social Security Administration

Big Day: Lyndon B. Johnson died on January 22nd, 1973, the same day the U.S. Supreme Court handed down the landmark *Roe v. Wade* decision. This ruling allowed a woman the right to terminate her pregnancy until the fetus is viable.

Mourners pay their respects at the Lyndon Baines Johnson Library and Museum
Lyndon Baines Johnson Library and Museum

Not Truman's Kitchen: While Harry S. Truman is credited by many with originating the line: "If you can't stand the heat, get out of the kitchen" Truman was actually quoting his military aide and confidant, Harry H. Vaughan.

Harry Vaughn
Harry S. Truman Library and Museum

A Pet Goat: When informed that a second plane hit the World Trade Center, George W. Bush was reading to elementary school pupils at Emma E. Booker Elementary School in Sarasota County, Florida. The name of the book he was reading from was: *A Pet Goat* by Siegfried Engelmann and Elaine C. Brune.

George W. Bush being informed by his Chief of Staff, Andrew Card, that the second plane had hit the World Trade Center
Official White House Photograph

Mr. Veto: Gerald R. Ford earned the nickname: "Mr. Veto" by vetoing 66 pieces of legislation given to him by the Democratic Congress in his 895 days in office. Fifty-Four of those vetoes were sustained, while the U.S. Congress overrode twelve of the vetoes.

Gerald R. Ford
Gerald R. Ford Presidential Library and Museum

Remembering Truman: In 1965, at the Harry S. Truman Library and Museum in Independence, Missouri, President Lyndon B. Johnson signed legislation establishing the Medicare system. Former President Harry S. Truman and former First Lady Bess Truman received the first Medicare registration cards, which were issued in 1966.

Lyndon B. Johnson signing Medicare Legislation as Harry and Bess Truman look on
Harry S. Truman Library and Museum

The Curse of the Whig Party: Both Whig Party nominees who were elected President, William Henry Harrison in 1840 and Zachary Taylor in 1848, died in office.

Beating Bill Clinton: Two Republicans have defeated Bill Clinton for political office in Arkansas. The first Republican was U.S. Representative John Paul Hammerschmidt, who defeated Clinton in his bid to unseat him in 1974. The second was Frank White, who defeated Clinton in his re-election bid as Governor of Arkansas in 1980 (Clinton came back and defeated White in 1982).

Bill Clinton as Governor of Arkansas
Butler Center for Arkansas Studies, Central Arkansas Library System

Old Hickory says "No:" Andrew Jackson vetoed twelve pieces of legislation during his eight years as President. His seven predecessors had vetoed only nine bills combined.

Andrew Jackson
Library of Congress

Republican Raises Taxes: Herbert Hoover signed legislation raising the top tax rate from 25% to 63%.

Herbert Hoover
Library of Congress

Nothing lasts like a Ford: Gerald R. Ford lived longer than any other President. He died at age 93.

Gerald R. Ford
Gerald R. Ford Presidential Library and Museum

Lincoln and _My American Cousin_: The play Abraham Lincoln was watching at Ford's Theater when he was shot was _My American Cousin_.

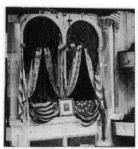

The Box at Ford's Theater where Abraham Lincoln was Assassinated
Library of Congress

The Ohio Tax Cutter: Warren G. Harding signed legislation resulting in the top tax rate dropping from 77% to 46%.

Warren G. Harding
Library of Congress

LBJ Proposes Longer Terms for House Members: In 1966, Lyndon B. Johnson proposed an Amendment to the *U.S. Constitution* to extend the terms of all members of the U.S. House of Representatives from 2 to 4 years. The proposal never came to fruition.

Lyndon B. Johnson
Lyndon Baines Johnson Library and Museum

No Malaise: Although Jimmy Carter's speech to the American people in 1979 warning of "a crisis of confidence" is referred in the annals of history as: *The Malaise Speech.* The term "malaise" was never used in the speech."

Jimmy Carter Delivering his *Crisis of Confidence* **Speech**

Last Bearded Man in the White House: Benjamin Harrison was the last President to sport a beard while in office.

Benjamin Harrison
Library of Congress

Reagan Breaks the Curse: Ronald Reagan broke "The Curse of the White House" (also referred to as the "Curse of Tippecanoe"). The American Indian Tenskwatawa ("The Prophet") cursed President William Henry Harrison and every U.S. President elected in a year that ends in zero (The Profit was protesting the treatment of Native Americans). Every Twenty years, Presidents elected in a year ending in zero died while in office. William Henry Harrison was elected in 1840 and died of pneumonia. Abraham Lincoln was elected in 1860 and was assassinated. James Garfield was elected in 1880 and was assassinated. William McKinley who was re-elected in 1900 was assassinated. Warren G. Harding was elected in 1920 and died of heart failure. Franklin D. Roosevelt was re-elected in 1940 and died of a cerebral hemorrhage. John F. Kennedy was elected in 1960 and was assassinated. Ronald Reagan, elected in 1980, broke the curse and even survived an assassination attempt.

The U.S. Presidency

From Janitor to President: While a student at Southwest Texas State Teachers College in San Marcos, Texas, Lyndon B. Johnson worked as a janitor at the school.

Lyndon B. Johnson, Right with fellow members of the Texas State Teachers College Debate Team
Lyndon Baines Johnson Library and Museum

A Young "Up and Coming" Writer: Thomas Jefferson penned the *Declaration of Independence* in 1776 at the young the age of 33.

Thomas Jefferson
Library of Congress

From the Peoples House to the White House: 18 U.S. Presidents were former members of the U.S. House of Representatives

Meanwhile Back at the Ranch: Of the approximately 1884 days Lyndon B. Johnson served as President, he spent 490 days in his home state of Texas, where he owned a ranch during his Presidency.

Lyndon B. Johnson: At his Ranch
Lyndon Baines Johnson Library & Museum

John F. Kennedy's Unlikely Friend: Anti-Communist U.S. Senator Joseph McCarthy (R-WI) had a close personal relationship with U.S. Senator John F. Kennedy (D-MA). In 1952, at the high water mark of his political popularity, McCarthy barnstormed the country supporting Republican U.S. Senate candidates. The only Republican he would not campaign for was U.S. Senator Henry Cabot Lodge Jr., Kennedy's opponent. In support of McCarthy, Kennedy stormed out of a Harvard Reunion dinner when a speaker extolled the fact that alleged American Communist Alger Hiss and Joseph McCarthy had never graduated from Harvard. Kennedy bellowed: "How dare you couple the name of a great American patriot with that of a traitor!"

Joseph McCarthy
Library of Congress

They're All Against Me: Richard M. Nixon's "Enemies List," written by aides Charles Colson and George T. Bell, included over 47,000 names.

Richard M. Nixon
Richard M. Nixon Library and Museum

Bill and Yasser: Bill Clinton met with Palestinian Liberation Organization (PLO) Leader Yasser Arafat 24 times. Clinton met with Arafat more than any other world leader.

Bill Clinton, Center, with Yasser Arafat Right, and Israeli Prime Minister Ehud Barack, Left
White House Photograph by Sharon Farmer

Tough Job: The average tenure for a Presidential Chief of Staff is less than 2.5 years.

Don't Listen to Richard Russell: When Lyndon B. Johnson signed the Civil Rights Act of 1964 in July of that year, U.S. Senator Richard Russell told him it would cost him the Presidential election. Four months later Johnson defeated Republican Barry Goldwater with 61% of the vote, winning 44 states and 486 electoral votes.

Lyndon B. Johnson and Richard Russell
Lyndon Baines Johnson Library and Museum

Sanction Diplomacy: During Bill Clinton's first term as President (1993-1997), the U.S. imposed sanctions 61 times on 35 nations.

Bill Clinton
Official Photograph

They All Had the Same Two Jobs: Presidents Thomas Jefferson, James Madison, James Monroe, John Quincy Adams, Martin Van Buren, and James Buchanan all served as U.S. Secretary of State prior to becoming President.

FDR, Not as Liberal as you might Think: Although Franklin D. Roosevelt is viewed today as a liberal, during his Presidency many liberals viewed him as too conservative. In fact, there was a movement amongst liberals to nominate U.S. Senator Huey Long (D-LA) instead of re-nominating Roosevelt in 1936 (This ceased upon the assassination of Long). During his second term, many liberals were further inflamed with FDR for his fiscal austerity measures, which included truncating federal spending. Many blamed FDR's austerity measures for prolonging the Great Depression.

Franklin D. Roosevelt
Franklin D. Roosevelt Presidential Library and Museum

Tennis Anyone? Theodore Roosevelt had the original tennis courts added to the White House property in 1902. Roosevelt was an avid tennis player.

Original White House Tennis Courts, circa 1909
White House Museum

Camp David Eisenhower: The Presidential retreat named Camp David was named after the son of President Dwight D. Eisenhower: Ike's son is named "David" Eisenhower.

David Eisenhower
The Eisenhower Presidential Library and Museum

Admit Your Mistakes: John F. Kennedy reached his high watermark in popularity after taking responsibility for the failed Bay of Pigs Invasion. In the invasion, U.S. government-supported Cuban commandos living in the U.S. attempted to take back their country of origin from Fidel Castro. The attempt ended in utter and miserable failure, resulting in much embarrassment for the Kennedy Administration. Because Kennedy was up front about the failure and admitted his mistake to the public, his job approval ratings went up to 82%.

John F. Kennedy with Leaders of the Cuban Brigade Invasion
John F. Kennedy Presidential Library and Museum

The Boy who Became Bill Clinton: Bill Clinton was born William Jefferson Blyth. Blyth was the surname of his birth father who died before Clinton was born. At age 15, Bill Clinton took the surname of his first stepfather, Roger Clinton, Sr.

Bill Blyth (Clinton)
Clinton Family Historical Collection

Last of the Whigs: Millard Fillmore was the last President who was a member of the Whig Party. He left office in 1853.

Millard Fillmore
Library of Congress

Old Hickory Honored by the Old Confederacy: Former President Andrew Jackson and Vice President John C. Calhoun are featured on the Confederate $1,000 bill.

Confederate $1,000 bill

Harding's Oratorical Legacy: The term: "Founding Fathers" was coined by then U.S. Senator Warren G. Harding (R-OH) during his keynote address at the 1916 Republican Convention.

Warren G. Harding
Library of Congress

The idea that started a trend: The first Presidential library, the Rutherford B. Hayes Presidential Center in Freemont, Ohio, was the brainchild of Webb Hayes, the son of President Rutherford B. Hayes. Webb was the founder of the chemical giant Union Carbide Corporation. The Presidential Library was opened in 1922.

Webb Hayes
Library of Congress

Mutts Need Not Apply: Twenty-three Presidents owned pure-bread dogs while in the White House.

Witnessing Eisenhower's late baptism: Although Dwight D. Eisenhower's parents were Mennonites who subsequently became followers of the Watch Tower Society (known today as the Jehovah Witnesses), he decided to be baptized as a Presbyterian in 1953, twelve days after being inaugurated as President.

Dwight D. Eisenhower
Harry S. Truman Library and Museum

No Monday Night Football for Ford: A star football player at the University of Michigan, Gerald R. Ford was offered contracts by both the Detroit Lions and the Green Bay Packers. He turned them down to attend Yale Law School instead.

Gerald R. Ford on the Gridiron
Gerald R. Ford Library & Museum

The Rule of Fours: Five Presidents have four-letter last names. They were James K. Polk, William Howard Taft, Gerald R. Ford, George H.W. Bush, and George W. Bush.

Listen to Your Speech Writer: The famous quote by Gerald R. Ford on his inauguration: "Our long national nightmare is over," referring to the Watergate affair, was written by White House speechwriter Robert T. Hartmann. Ford thought the language was too dramatic. Hartmann insisted the phrase stay in the speech and persuaded Ford not to remove the phrase from the address.

Gerald R. Ford
Gerald R. Ford Presidential Library and Museum

Ronald Reagan Saves 77 Lives: In 1926, Ronald Reagan saved 77 lives during a stint as a lifeguard at the Rock River in Lowell Park in Dixon, Illinois.

Ronald Reagan as a Life Guard
Reagan Presidential Foundation and Library

Product of a Corrupt System Moves Political Mountains to Reform it: In 1883, President Chester A. Arthur signed into law the *Pendleton Civil Service Reform Act,* which requires the hiring and promotion of federal employees to be based on merit rather than on political connections. In addition, the law makes it a crime to raise political money on federal property. Ironically, Arthur had been the archetypical party hack for much of his political life. In fact, he was a member of the "Stalwart" faction of the Republican Party, which opposed Civil Service Reform and was "the patronage wing" of the GOP. He was chosen as the Vice President to propitiate that wing of the party. The Presidential nominee was James Garfield, a "mugwamp" He supported Civil Service Reform and open government. When Arthur succeeded to the Presidency upon the assassination of Garfield, Arthur changed his prior position and became a vociferous exponent of Civil Service Reform, shepherding the *Pendleton Civil Service Reform Act* through the U.S. Congress, requiring civil service employees to be chosen on merit. This inflamed U.S. Senator Roscoe Conkling (R-NY), Arthur's political mentor. As a result, Arthur did not receive "Stalwart" backing in the 1884 nomination contest and did not receive the GOP nomination.

Campaign Poster for James Garfield and Chester A. Arthur
Library of Congress

With Friends Like These: In 1940, Franklin D. Roosevelt sought an unprecedented third term as President. His Vice President, John Nance Garner, and James Farley (the former Democratic National Committee Chairman and Post Master General), ran against him for the Democratic nomination. In the past, Farley had managed Roosevelt's successful campaigns for Governor of New York and for President. Gardner, a business-oriented conservative Democrat from Texas, thought that Roosevelt had veered too far to the left ideologically. Farley asserted that no President should serve more than two terms. Roosevelt easily won the nomination and went on the win his third term.

Franklin D. Roosevelt
Franklin D. Roosevelt Presidential Library and Museum

TR'S Axiom: The West African proverb: "Speak softly, but carry a Big Stick" was popularized in the U.S. by then Vice President Theodore Roosevelt in 1901 during an oration at the Minnesota State Fair.

Theodore Roosevelt
Library of Congress

The Ford-Dubya. Connection: Both former Vice President Dick Cheney and Secretary of Defense Donald Rumsfeld were Chiefs of Staff under President Gerald R. Ford. Rumsfeld served in that post from 1974-1975, while Cheney served from 1975-1977.

Gerald R. Ford
Baseball Hall of Fame

JFK and Affirmative Action: The term: "Affirmative Action" entered into the American lexicon in 1962 when President John F. Kennedy signed *Executive Order 10925*, mandating federal contractors "take affirmative action to ensure that applicants are employed, and that employees are treated during employment, without regard to their race, creed, color, or national origin."

John F. Kennedy
John F. Kennedy Presidential Library and Museum

A Panoply of Pens: When signing legislation, Presidents use many pens. The pens are usually given to individuals who worked to get the bill passed through the U.S. Congress.

Lyndon B. Johnson with Panoply of Pens as he Signs the Housing and Urban Development Act of 1965
Lyndon Baines Johnson Library and Museum

Gerald R. Ford's Amazing Adventure: Gerald R. Ford never received more than 131,461 votes prior to assuming the Presidency in 1974. The U.S. House Member from the Fifth Congressional District of Michigan who ascended to House Minority Leader was nominated by Richard M. Nixon and confirmed by the U.S. Senate to serve out the remainder of the term of Spiro Agnew (who resigned as Vice President after pleading *nolo contender* (no contest) to charges of not reporting income). He assumed the Presidency a year later upon the resignation of Richard M. Nixon. He did this having never been elected to any office outside of his Michigan Congressional District.

Gerald R. Ford
Gerald R. Ford Presidential Library and Museum

Hope Springs Eternal: Although Bill Clinton is known as: "The Man From Hope," he actually spent only his first four years as a resident of the town before moving to Hot Springs, Arkansas, in 1950.

Bill Clinton in Hope Arkansas
William J. Clinton Presidential Library

Veto-rama: In his first term, Grover Cleveland vetoed 414 pieces of legislation. That is more than all of his predecessors combined.

Grover Cleveland
Library of Congress

Fifteen Must be President Obama's Lucky Number: Barack Obama is the fifteenth Democrat to hold the office of President.

Barack Obama
White House Photograph by Pete Souza

Ulysses "Grants" Freedom: Ulysses S. Grant inherited one slave from his father-in-law. Grant freed him.

Ulysses S. Grant
Library of Congress

Nixon the Sportscaster: In a 1971 interview with sportscaster Frank Gifford, President Richard M. Nixon said: "I have often thought that if I had my life to live over again and did not go into politics I would like to have your job, you know, be a sportscaster or writer."

Richard M. Nixon
Richard M. Nixon Presidential Library and Museum

Popular Presidential Retreat: Three U.S. Presidents have vacationed on the Massachusetts island of Martha's Vineyard while in office. They were Ulysses S. Grant, Bill Clinton, and Barack Obama.

Remarkable Feat: Theodore Roosevelt read one book every day, even while he was President.

Theodore Roosevelt
Library of Congress

Bush at Play: At Yale University, George W. Bush was a fullback for the Club Rugby team.

George Bush delivers illegal, but gratifying right hook to opposing ball carrier.

George W, Bush at Rugby
1969 Yale College Yearbook

Presidential Legacies: There are four state capitals named after U.S. Presidents: Jackson, Mississippi (Andrew Jackson), Jefferson City, Missouri (Thomas Jefferson), Lincoln, Nebraska (Abraham Lincoln) and Madison, Wisconsin (James Madison).

Prominent Dog in White House: Theodore Roosevelt owned a Chesapeake Bay Retriever named "Sailor Boy." The dog was a descendent of one of General Armstrong Custer's dogs, which had followed Custer into battle.

Theodore Roosevelt
Library of Congress

Hoover Gives Back: President Herbert Hoover, who made a fortune in the mining industry, donated his entire Presidential salary to charity.

Herbert Hoover
Library of Congress

England was once a Stepping-Stone to the Presidency: Future Presidents John Adams, James Buchanan, James Monroe, John Quincy Adams, and Martin Van Buren were former U.S. Ambassadors to the Court of Saint James (England).

Serving LBJ and Obama: Jeremiah Wright, the former pastor of the Trinity Church of Christ in Chicago to which Barack Obama belonged while a resident of Chicago, served as a Navy Hospital corpsman and assisted with the medical care of President Lyndon B. Johnson.

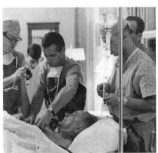

Jeremiah Wright at Right tending to Lyndon B. Johnson
Federal Government Photograph

Not Present for the Constitutional Convention: Future Presidents Thomas Jefferson and John Adams did not attend the Constitutional Convention of 1787. Jefferson was in France, where he was serving as U.S. Minister to France. Adams was in England, where he was serving as U.S. Ambassador to Great Britain.

Bush rakes in the Cash: In 1989, George W. Bush paid $800,000 to be part owner of the Texas Ranger's Baseball Franchise. Nine years later, while serving as Governor of Texas, Bush sold his shares for $15 million.

Texas Rangers Official Logo

Rich Man: George Washington was worth half a billion dollars in today's money. He owned a Virginia plantation called Mount Vernon with crops on about 8,000 acres of farmland run by about 300 slaves.

George Washington at Mount Vernon
Library of Congress

Show Me the Money: Barack Obama enjoys a net worth of over $5 million. Much of this fortune comes from royalties from the two books he authored, *Dreams of My Fathers* and *The Audacity of Hope.*

Barack Obama
White House Photograph by Pete Souza

Harry and Gerry: Both Harry S. Truman and Gerald R. Ford died the day after Christmas; Truman in 1972, and Ford in 2006.

Truman to Fulbright: You're a "Half-Bright:" After Democrats suffered an electoral shellacking in 1946, losing both the U.S. House of Representatives and the U.S. Senate (due in part to the unpopularity of President Harry S. Truman), prominent Democrat U.S. Senator J. William Fulbright came up with a scheme wherein Truman would nominate U.S. Senator Arthur Vandenberg (R-MI) as U.S. Secretary of State. Vandenberg shared President Truman's international proclivities. Fulbright's plan was that once the Republican Controlled U.S. Senate confirmed Vandenberg as Secretary of State, Truman would then resign and Vandenberg would become President (At the time, the Vice Presidency was vacant and there was no Constitutional procedure to fill the office until the next Presidential election, and the Secretary of State would be next in line to the Presidency). Thinking Truman was a lame duck with no chance of keeping the Presidency in 1948, Fulbright said: "It will place the responsibility of running the Government on one party and prevent a stalemate." Truman derided Fulbright as being: "Halfbright" and won the 1948 Presidential election in an historic upset.

Harry S. Truman & J. William Fulbright (left)
Harry S. Truman Library and Museum

First Stanford Class: Herbert Hoover graduated from Stanford University in 1895. That was the first class to graduate from this West Coast University.

Herbert Hoover
Library of Congress

Grant's Linguistic Legacy: The term "lobbyist' was coined by Ulysses S. Grant. He called those individuals "lobbyists" who represented special interest groups and who bothered him while he attempted to rest in the "lobby" of the Willard Hotel in Washington, DC.

The Original Willard Hotel
Library of Congress

The $688 Million Man: During the 2008 Presidential campaign, Democrat Barack Obama broke the all-time fundraising record by raising $688 million.

Barack Obama
White House Photograph

Going Once, Going Twice: Chester A. Arthur sent the surplus unfashionable White House furniture to be sold at auction.

Chester A. Arthur
Official Portrait

This Ford Floats: Gerald R. Ford enjoyed swimming laps in the White House pool. He once held a press conference while in the pool.

**Gerald R. Ford Swims
In the White House Pool**
Gerald R. Ford Presidential Library and Museum

Washington and Monroe: The capitals of two countries are named after U.S. Presidents. Washington, D.C. is named after President George Washington, and Monrovia, Liberia is named after President James Monroe. As President, Monroe supported repatriation of freed slaves in America to colonize Liberia.

Nixon the Bowler: Richard M. Nixon, with the help of private donations, had a one-lane bowling ally built in the White House.

Richard M. Nixon Bowling
Richard M. Nixon Library

Birthday Present to All Visitors: The William J. Clinton Presidential Library and Museum in Little Rock, Arkansas offers free admission on August 19, the President's birthday.

William J. Clinton Presidential Library and Museum
William J. Clinton Presidential Library and Museum

Popular Presidential Last Names: Five Presidents share a last name with another President. They are President Adams (President John Adams and John Quincy Adams), President Harrison (President William Henry Harrison and President Benjamin Harrison), President Johnson (President Andrew Johnson and President Lyndon B. Johnson), and President Bush (President George Herbert Walker Bush and President George Walker Bush).

Young Man Speaks: At age 26, future President Franklin Pierce was elected Speaker of the New Hampshire House of Representatives.

Franklin Pierce
Library of Congress

The Virginia Dynasty: A Virginian was President for all but four years from 1789-1825.

Bush Gave a Rapper a Break: In his last months in office, George W. Bush commuted the sentence of rapper John Forte who had been convicted in 2000 for "possession with intent to distribute cocaine and conspiracy to distribute." Forte was to serve 14 years in jail. Because of Bush's actions, he was released after about eight years in prison.

George W. Bush
White House Photograph by Pete Souza

Getting Into the Oil Business: The enduring relationship between the U.S. and Saudi Arabia began during World War ll. Franklin D. Roosevelt asserted it was in America's interests to protect the oil rich kingdom and made Saudi Arabia eligible for aid under the *Lend-Lease Act* (including military assistance and training). In 1945 Franklin D. Roosevelt and Saudi King Abd Al Aziz secured the alliance in a meeting aboard the *USS Quincy*.

USS Quincy
Library of Congress

No More Hits: In 1975, President Gerald R. Ford signed *Executive Order 11905,* barring the U.S. government from assassinating foreign leaders.

Gerald R. Ford
Lyndon Baines Johnson Library and Museum

No Pardons: William Henry Harrison and James Garfield are the only Presidents who did not issue any pardons. Both men died during their first year in office.

LBJ the Mechanic: After graduating from High School, Lyndon B. Johnson and five friends moved from Texas to California where they performed odd jobs. Johnson worked as an auto mechanic before hitchhiking back to Texas where he attended Texas State Teachers College.

Lyndon B. Johnson as a Young Man
Lyndon Baines Johnson Library and Museum

When Ronald Reagan was a Reagan Democrat: Ronald Reagan was a member of the Democratic Party until switching his partisan affiliation, becoming a Republican in 1962. He was a supporter of the Presidential campaigns of Democrats Franklin D. Roosevelt and Harry S. Truman. Reagan remained a Democrat in the 1950's and in the early 1960's, despite the fact that he supported Republican Dwight D. Eisenhower and Richard M. Nixon in their Presidential quests.

Ronald Reagan
Ronald Reagan Presidential Foundation

When Ruth Met Bush: In 1948, George H.W. Bush was captain of the Yale University Baseball team. As captain, he officially accepted a donation from Baseball Hall of Famer Babe Ruth. Ruth donated the manuscript of his autobiography, *The Babe Ruth Story*, to the Yale University Library.

Babe Ruth with George H. W. Bush
National Archives and Records Administration

Constricted use of the Veto Power: George Washington vetoed all legislation he believed to be unconstitutional, not because he had policy objections to it.

George Washington
Portrait by Gilbert Stuart

Praying Presidents: Every President since Dwight D. Eisenhower has attended at least one National Prayer Breakfast.

Do You Want White or Dark Meat?
The day before Thanksgiving the President is presented with a turkey raised in the United States. George H.W. Bush began the tradition of pardoning the turkey. President Dwight D. Eisenhower was the first President to be presented with a live Thanksgiving turkey. He ate it.

Lyndon B. Johnson is presented with a Thanksgiving Day turkey in 1967
Lyndon Baines Johnson Library and Museum

Reagan Assiduously Cultivates the Religious Right: Ronald Reagan met in the Oval Office with conservative Pastor and Liberty University founder Jerry Falwell more than any other religious leader.

Jerry Falwell
Library of Congress

White House Goes Solar: During the energy crisis, President Jimmy Carter ordered 32 solar heating panels to be installed on the White House roof. His successor, Ronald Reagan, ordered them removed when maintenance was being performed. They were never put back up on the White House roof. Most of these original solar panels are now owned by Unity College in Unity, Maine.

Jimmy Carter with the White House Solar Panels
White House Museum

The Man of Eights: Martin Van Buren was both the eighth Vice President (1833-1837) and the eighth President (1837-1841).

Martin Van Buren
Library of Congress

Bi-partisan support for Puerto Rico: Every President from Harry S. Truman to Barack Obama has supported allowing Puerto Rico the right to choose Statehood, Independence, or their current Status as a Commonwealth.

Bush Wins: First Time out of the Gate:
In 2000, Republican George W. Bush won the Presidency in his first attempt at winning the highest office in the nation. The last Republican to achieve this feat was Dwight D. Eisenhower in 1952.

George W. Bush
White House Photograph by Eric Draper

If that Bible could only Talk: In 1989, George H.W. Bush was inaugurated as President on the same Bible used to inaugurate George Washington in 1789.

George H. W. Bush at his Inauguration
Official Federal Government Photograph

Pardon Me: On his last two days in office, President Bill Clinton pardoned 177 people, 27 of them were from Arkansas.

Bill Clinton
William J. Clinton Presidential Library

Move Over Columbus Day: In 1964 President Lyndon B. Johnson signed a proclamation declaring October 9th "Leif Ericson Day" in commemoration of the Norse explorer being the first European to discover America. The U.S. Congress approved the proclamation unanimously. October 9 was the day chosen to commemorate this event because October 9, 1825 represents the start of organized immigration from Scandinavia to the United States.

Leif Ericson
Library of Congress

The Kansas Cyclone: As a running back at the United States Military Academy at West Point, future U.S. President Dwight D. Eisenhower was known as "The Kansas Cyclone."

Dwight D. Eisenhower as a West Point Student
Eisenhower Presidential Library and Museum

Lyndon Baines Johnson Day: August 27 is a legal state holiday in Texas to commemorate the birthday of native son Lyndon B. Johnson. The holiday is optional for state workers.

Lyndon B. Johnson
Lyndon Baines Johnson Library and Museum

When Ford was King: Gerald R. Ford's birth name was Leslie Lynch King Jr. (named after Ford's paternal father, Leslie Lynch King Sr.). The senior Ford divorced Ford's mother Dorothy before Gerald was a year old. Dorothy Gardner eventually married Gerald Rudolf Ford Sr. Gerald took his stepfather's name.

Gerald R. Ford when he was Leslie Lynch King Jr.
Gerald R. Ford Presidential Library and Museum

The land of Leaders: Virginia is the birthplace of eight Presidents, more than any other state.

White House on the World Wide Web: Bill Clinton officially launched The White House Web Site in 1994.

Bill Clinton
William J. Clinton Presidential Library and Museum

Congress Rubber Stamps President: In 1965, Lyndon B. Johnson sent eighty-seven pieces of proposed legislation to the Democratically-controlled U.S. Congress. They passed, and the President signed eighty-four of the eighty-seven proposals into law.

Lyndon B. Johnson after Signing the Highway Beautification Act of 1965
Lyndon Baines Johnson Library and Museum

Unpopular Decision for new President: After pardoning his predecessor Richard M. Nixon, Gerald R. Ford received 273,331 letters, most of them negative.

Gerald R. Ford
Lyndon Baines Johnson Library and Museum

Emancipation 48 Times Over: In 1863, Abraham Lincoln signed 48 copies of the *Emancipation Proclamation*. This historic Proclamation ordered all slaves in the Old Confederacy to be free. These 48 copies of the Proclamation were sold to private buyers, with the proceeds going toward medical care for Union soldiers. In 1963, U.S. Attorney General Robert F. Kennedy purchased one of these copies for $9,500. In 2010, this copy was purchased at a Sotheby's Auction for $3.7 million by an anonymous buyer.

Robert F. Kennedy
Lyndon Baines Johnson Library and Museum

"Mark Twains New Deal:" The term "New Deal" which was used to refer to Franklin D. Roosevelt's domestic policy was first used by author Samuel Clemens (a.k.a., Mark Twain in the 1889 novel: *A Connecticut Yankee at the Court of King Arthur*.) In the book, Twain asserted: "It seemed to me that what the nine hundred and ninety-four dupes needed was a new deal."

Mark Twain
Library of Congress

Electrician "Ushers" in New Era at The White House: The longest serving White House usher was Irwin H. Hoover who served from 1891 until his death in 1933. Hoover began working in the White House in 1891, when he was hired as an electrician to install the first electric lights in the White House. He stayed in the White House monitoring the new invention until President William McKinley appointed him as Chief Usher.

Presidential Card-Carrying Members of the NRA: Nine Presidents have been National Rifle Association (NRA) members. They are: Ulysses S. Grant, Theodore Roosevelt, William Howard Taft, Dwight D. Eisenhower, John F. Kennedy, Richard M. Nixon, Ronald Reagan, George H.W. Bush, and George W. Bush. They all were Republicans except for Kennedy. George H.W. Bush resigned his membership in protest after a fundraising letter was sent out branding some federal law enforcement officials as: "Jack-booted thugs."

Nixon Proposed Obama-Care before Obama: In 1974, Richard M. Nixon proposed a comprehensive Health Insurance Reform Program, which would mandate all Americans to have Health Insurance, with the federal government subsidizing those who could not afford it. Nixon said in his 1974 State of the Union Address: "The time is at hand to bring comprehensive, high quality health care within the reach of every American." The Democratic Congress did not move on Nixon's plan, arguing that it would be a boon for the insurance companies.

Richard M. Nixon
Library of Congress

Fraternal Presidents: Fourteen U.S. Presidents have been Free Masons.

Harry S. Truman in Mason Regalia
Harry S. Truman Library and Museum

Old Blue Eyes: The only Presidents with brown eyes were: John Quincy Adams, Andrew Johnson, Chester A. Arthur, Lyndon B. Johnson, Richard M. Nixon, and Barack Obama.

The Presidential Office

Compensating the President: George Washington's salary was $25,000 a year. Today the President earns $400,000 a year.

George Washington
Library of Congress

POTUS: The official acronym for the President **O**f **T**he **U**nited **S**tates is POTUS.

Constitutional Requirements: The *U.S. Constitution* has three requirements for a person to become President of the United States. He/she must be 1) a Natural-Born American Citizen, 2) at least 35 years old, and 3) must have been a U.S. resident for at least 14 years.

"Doing All Right:" The President gets an annual expense account of $150,000 and $19,000 to pay for entertainment and $100,000 for travel.

The President's Jobs Program: The Presidential Administration employs more than 350,000 Americans.

The President does it All: The U.S. system is rare in that the President is both the Chief of State and the Head of the Government.

Presidential Resignations: When the President of the United States resigns from office, the resignation is issued to the U.S. Secretary of State. The only time this happened in U.S. history was (During the Watergate Affair) when Richard M. Nixon wrote a letter stating: "Dear Mr. Secretary: I hereby resign the office of President of the United States."

Richard M. Nixon
Harry S. Truman Library and Museum

The Oath: Every federal employee, excluding the President, takes the following oath: "I, (the Persons name) do solemnly swear (or affirm) that I will support and defend the Constitution of the United States against all enemies, foreign and domestic; that I will bear true faith and allegiance to the same; that I take this obligation freely, without any mental reservation or purpose of evasion; and that I will faithfully discharge the duties of the office on which I am about to enter. So help me God." The phrase: "So help me God" is not officially part of the Presidents oath, although most Presidents say it.

"You've Got Mail:" The President receives about 40,000 pieces of mail per day.

Presidential Succession: Under the Presidential Succession Act of 1947 (signed by Harry S. Truman), in the event the President is forced to leave office, resigns, or becomes incapacitated, the Vice President assumes the Presidency. Beyond that, the line of Presidential succession goes to the Speaker of the U.S. House of Representatives, the President pro tempore of the U.S. Senate, then Federal cabinet officers, beginning with the U.S Secretary of State. But they must meet the Constitutional requirements to assume the office.

Treaties and Executive Agreements: The President has many diplomatic tools at his disposal in foreign policy. Two are "Treaties" and "Executive Agreements." Treaties are similar to contracts and once in force, bind the country to the terms of the treaty through succeeding administrations. The President negotiates the terms of a treaty and the U.S. Senate reviews the treaty and takes a vote on whether or not to ratify it. A treaty must pass a two-thirds vote in the U.S. Senate to be ratified. In contrast to a treaty, which needs approval in the U.S. Senate and binds the country through successive administrations, Executive Agreements are less formal agreements and can be used by the President to form agreements and understandings with foreign nations. Executive Agreements do not bind the parties, but instead obligate them to respect the terms of the Agreement. Unlike Treaties, Executive Agreements do not require U.S. Senate approval and do not bind succeeding administrations.

Protecting Former Presidents: Former presidents and their spouses receive Secret Service protection for 10 years from the date they leave office.

Part II: U.S. Presidential Elections

When Republicans were Democrats: In 1888, Republican Presidential nominee Benjamin Harrison defeated incumbent Democratic President Grover Cleveland by advocating what are now considered Democratic proposals. He pledged to expand the money supply, expand the protective tariff, and to increase funding for social services.

Benjamin Harrison
Library of Congress

Driving the Campaign: In 1896, Democratic Presidential nominee William Jennings Bryan became the first Presidential candidate to campaign in a car. While campaigning in Decatur, Illinois, he rode in a Mueller automobile which was made in Decatur.

William Jennings Bryan
Library of Congress

First Man to Beat a Kennedy: The first time a Kennedy was beaten in any election was in 1968, when U.S. Senator Eugene McCarthy (D-MN) defeated U.S. Senator Robert F. Kennedy (D-NY) in the Oregon Presidential primary. McCarthy garnered 44.7% of the vote. Kennedy mustered 38.8% of the vote.

Eugene McCarthy on the Cover of *Time* *Magazine*

80-year-old VP Nominee: West Virginia businessman and former U.S. Senator Henry G. Davis (D-WV) is the oldest person ever to be nominated by a major party on a national ticket. At age 80, he garnered the Democratic Party nomination as the running mate for Alton B. Parker in 1904. The ticket lost in a landslide to Republican President Theodore Roosevelt and his running mate Charles Fairbanks.

Henry G. Davis
Library of Congress

First Woman Presidential Candidate: In 1872, the Equal Rights Party nominated Women's Suffrage proponent Victoria Woodhull as their Presidential candidate. Woodhull was the first female to be nominated by an American political party. She garnered just over 2,000 popular votes.

Victoria Woodhull
Associated Press

Can't Get from Big House to White House: In 1920, Eugene V. Debs, the Presidential nominee of the Socialist Party of America, ran for President from prison. He was incarcerated for urging Americans to defy the military draft. He garnered 920,000 votes.

Eugene V. Debs
Library of Congress

Conservative Hillary, Liberal Newt: During the 1964 Republican nomination process, Newt Gingrich supported liberal Nelson Rockefeller while Hillary Clinton backed his conservative opponent Barry Goldwater.

First African-American to Receive Votes at a Major Party Convention: In 1880, U.S. Senator Blanche Kelso Bruce (R-MS) became the first African-American to garner votes at a national political convention by a major political party. Bruce, a former slave, mustered eight votes for the Republican nomination for Vice President. The winner was former Collector of the Port of New York, Chester A. Arthur. For his loyalty to the Republican Party, Bruce was appointed Register of the Federal Treasury in 1881 by President James A. Garfield.

Bruce Kelso Blanche
Library of Congress

Voter Turnout Rates: The District of Columbia and Minnesota recorded the highest turnout in the 2008 Presidential election with 75% of registered voters casting ballots. By contrast, Utah and Hawaii recorded the lowest numbers with just 52% of registered voters casting ballots.

Vital Sunshine State: Since 1924, no Republican has captured the Presidency without winning in Florida.

No Winners Here: No Republican Presidential nominee has won any of the 14 counties comprising Massachusetts since 1988.

The Winds of Political Change: In the 1922 mid-term elections, the Republican Party, with Warren G. Harding as President, lost 77 seats in the U.S. House of Representatives. Two years later, Republican Calvin Coolidge, who had assumed the Presidency after Warren G. Harding's death, won a full term in a landslide victory, winning by 25.2% and losing just one state outside of the South.

Warren G. Harding (left) with Calvin Coolidge (right)
Library of Congress

"W" wins the Mountain State: In 2000, George W. Bush became the first non-incumbent Republican Presidential nominee to win the state of West Virginia since 1928.

George W. Bush
White House Photograph

Run Lyndon, Run and Run Again: Democrat Lyndon LaRouche has sought the Democratic Nomination for the Presidency seven times.

Who is Wheeler? In 1876, upon hearing that U.S. Representative William A. Wheeler (R-NY) had secured the Republican Nomination for Vice President, the party's Presidential nominee, Ohio Governor Rutherford B. Hayes, replied: "I am ashamed to say: Who is Wheeler?"

Rutherford B. Hayes and William Wheeler Presidential Campaign Poster
Library of Congress

Peanut Power: Jimmy Carter called his 1976 Presidential Campaign plane "Peanut One."

Jimmy Carter Egresses from Peanut One
Library of Congress

No Incumbent on the Ticket: In twenty-five out of fifty-six Presidential elections, no incumbent President's name appeared on the general election ballot.

If at First You Don't Succeed? Minnesota Governor Harold E. Stassen (1939-1943) ran a record nine times for the Republican Presidential nomination (all of them unsuccessful).

Harold E. Stassen
Official Photograph

I'll Win this Time. I Promise: Thomas E. Dewey and Richard M. Nixon were the only two Republican Presidential nominees who lost in the general election and were re-nominated to run again. Dewey, who lost the election in 1944 was re-nominated in 1948, and lost again. Nixon, who lost the election in 1960, was re-nominated in 1968, and won the Presidency.

Obama's Benefactors: Employees of the Goldman Sachs Group Inc. donated $994,795 to Barack Obama during his 2008 Presidential campaign. They were his highest contributors.

Barack Obama
White House Photograph

Untimely Death: On October 30, 1912, Vice President James S. Sherman died. This was just one week before he and his running mate, President William Howard Taft, were up for re-election. Taft chose Columbia University President Nicholas Butler to supplant Sherman on the ticket. The ticket mustered just eight electoral votes, winning only Vermont and Utah.

James S. Sherman
Library of Congress

Bellwether State: Missouri has voted for the winning presidential candidate since 1904 except in 1956 when it chose Democrat Adlai Stevenson over President Dwight D. Eisenhower, and in 2008 when it selected Republican John McCain over Democrat Barack Obama.

Just Can't Wait to Vote: In the 2008 Presidential election, 30% of all voters cast their ballots prior to Election Day.

It's All in the Name: With the exception of 1964, between 1952 and 2004, the Republican Party has nominated either a Nixon, a Dole, or a Bush for either President or Vice President.

Lone Star Shines Bright for McCain: In the 2008 Presidential election, four of the ten Congressional Districts where Republican John McCain performed best are in Texas.

Okies for Socialist Debs: In 1916, Eugene V. Debs, the Presidential nominee of the Socialist Party of America, did better in Oklahoma than in any other state, garnering 15% of the vote.

Eugene V. Debs
Library of Congress

Volatile South: In 1976, Presidential candidate Jimmy Carter won every state in his native South except for Virginia. In 1980, when running for re-election, President Carter lost every Southern state except for his home state of Georgia.

Jimmy Carter
Official Photograph

Show me the Differences: Missouri is the only state that voted for Republican Dwight D. Eisenhower in 1952 and for his opponent, Democrat Adlai Stevenson, in 1956.

GOP Catholic VP Nominee: The only Catholic to be nominated by the GOP on a national ticket was U.S. Representative William E. Miller (R-NY 1953-1965). He ran as the Vice Presidential nominee with Presidential candidate Barry Goldwater, in 1964.

William E. Miller
Official Photograph

Showdown Silver State: Since 1912, Nevada has voted for the winner in every Presidential Election except in 1976, when it chose Gerald R. Ford over Jimmy Carter.

Dems take Golden State from GOP: Between 1952 and 1992, California went Republican in every Presidential election except for 1964 when it elected Lyndon B. Johnson. Since 1992, it has gone for only Democratic presidential candidates.

Must-Win State: No Republican has ever won the Presidency without carrying Ohio.

Beginning of the end of the Solid Democratic South: Between 1880 and 1920, all 11 states of the "Old Confederacy" voted for the Democratic Presidential candidate. Tennessee broke this streak in 1920 by voting for Republican Presidential Candidate Warren G. Harding.

He Shouldn't have Listened to Roscoe Conkling: U.S. Senator Roscoe Conkling (R-NY 1867-1881), a steadfast opponent of James Garfield (the 1880 Republican Party nominee), successfully urged Levi Morton (the Party's first choice for Vice President) not to accept the position. Morton wanted someday to be President. Conkling, the most feared party boss of the era, also tried to persuade the party's second choice, Chester A. Arthur, not to accept the position. He asserted that James Garfield would lose the election. Arthur defied Conkling and accepted his Party's nomination for Vice President. James Garfield won the Presidential election. Just nine months into his term, Garfield died. Chester A. Arthur succeeded him to the Presidency. Levi Morton came ever so close to realizing his dream of becoming President.

Roscoe Conkling
Library of Congress

Election Without President or Vice President Running: 2008 was the first Presidential election since 1928, in which no incumbent President or Vice President was seeking the Presidency.

Republican Lock: The same twenty-four states voted Republican in every Presidential election between 1972 and 1988. This voting block comprised 219 of the requisite 270 electoral votes needed to clinch a Presidential election.

McCain's Best District: In the 2008 Presidential Election, John McCain's best electoral showing was in Texas' 13th Congressional District located in the Texas Panhandle, (which includes the city of Amarillo). McCain garnered 76% of the vote in this district.

John McCain
Official Photograph

Utah's Shifting Political Allegiances: Between 1932 and 1948, Utah went for the Democratic Presidential nominee in every election. Since 1952, it went for the Democratic nominee only one time, in 1964, when Lyndon B. Johnson trounced Barry Goldwater.

The Last Cabinet Officer to Capture the Presidency: Herbert Hoover was the last sitting Cabinet Secretary to be elected President. He was elected in 1928. Hoover served for eight years as U.S. Commerce Secretary under Presidents Warren G. Harding and Calvin Coolidge.

Herbert Hoover
Library of Congress

Bowdoin Buddies: President Franklin Pierce and writer Nathaniel Hawthorne were classmates and friends at Bowdoin College in Brunswick, Maine. In 1852, Hawthorne authored a biography titled *The Life of Franklin Pierce* praising presidential candidate Pierce (1852).

Nathaniel Hawthorne
Library of Congress

The Bronx Cheers for Obama: In the 2008 Presidential election, Barack Obama's best showing was in New York's 16th Congressional District, which is based in the Bronx section of New York City. Obama scored 95% of the vote in that Congressional District.

Barack Obama
White House Photograph by Pete Souza

Every Vote Counts; The U.S. Census Bureau reports that about 131 million voters cast ballots in the 2008 Presidential election.

Taft Loses Primaries, But Garners GOP Nomination: Of the twelve Republican Presidential primaries in 1912, incumbent President William Howard Taft won only one, Massachusetts. He even lost his home state of Ohio to former President Theodore Roosevelt. However, Taft garnered the Party's nomination by winning enough delegates at the Republican National Convention in Chicago, Illinois. Roosevelt, who won nine Republican primaries, bolted the party and formed the Progressive Party, a.k.a. the Bull Moose Party, and won 86 electoral votes in the General Election. Taft won just eight. The Democratic nominee, New Jersey Governor Woodrow Wilson, mustered 435 and won the Presidential Election.

William Howard Taft
Library of Congress

Veep runs Against Pres: The 1800 Presidential election was the only election to pit an incumbent Vice President (Thomas Jefferson) against an incumbent President (John Adams). Jefferson won.

Contradictory Virginia: Since 1977, the party that holds the White House has lost the Virginia Governorship in every off-year election.

Eisenhower's Popularity among New England African-Americans: In 1956 President Dwight D. Eisenhower garnered 70% of the African-American vote in the Northeast.

Dwight D. Eisenhower
Dwight D. Eisenhower Presidential Library and Museum

Mormons Come Out for Mitt: Mormon Mitt Romney garnered over 90% of the vote in the Utah Republican Presidential Primary in 2008. About 60% of Utah residents share Romney's Mormon religion.

Mitt Romney
Official Photograph

The Real First Nixon-Kennedy Debate: Richard M. Nixon and John F. Kennedy debated more than 13 years before the famous 1960 Presidential debates. In 1947, the two Freshmen Congressmen debated The Taft-Hartley Labor-Management Relations Act at the Penn McKee Hotel in McKeesport, Pennsylvania. Nixon favored the Act while Kennedy opposed it. (The act regulates the power of labor unions)

Cleveland-Bryan Rift: In the 1896 Presidential election, Democratic President Grover Cleveland did not support William Jennings Bryan, the Democratic nominee to succeed him. This was because Bryan was opposed to the Gold Standard. Cleveland placed his support with Third Party Candidate, John M. Palmer, of the Pro-Gold Standard National Democratic Party. Palmer garnered less than 1% of the vote in that election. The winner of the election was the Republican nominee William McKinley. The National Democratic Party dissolved in 1900.

John M. Palmer
History of The Republican Party in Illinois 1854-1912 by Charles A. Church

Oklahoma Dichotomy: In Oklahoma, Democrats outnumber Republicans by more than ten percent. Yet at the Presidential level, Republican John McCain mustered 65.7% of the vote in 2008.

New States: The 1960 Presidential election was the first to include the electoral votes of Alaska and Hawaii. Democrat John F. Kennedy carried Hawaii while Republican Richard M. Nixon captured Alaska.

Economic Danger Zone: No President since WWII has won re-election with the official unemployment rate over 7.2%.

110

Maverick Millard: In 1856, former U.S. President Millard Fillmore (1850-1853), who had been a Whig, ran for President as the nominee of the American Party (a.k.a. "Know Nothing Party"). He garnered just 21% of the vote and won just one state, Maryland, with eight electoral votes.

Campaign Poster for Millard Fillmore in 1856
Library of Congress

Not Within the Margin of Error: In 1936, a poll taken by *Literary Digest* predicted that Republican Presidential nominee Alfred Landon would win the Presidential election with 370 electoral votes. He lost in a landslide to the Democratic Nominee, President Franklin D. Roosevelt. Landon collected just 8 electoral votes.

Mississippi Blues: In 1964, Lyndon B. Johnson won the Presidential election with 60.6% of the popular vote nation-wide. However, his Republican opponent Barry Goldwater trounced Johnson in Mississippi, mustering 87% of the vote.

Democratic Votes in Utah: Though Republican Presidential nominee John McCain won Utah by almost 30 points in the 2008 Presidential Election, he became the first Republican nominee to lose the state's most populous county, Salt Lake County.

The Battle of Barack Run: Barack Obama made his last campaign stop of the 2008 Presidential election in Manassas, Virginia (A northern Virginia City with a population of about 35,000). It was also the place where the first major battle of the Civil War took place. The Battle of Bull Run was fought in 1861.

Barack Obama
U.S. Air force Photograph

Stevenson Loses Home State Two Times: Illinois resident Adlai Stevenson lost his home state when he ran for President in 1952 and again in 1956. In 1952 he was the state's sitting Governor.

Adlai Stevenson
Library of Congress

Primary Version of the Electoral College: In the 1972 Democratic Presidential primaries, U.S. Senator Hubert Humphrey (D-MN) garnered more popular votes than U.S. Senator George McGovern (D-SD), yet McGovern won more delegates and mustered the Party's nomination.

Obama Youth Movement: In the 2008 Presidential Election, Democrat Barack Obama beat Republican John McCain by a margin of 66% to 32% amongst voter under 30 years of age.

Barack Obama
Official Photograph

Bush Sr.'s Revenge: In 1970 Lloyd Bentsen defeated Republican George H.W. Bush in the U.S. Senate race in Texas. In 1988 the two met again when Bush was the Republican Presidential nominee and Bentsen was the Democratic Vice Presidential nominee. This time, Bush won the race.

George H.W. Bush Campaigning in 1988
George Bush Presidential Library and Museum

Catholic Vote: In 2004, George W. Bush defeated Democrat John Kerry amongst Catholic Voters 52-47% (Kerry is Catholic). In 2008, Democrat Barack Obama (who is not Catholic, but a member of the United Church of Christ) defeated Republican John McCain among Catholic voters, 54%-45%.

Throwing the VP Selection to the Convention: The last time a major party Presidential candidate allowed the party's convention delegates to decide on the Vice Presidential nominee was in 1956, when Democrat Adlai Stevenson opened the choice to the convention. Their choice was U.S. Senator Estes Kefauver (D-TN).

Estes Kefauver
Harry S. Truman Library and Museum

Former Democratic Citadels Trending Republican: Tennessee and Arkansas are the only states where the percentage of the vote for Republican Presidential candidates has increased in each of the last four elections.

Weird Political Dichotomy: The two states where 2008 Republican Presidential nominee John McCain performed the best were Oklahoma and Wyoming. Ironically both states had Democratic Governors. Conversely, the two states where Democrat Barack Obama performed the best were Hawaii and Vermont. Both states had Republican Governors.

Al Smith and the Pope: After learning that he had lost the Presidential election in 1928, Democrat Al Smith, the first Catholic nominated to a major party ticket, telegrammed Pope Pius XI a message stating: "Unpack."

Al Smith
Library of Congress

Educational Breakdown: In 2008, Barack Obama carried 78 of the 100 U.S. counties with the highest education levels, while Republican John McCain carried 88 of the nation's 100 counties with the lowest education levels.

Reagan Landslide: In 1984, President Ronald Reagan won 49 states. The only state he lost was Minnesota, the home state of his Democratic opponent, Walter Mondale. Reagan lost Minnesota by just 3,761 votes. (Mondale also won the District of Columbia)

Ronald Reagan
Ronald Reagan Presidential Library and Museum

The Origin of Booze: Whisky distiller E.G. Booze supported William Henry Harrison's 1840 Presidential campaign. In promoting Harrison, he sold whisky in log-cabin-shaped bottles. This is where the word Booze came from.

William Henry Harrison
Library of Congress

When Ohio Took the National Political Stage: In 1920, both the Republican and Democratic Presidential nominees were elected officials from Ohio. U.S. Senator Warren G. Harding defeated the state's Governor, James M. Cox, in a 60.3% - 34.1% landslide nationally. Harding won Ohio 58.47% - 38.58%.

Independent Streak: Democratic Presidential nominee Barack Obama garnered 52% of the Independent vote in 2008.

Barack Obama
White House Photograph

Razor-thin Victory in Keystone State- Congressional District: Republican Presidential Candidate John McCain eked out a victory over Democratic nominee Barack Obama in the Erie-based Third Congressional District of Pennsylvania by just 17 votes.

John McCain
Official Photograph

The Bush Factor: In 2008, Republican Presidential nominee John McCain won every state where President George W. Bush's job approval rating was above 35%.

George W. Bush
White House Photograph by Eric Draper

Dare to Explore: Before declaring their Presidential candidacies, most prospective candidates test the waters by establishing an "exploratory committee" which allows them to raise more than $5,000 without disclosing their sources to the Federal Election Commission (FEC). The stipulation is that they cannot refer to themselves as a candidate for President.

Age Dichotomy: In 2008, Presidential candidate Barack Obama won voters who were over 30 years of age by just one percentage point, 50%-49%.

Barack Obama
White House Photograph

First for the Maverick: In 2007, Minnesota Governor Tim Pawlenty was the first Governor to endorse U.S. Senator John McCain (R-AZ) in his bid for the Republican Nomination for President.

Tim Pawlenty
Official Photograph

Buckeye Bellwether: Ohio has voted for the winner of every Presidential election since 1960.

Keystone State Anomalies: The Twelfth Congressional District of Pennsylvania is the only Congressional District where Democratic nominee John Kerry won in 2004, but Democratic nominee Barack Obama lost in 2008.

He'll Always Have Vermont: The first third-party Presidential candidate to win a state was William Wirt. The former U.S. Attorney General was the nominee of the American Party, a.k.a. the Know Nothing Party, in 1832. He won Vermont, picking up seven electoral votes.

William Wirt
Library of Congress

Obama Loves New York: The Four Congressional Districts where Democrat Barack Obama performed the best in 2008 are all urban districts in New York.

Barack Obama
White House Photograph by Pete Souza

Catholics Turn Out for One of Their Own: In 1960, John F. Kennedy won 80% of the Catholic vote, helping him to win the Presidential election and to become the first and only Catholic President.

John F. Kennedy
John F. Kennedy Presidential Library and Museum

Maverick-Minded-Maine: In 1992, Independent Presidential Candidate H. Ross Perot's best electoral performance was in Maine, where he garnered 30% of the vote. Two years later, Maine elected Independent Angus King as its Governor.

Ronald Reagan's Electoral Appeal in the Bay State: Since 1956, Republican Presidential Candidates have won Massachusetts twice. Ronald Reagan carried the state in 1984 as well as in 1988.

Ronald Reagan
Ronald Reagan Presidential Foundation and Library

Presidential Candidate was Ahead of his Time: The first Presidential Candidate to run on a platform in opposition to the expansion of slavery in the Western Territories was U.S. Senator John P. Hale of New Hampshire. He ran as the nominee of the Free Soil Party in 1852. Hale garnered just 4.9% of the vote. His fellow New Hampshire native, Democrat Franklin Pierce, won the election.

John P. Hale
Library of Congress

Loyal to Obama: Barack Obama won the African-American vote 24-1 in the 2008 Presidential election.

Barack Obama
White House Photograph

No Limits: There is no maximum amount a Presidential candidate can spend on their campaigns, unless they accept federal matching funds.

He'll Always Have Mississippi: In the 1992 general election campaign, George H.W. Bush did not win a majority of the votes in any state. He came the closest in Mississippi, garnering 49.7% of the vote.

George H.W. Bush
George Bush Presidential Library and Museum

End of the Ninth: President Gerald R. Ford developed a close friendship with former Major League Baseball player and broadcaster Joe Garagiola. Garagiola appeared in advertisements for Ford in his 1976 Presidential campaign and watched election returns with Ford on election night.

Gerald R. Ford with Joe Garagiola
Watching Election Returns
Gerald R. Ford Presidential Library

The Bill Clinton and Jerry Brown Soap Opera: After Bill Clinton lost in his re-election bid as Governor of Arkansas in 1980, California Governor Jerry Brown offered Bill Clinton a job on his staff. Clinton turned it down and won back the Arkansas Governorship in 1982. Ironically, in 1992 Clinton defeated Jerry Brown in the Democratic Presidential primary.

Clinton supports a losing Cause: In 1972, Bill Clinton served as Co-chairman of Democrat George McGovern's 1972 Presidential Election Campaign in Texas. McGovern garnered just 33.24% of the vote in the Lone Star State, losing to Republican President Richard M. Nixon.

George McGovern
Library of Congress

High Watermark for Voter Turnout: The 1876 Presidential election recorded the highest voter turnout on record. Of eligible voters, 81.8% voted in the election, which pitted Republican Rutherford B. Hayes against Democrat Samuel Tilden. Hayes was declared the winner.

Peach State Represented: The 1976 Presidential campaign included two former Governors of Georgia. The Democratic nominee was Jimmy Carter, who had served as the Peach State's Chief Executive from 1971-1975. He won the Presidential election, garnering 50.1% of the popular vote. Lester Maddox had served as Georgia Governor from 1967-1971. He was the nominee of the American Independence Party. He garnered less than 1% of the vote.

Electors got to vote Twice: In the first four Presidential elections, members of the Electoral College were permitted to select two candidates. The candidate with the most votes became President, while the candidate with the second most votes became Vice President.

$11 Million Lady: Former Texas Governor and U.S. Treasury Secretary John Connally spent $11 million dollars on his 1980 campaign for the Republican Presidential nomination. All that money garnered him just one convention delegate, Ada Mills of Arkansas.

John Connally
Official Photograph

Supporting the Insurgent: In the 1976 Republican Presidential primary, only two Republican U.S. Senators supported the failed insurgency candidacy of former California Governor Ronald Reagan over President Gerald R. Ford. They were Republicans Jesse Helms of North Carolina and Paul Laxalt of Nevada.

Ronald Reagan
Ronald Reagan Presidential Foundation and Library

117

Governors for Jimmy: In the 1980 Democratic Presidential Primary, President Jimmy Carter garnered the support of 20 Governors. His challenger, U.S. Senator Edward M. Kennedy (D-MA), mustered the support of just four Governors.

Jimmy Carter
Library of Congress

Campaigning in a Foreign Language: In 1880, Republican Presidential nominee James Garfield, fluent in German, delivered a campaign speech to a group of German-Americans in German. This was the first time a major Party Presidential nominee campaigned in a foreign tongue.

James Garfield
Library of Congress

Supporters for a Perennial Presidential Candidate: In the 2004 election cycle, Democratic Presidential candidate Lyndon LaRouche, in his eighth run, received 7,834 individual donations.

Very Short Coattails: In the 1984 election, while Ronald Reagan cruised to a 49 state landslide, his coattails extended to just one Democratic U.S. Senator losing his seat. Walter Huddleston lost to Republican challenger Mitch McConnell.

Walter Huddleston
Official Photograph

No Opposition: George Washington was the only President to be unanimously selected by the Electoral College. He won all 69 Electoral votes.

George Washington
Library of Congress

Repubizona: Arizona has voted for the Republican Presidential nominee every year since 1952, except in 1996 when Democrat Bill Clinton carried the state.

Taken to the Congressional Woodshed and Kicked Out of the Caucus: In 1912, twelve Republican members of the U.S. House of Representatives supported the Presidential candidacy of Progressive Party Nominee Robert M. La Follette Sr. against the Republican Party nominee Calvin Coolidge. La Follette won only his home state of Wisconsin. Coolidge won the election in a landslide victory. These unlucky twelve contrarians were expelled from the Republican caucus by U.S. House Speaker Nicholas Longworth (R-OH) and stripped of their seniority.

Robert M. La Follette Sr.
Library of Congress

Razorbacks support Favorite Son: In the 1992 Presidential election, Democratic Presidential nominee Bill Clinton won a majority of the vote in just one state, his home state of Arkansas. He garnered 53.2% of the vote in the Razorback State.

Bill Clinton
William J. Clinton Presidential Library and Museum

The 103rd Ballot: In 1924, former U.S. Solicitor General and U.S. Ambassador to the United Kingdom John W. Davis won the Democratic Presidential Nomination on a record 103rd ballot. But all was for not, as Davis lost the general election to Republican President Calvin Coolidge.

John W. Davis
Library of Congress

Van Buren and G.H.W. Bush: In 1988, President George H.W. Bush became the first sitting Vice President to be elected President since Martin Van Buren in 1836.

George H.W. Bush
George Bush Presidential Library

First For Obama: U.S. Senator Dick Durbin (D-IL) was the first Senator to endorse Barack Obama in his 2008 Presidential run.

Dick Durbin
Official Photograph

Kerry's Base: In the 2004 Presidential election, Democratic nominee John Kerry won just one age demographic, the 18 to 29-year-olds.

John Kerry
Official Photograph

Dixie Trends Republican: In the Presidential Election of 2008, Arkansas, Louisiana, Tennessee, Oklahoma, and West Virginia were the only states where the Democratic Presidential nominee, Barack Obama, scored a lesser percentage of the vote than Democratic nominee John Kerry in 2004.

Sorry Adlai: In 1952, US. Senator Paul Douglas (D-IL) supported U.S. Senator Estes Kefauver (D-TN) in the Democratic Presidential Primaries over his state's Governor, Adlai Stevenson.

Paul Douglas on the Cover of *Time Magazine*

Cotton State Defies National Trend: In 1964, Alabama elected five Republicans to the U.S. House of Representatives. Republican Presidential nominee Barry Goldwater won the state with 69% of the vote. He became the first Republican to carry the state since Reconstruction. Nationally, Lyndon B. Johnson won the Presidency with 61% of the vote and the Democrats picked up 36 U.S. House seats.

Arizona Republican eschews Favorite Son: In 2000, Arizona Republican Governor Jane Hull supported Texas Governor George W. Bush over her home states Senator John McCain in the Republican Presidential Primary.

Jane Hull
Official Photograph

Former Segregationist Endorses Civil Rights Activist for President: Arkansas Governor Orval Fabus (1955-1967), known for sending the Arkansas National Guard to Central High School in Little Rock to prevent nine African-American students from entering the building, endorsed Civil Rights leader Jesse Jackson in his 1984 Presidential bid for the Democratic Presidential nomination.

Jesse Jackson
Library of Congress

Women Vote for Obama: In the 2008 Presidential election, Democrat Barack Obama garnered 56% of the female vote, but just 49% of the male vote.

Barack Obama
White House Photograph by Pete Souza

Okies Muster Big Support for McCain: In the 2008 Presidential election, Republican John McCain won all 77 counties in Oklahoma.

Once in an Electoral College Lifetime: The Vice Presidential Clause of the U.S. Constitution stipulates . . . "if no person have a majority, then from the two highest numbers on the list, the Senate shall choose the Vice-President." The only time this clause was utilized was in 1836. With no candidate garnering a majority, the U.S. Senate chose Democrat Richard M. Johnson (the running mate of Martin Van Buren) over Whig Francis Granger (the running mate of William Henry Harrison). Johnson did not win a majority outright because the Virginia electors voted for Van Buren but not for Johnson. They were offended that Johnson's late common-law wife was African-American and had been one of his father's slaves. The Johnson's had two children.

Richard M. Johnson
Library of Congress

Please Vote for Me because I can't Vote: In Virginia, convicted felons are disallowed from voting even after serving their sentence. Lyndon LaRouche, after serving a sentence for credit card fraud and obstruction of justice, was legally barred from voting in his last three Presidential bids in 1996, 2000, and 2004.

Surreptitious Job Offers: Prior to winning the 2008 Presidential election, the Barack Obama Presidential campaign secretly hired over 600 people to serve on his transition team.

Barack Obama
White House Photograph by Pete Souza

Dramatic Electoral Shift in the Magnolia State: In 1972, Republican Presidential nominee Richard M. Nixon won Mississippi with 78% of the vote. Just four years later, in 1976, Democratic nominee Jimmy Carter won the state, garnering 49.96% of the vote.

Jimmy Carter
Campaigning for President in 1976
Jimmy Carter Library and Museum

My Colleague, "The Whip:" In 2008, the Democratic Presidential nominee was U.S. Senator Barack Obama from Illinois. The state's other U.S. Senator, Dick Durbin, served as Democratic Whip. The Republican nominee was U.S. Senator John McCain of Arizona. Arizona's other U.S. Senator, John Kyle, served as Republican Whip.

Wallace Country: The Democratic Presidential Nominee "nationally" in 1968 was Vice President Hubert Humphrey. However, in Alabama, native son George C. Wallace was the nominee of the American Independence Party, which was ironically listed on the ballot as the "official" Democratic Candidate. Wallace won the state with 65.86% of the vote. Humphrey garnered just 18.72% of the vote in Alabama.

George C. Wallace
Library of Congress

Born Not in the Continental USA: In 2008, both of the major Party Presidential nominees were born outside of the continental United States. Democrat Barack Obama was born in Hawaii, while Republican John McCain was born in the Panama Canal Zone.

Clinton Not Feeling the Love in The Beehive State: In 1992, Utah was the only state where Democrat Bill Clinton finished in third place behind President George H. W. Bush and Texas Businessman H. Ross Perot.

Bill Clinton
William J. Clinton Presidential Library

President's Electoral Embarrassment: William Howard Taft's performance in the 1912 Presidential election garnering just 23.2% of the popular vote and just eight electoral votes. This was the worst showing for any incumbent President in a re-election bid.

William Howard Taft
Library of Congress

Cheney and Betty Concede to Carter: After the grueling last days of the 1976 Presidential campaign, Republican President Gerald R. Ford lost his voice and was unable to concede to the winner, Democratic nominee Jimmy Carter. He had his Chief of Staff Dick Cheney read a concession statement to Carter over the telephone. Ford's wife Betty read the Concession speech to the nation.

Betty Ford reads her Husbands Concession Speech
Gerald R. Ford Presidential Library and Museum

Bluegrass Bellwether: Between 1964 and 2004, Kentucky voted for the winner of the Presidential race every year.

All Hail Massachusetts: In 1988, both Democratic and Republican Presidential candidates were born in Massachusetts. Democrat Michael Dukakis was born in Brookline, Massachusetts. He lived most of his life in the Bay State and won three terms as the state's Governor. Republican George H.W. Bush was born in Milton, Massachusetts. His family moved to Connecticut before his first birthday, but Bush came back to the state for his High School years, where he attended Philips Academy in Andover, Massachusetts.

George H. W. Bush and Michael Dukakis
George Bush Presidential Library and Museum

Not beholden to large Donors: During his unsuccessful campaign for the Democratic Presidential nomination in 1992, former California Governor Jerry Brown did not accept donations of over $100.

Jerry Brown in 1992
www.Jerrybrown.org

Don't Believe Everything You Read: Republican Presidential nominee Thomas E. Dewey was heavily favored to defeat Democrat Harry S. Truman in the 1948 Presidential election. In fact, the *Chicago Dailey Tribune* prematurely published the blazing headline: "Dewey Defeats Truman." Truman stunned political prognosticators by defeating Dewey handily, garnering 114 more electoral votes than Dewey.

Harry S. Truman Holds Up False Headline
Chicago Tribune

The Vanishing GOP Female Vote: In 2004, Republican Presidential nominee George W. Bush garnered 48% of the female vote in his successful campaign for re-election. In 2008, Republican John McCain, with Sarah Palin as his running-mate, mustered just 43% of the female vote.

Democrats Elected in McCain Country: In 2008, 49 Democrats won seats or were re-elected to the U.S. House of Representatives in Congressional Districts won in 2008 by Republican Presidential nominee John McCain.

Dems break the Electoral Lock: In 1992, Republican President George H.W. Bush lost 22 of the 40 states he had carried in 1988.

Recruiting Magnet for College Admissions Office: Both U.S. Senate Majority Leader Robert J. Dole (R-KS 1995 - 1996) and Arthur Allan Fletcher, an advisor in Republican Presidential administrations, are alumni of Washburn University in Topeka, Kansas. Both men ran for the Republican nomination for President. Dole won.

Washburn University Official Symbol

Winning the New Hampshire Primary is becoming less of a Precursor to the Presidency: Prior to 1992, no Presidential candidate who had lost the New Hampshire Presidential Primary went on to win the Presidential election. Since 1992, the last three Presidents, Bill Clinton, George W. Bush, and Barack Obama lost the New Hampshire Primary, but were elected President.

The Phil Gramm Effect: Both of the top finishers in the 2000 Republican Presidential primary, George W. Bush and John S. McCain, had endorsed then U.S. Senator Phil Gramm (R-TX) in his failed bid for the GOP nomination for President in 1996.

Michigan Pendulum Swings: From 1968-1988, Michigan voted for the Republican Presidential nominee in every Presidential election. To the contrary, it has voted for the Democratic Presidential candidate every year since 1992.

Shivercrats: In 1952 some conservative Texas Democrats, including Governor Allan Shivers, endorsed Republican Presidential nominee Dwight D. Eisenhower over Democrat Adlai Stevenson. The more liberal bloodline of the Texas Democratic Party mocked these Democrats as "Shivercrats."

Allan Shivers
Texas State Library and Archives

The Primogeniture Republican Party: In 1976, President Gerald R. Ford won the Republican Presidential nomination. Former California Governor Ronald Reagan came in second. In 1980, Ronald Reagan won the nomination with former CIA director George H.W. Bush finishing in second place. In 1988, George H.W. Bush garnered the party's nomination with U.S. Senate Minority Leader Robert J. Dole (R-KS) coming in second. In 1996, Robert J. Dole mustered the party's nomination. Breaking the pattern. Patrick J. Buchanan finished in second place in 1996 and did not win the nomination in 2000. The nomination instead went to Texas Governor George W. Bush, with U.S. Senator John McCain (R-AZ) coming in second place. The pattern continued in 2000, with John McCain winning the GOP nomination in 2008.

Don't Blame Me. I'm From Massachusetts: Massachusetts was the only state carried by Democrat George McGovern in the 1972 Presidential Election. Republican President Richard M. Nixon took every other state including McGovern's home state of South Dakota. During and after the Watergate Affair, some Massachusetts residents donned bumper stickers exclaiming: "Don't blame me. I'm From Massachusetts."

George McGovern
Library of Congress

Four Way Race and the Electoral College: In the 1860 Presidential election, Northern Democrat Stephen A. Douglas won 29.5% of the popular vote, yet garnered just 12 electoral votes. By contrast, Southern Democrat John C. Breckinridge garnered just 18.1% of the vote yet garnered 72 electoral votes. The Constitutional Union candidate John C. Bell mustered just 12.6% of the vote, yet won 39 electoral votes. Accordingly, Douglas finished second in the popular vote behind the winner, Republican Abraham Lincoln, yet finished fourth in the Electoral College.

JB: In 1860 two of the major Presidential Nominees had the same initials. These individuals were Southern Democrat John Breckenridge and John Bell of the Constitutional Union Party.

125

Sock it To Me: In 1968, both the Republican and Democratic nominees, Richard M. Nixon and Hubert Humphrey, were invited to appear on the television show *Rowan and Martin's Laugh-In.* Nixon scored political points by showing his humorous side by declaring: "Sock it to Me." This was a catchphrase on the program. Under normal circumstances the person saying this suffered the fate of having water poured on them. Nixon did not suffer that fate. Humphrey declined to appear on the program and later said it may have cost him the election.

Richard M. Nixon on *Rowan and Martin's Laugh-In*

Carter Political Operative Wrestles Reptile for Money: In 1980, Terry McAuliffe, the National Finance Director for Jimmy Carter's re-election campaign, wrestled a 260-pound alligator in return for a contribution of $15,000 from Seminole chief Jim Billie.

Clinton and Perot Born Near Each Other: Two of the three major candidates for President in 1992 were born in municipalities just 30 miles from each other. Democratic nominee Bill Clinton was born in Hope, Arkansas, while Independent H. Ross Perot was born in Texarkana, Texas.

Presidential Candidate Stands by his Principles: U.S. Senator Stuart Symington (D-MO 1953-1976) refused to speak to racially segregated audiences during his failed 1960 bid for the Democratic Presidential nomination.

Stuart Symington
Harry S. Truman Library and Museum

Peculiar Coincidence: Both of the Democratic Presidential nominees in 1988 and in 1992 were incumbent Governors who had lost their first try at re-election. Michael Dukakis was elected as Governor of Massachusetts in 1974 but he lost renomination to Ed King in 1978. Dukakis came back in 1982 and beat King for the nomination, then won the general election. Bill Clinton won the Governorship of Arkansas in 1978 but was dislodged in 1980 by Republican Frank White (At the time Arkansas had 2-year terms), after a tough, hard-hitting primary, Bill Clinton won the nomination of the Democratic Party in 1982, and then beat White in a rematch for the Governorship.

New York, New York: In 1944, the Democrats nominated Franklin D. Roosevelt for a fourth term as President. Roosevelt was also a former Governor of New York. The Republicans nominated Thomas E. Dewey to run against Roosevelt. Coincidentally, Dewey was the incumbent Governor of New York.

High Water Mark for the American Communist Party: In 1932, William Z. Foster, the Presidential nominee of the Communist Party USA, garnered 102,000 votes, finishing in fourth place: the best showing for any Communist Party in a U.S. Presidential election.

William Z. Foster
Library of Congress

McCain Outperforms low Bush Job Approval Rating: On Election Day of 2008, outgoing Republican President George W. Bush suffered from a job approval rating of just 28%. The Party's nominee, John McCain, won 45.7% of the vote.

George W. Bush with John McCain and Cindy McCain
White House Photograph by Chris Greenberg

Young Man for a Big Job: Terry McAuliffe became the National Finance Director for President Jimmy Carter's 1980 re-election campaign, at the young age of 22.

The "Free" Republican Candidate: The first Republican Nominee for President was former Military Governor and U.S. Senator John C. Fremont of California. Freemont lost the 1856 Presidential election to Democrat James Buchanan, but he had an inimical catch phrase: "Free Soil, Free Men, Fremont."

John C. Freemont
Kansas Historical Society

Big Name Senators Lose Re-Election bids: In 1980, two of the candidates for the Democratic Presidential nomination in 1976 lost their re-election bids in the U.S. Senate. They were U.S. Senators Birch Bayh (D-IN) and Frank Church (D-ID).

The Battle of the Speakers: In 1844, the two major party nominees for President, Democrat James K. Polk and Whig Henry Clay, were both former Speakers of the U.S. House of Representatives. Whig Henry Clay served as Speaker from 1821-1823. Polk served as Speaker from 1835-1839. Polk won the race and remains the only former Speaker of the House to become President.

CREEP: Richard M. Nixon's 1972 re-election campaign committee, "The Committee for the Re-election of the President," had the unfortunate acronym, "CRP." His critics mockingly put two ee's after the r and called the committee "CREEP."

Richard M. Nixon
Richard M. Nixon Library and Museum

Reagan Tries to Balance the Ticket: In 1976, former California Governor and Presidential Candidate Ronald Reagan inflamed many of his conservative supporters before the Republican National Convention. He announced that if he garnered the Presidential nomination he would select U.S. Senator Richard Schweiker (R-PA), a moderate, as his running mate. This was a move to propitiate establishment Republicans, who were afraid Reagan would be too conservative to win the general election. Reagan lost the nomination to President Gerald R. Ford.

Richard Schweiker
Official Photograph

The Elephant in the Room: In John McCain's 2008 Acceptance Speech at the Republican National Convention, he never mentioned the name of the incumbent Republican President, George W. Bush.

George W. Bush
White House Photograph by Eric Draper

William Jennings Bryan finally gets it: After losing the Presidency for a third time in 1908, Democratic nominee William Jennings Bryan deadpanned: "I'm beginning to think those fellows don't want me in there."

William Jennings Bryan
Library of Congress

Free-For-All At The Electoral College: In 1872, Horace Greeley, the nominee of the Liberal Republicans and the Democratic Party, died before the Electoral College met to cast their votes. Greeley had lost the election, mustering just 66 electoral votes. Four non-candidates received the votes of the electors pledged to Greeley. The leading vote-getter was the newly-inaugurated Governor of Indiana, Thomas Andrews. Ulysses S. Grant was re-elected to a second term.

Horace Greeley
Library of Congress

Money Don't "Always" Buy You Electoral Votes: U.S. Senator George McGovern (D-SD), the Democratic Presidential nominee in 1972, spent more than four times as much money as the party's 1968 nominee, Vice President Hubert Humphrey. However, Humphrey won 191 electoral votes, while McGovern secured just 17 electoral votes.

Ignominious Distinction: The only two Republican Presidential nominees to lose the election between 1860 and 1912 were former Secretary of State James G. Blaine in 1884, and President Benjamin Harrison in 1892. Both men lost to Grover Cleveland.

"Anybody But Grant" Strategy Fails: 1872 was the only year since it's founding that the Democrats did not nominate their own Presidential candidate. A third-party, known as the Liberal Republicans, which had a similar platform to the Democrats, nominated a redoubtable candidate Horace Greeley, the Publisher of the *New York Tribune*. The Democrats did not want to split the anti-Grant vote (Republican President and Republican nominee Ulysses S. Grant), so they joined the Liberal Republicans in nominating Greeley. Greeley lost the election.

Ulysses S. Grant
Library of Congress

Deep Southern States Shift Partisan Loyalties: Alabama and Mississippi voted for the Democratic Presidential candidate every year between 1876 and 1964. However, since 1964, both states have voted for the Republican Presidential nominee every year excluding 1976 when southerner Jimmy Carter was the Democratic nominee.

Going Green in Spirit Only? Although Consumer Advocate Ralph Nader was the Presidential nominee of the Green Party in both 1996 and in 2000, he was never a registered member of the party. In fact, he was registered as an Independent.

You can pick on my family, but not on my Dog: Franklin D. Roosevelt had a Scottish Terrier named Fala. His beloved pet was mistakenly left behind when he departed the Aleutian Islands. Not willing to lose his companion, Roosevelt used taxpayer's money to send a ship back to retrieve his dog. The Republicans made political hay out of this in 1944, when Roosevelt was seeking an unprecedented fourth term as President. Roosevelt had no apologies, saying: "You can criticize me, my wife and my family, but you can't criticize my little dog. He's Scotch and all allegations about spending all this money have just made his little soul furious." This is now referred to as "The Fala speech." Roosevelt won that election. The Franklin D. Roosevelt Memorial in Washington, D.C. includes a statue of Fala.

Franklin D. Roosevelt Memorial
National Parks Service

Like Father, Unlike Son: In 1940 Joseph Kennedy Sr. supported Franklin D. Roosevelt in his bid to win an unprecedented third term as President. Kennedy's oldest son, Joseph Kennedy Jr., was a delegate to the Democratic National Convention for James Farley, who was running against Roosevelt for the nomination. Roosevelt garnered the nomination by winning the support of 946 delegates, while Farley mustered just 72 delegates.

Dichotomy Between Electoral College and Popular Vote: In the 1968 Presidential election, Republican Richard M. Nixon defeated Democrat Hubert Humphrey by less than one percentage point in the popular vote, yet in the Electoral College, Nixon won by over 100 electoral votes.

Richard M. Nixon
Executive Office of the President

Mugwamps Make History: In 1884, New York Governor Grover Cleveland, the Democratic nominee for President, won his home state by just 1,149 votes. New York was the deciding state in this extremely close election. Cleveland secured his home state in part due to support from "clean-government" minded Republicans who saw Cleveland as a Governor who had challenged the corrupt New York political system. They harbored an aversion to their party's nominee, James G. Blain, because of allegations of corruption. These Democratic defectors were known derisively as "Mugwamps" (Algonquian term for important person). *New York Sun* editor Charles Anderson Dana used the term satirically, comparing them to self-appointed moralists.

Electoral Microcosm: Delaware voted for the winner of the Presidential election every year from 1952 to 1996.

Watch who you praise: In 1920, Franklin D. Roosevelt praised Herbert Hoover for his role as U.S. Food Administrator during WWI. "He Certainly is a Wonder, and I wish we could make him President. There couldn't be a better one." Hoover went on to become President in 1929 and lost his re-election bid to Roosevelt in 1932.

Herbert Hoover and Franklin D. Roosevelt
Library of Congress

The Presidency is No Big Deal: In the 1900 Presidential election, Democratic activists convinced the enormously popular U.S. Navy Admiral George Dewey to seek the Democratic Presidential nomination. The Admiral was fresh from victory in the Spanish-American War. However, Dewey's candidacy imploded when he said publicly: "I am convinced that the office of the President is not such a very difficult one to fill."

Admiral George Dewey
Library of Congress

Cornhusker Pioneer: In 1940, U.S. Senator Gladys Pyle (R-NE 1939-1940) became the first female to nominate a Presidential candidate at a major political party's convention. She nominated the eventual Republican nominee, Utilities executive Wendell Willkie.

Gladys Pyle
Library of Congress

Garden State Disses Favorite Son: In 1916, Woodrow Wilson was re-elected as President, despite losing his home state of New Jersey. Wilson had been Governor of the Garden State just four years earlier.

Woodrow Wilson
Official Portrait

Empire State Loses Electoral Hegemony: From 1812-1968, New York had the most electoral votes. Its high watermark was 47 in the 1930's. It has since been supplanted by California, which gave its record 55 electoral votes to Barack Obama in 2008.

The Staph Infection that May have Changed the World: Richard M. Nixon blamed his narrow loss in the 1960 Presidential election on a staph infection he suffered after bumping his knee on a car door while campaigning in Greensboro, North Carolina. The malady took Nixon off of the campaign trail for two weeks. He was still recovering during the first Presidential debate against John F. Kennedy and many viewers thought he appeared ill.

Richard M. Nixon
Library of Congress

The Top Team Re-elected: In 1916, Woodrow Wilson and Thomas Riley Marshall became the first President and Vice President to be re-elected since James Monroe and Daniel D. Tompkins in 1820.

Campaign Poster for Woodrow Wilson and Thomas Riley Marshall
Library of Congress

African-American Political Pioneer: The first African-American to be nominated for President of the United State by a political party was Wisconsin Labor Publisher George Edwin Taylor. He captured the nomination of the National Negro Liberty Party, which advocated for the rights of African-Americans and other minorities.

George Edwin Taylor
The Quincy Daily Journal of Quincy, Illinois, on August 25, 1897

Prior to the Republican-Democratic Hegemony: The last Presidential election where the winner was neither a Republican nor a Democrat was in 1848, when the Whig Party ticket of Presidential nominee Zachary Taylor and Vice Presidential nominee Millard Fillmore were elected.

Campaign Poster for Taylor and Fillmore
Library of Congress

Father-in-Law Issues: In 1912, former President Theodore Roosevelt left the Republican Party and ran for President as the nominee of the Progressive Party (a.k.a. Bull Mouse Party). Roosevelt's Son-and-Law, Nicholas Longworth, who was married to Roosevelt's daughter Alice Roosevelt, was a Republican member of the U.S. House of Representatives from Ohio. Longworth supported the Republican nominee, which was William Howard Taft. Both Roosevelt and Taft lost the election to Democrat Woodrow Wilson.

Alice and Nicholas Longworth
Library of Congress

They were "a part of it:" From 1920-1944, the Democratic Party nominated a New York resident to every national ticket save one. In 1920, Franklin D. Roosevelt was the Vice Presidential nominee. In 1928, New York Governor Al Smith topped the ticket as the Presidential nominee. Franklin D. Roosevelt topped the ticket in 1932, 1936, 1940, and 1944. The only year a New Yorker failed to make the ticket was in 1924, when the party nominated John W. Davis of West Virginia, and Charles W. Bryan of Nebraska.

New York State Flag

An Assassination Attempt Will Not Stop a Bull Moose: In 1912, before a campaigning stop in Milwaukee, former President Theodore Roosevelt (the nominee of the Progressive Party, a.k.a. the Bull Moose Party) was shot in the chest by tavern operator John Schrank, a manic-depressive. While aids urged Roosevelt to go immediately to the hospital, he insisted on first delivering his scheduled speech. Roosevelt was not coughing blood, and the bullet had not infiltrated his chest, but blood was seeping though his chest. He gave a ninety-minute oration, opening by telling the crowd " . . . I have just been shot; but it takes more than that to kill a Bull Moose." That was the last campaign event he made, spending the rest of the election season recovering from the wound. The bullet was never dislodged from Roosevelt's chest due to the fact that the doctors believed the process of removing the bullet could be fatal.

Theodore Roosevelt
Library of Congress

Hoosiers Swing: The state with the biggest electoral divergence between 2004 and 2008 was Indiana. Republican George W. Bush won the state with a formidable 60% of the vote in 2004. In 2008, Democrat Barack Obama won it with 50% of the vote.

FDR Stabbed in the Back: In 1924, Franklin D. Roosevelt supported the re-election bid of his fellow Democrat, New York Governor Al Smith, over Roosevelt's cousin, Republican nominee Theodore Roosevelt Jr. He gave a nominating speech that year at the Democratic National Convention, nominating Smith for President. However, Smith did not return the favor. In fact, during Roosevelt's Presidency, Smith became a critic of Roosevelt and Roosevelt's domestic program: the New Deal, and even endorsed his Republican opponents in 1936 and 1940 (Alfred Landon and Wendell Willkie respectively).

Franklin D. Roosevelt with Al Smith
Franklin D. Roosevelt Presidential Library and Museum

When New England was Republican Country: In the 1932 Presidential election, Republican President Herbert Hoover won just six states, five of which were in the Northeast.

Herbert Hoover campaigning for re-election in 1932
National Archives and Records Administration

Party Pooper Pays Price for Crossing Party Line: U.S. Representative John Bell Williams (D-MS) defied his party in 1964 and endorsed Republican Presidential nominee Barry Goldwater over Democratic nominee, Lyndon B. Johnson. For this betrayal, the Democratic leadership stripped Williams of the eighteen years of seniority he had accumulated. Nevertheless, Williams remained a Democrat and in 1967 was elected as Governor of Mississippi. Throughout his life Williams continued to support Republican nominees at the Presidential level.

John Bell Williams
Official Photograph

Barrack's "Got Game:" Ritualistically, Barack Obama plays basketball with friends on Election Days.

Barack Obama on the Basketball Court
U.S. Navy Photograph

President Calls Opponents Bozos: At a 1992 campaign rally in Warren, Michigan, President George H.W. Bush lashed out at his Democratic opponents Bill Clinton and Al Gore saying: "My Dog Millie Knows More About Foreign Affairs than these two bozos." Bush lost the election.

Millie
George Bush Presidential Library and Museum

No Opposition: Two Presidents have been re-elected without opposition. They were George Washington in 1792, and James Monroe in 1820. Only Washington won the votes of all electors in the Electoral College. In 1820, a New-Hampshire elector who had been pledged to Monroe selected Secretary of State John Quincy Adams instead. The New Hampshire elector believed that George Washington should be the only President to sweep the Electoral College.

Mountaineer State Disconnect with the National Democratic Party: In 2008, Republican John McCain defeated Democrat Barack Obama in West Virginia by 13-percentage points. In contrast, Democrats in West Virginia won every constitutional office and gained seats in the Democratically-controlled State Senate.

Texas No Longer Vital to Democrats: Prior to 1992, no Democrat had won the Presidency without carrying Texas. Since then, Democrats Bill Clinton in 1992 and 1996 and Barack Obama in 2008 both won the Presidency handily without carrying the Lone Star State.

If only Reagan had campaigned harder for Me: During the summer of 1976, Democratic Presidential nominee Jimmy Carter held a 34-point lead over Republican President Gerald R. Ford. Ford almost closed the gap, just losing the election by two percentage points. Ford believed that had former California Governor Ronald Reagan campaigned for him with conservative Democrats in the South that he would have won the election. Reagan had challenged Ford in the Republican Primary and was popular with the conservative base. To Ford's dismay, Reagan had other commitments and spent limited time on the campaign trail.

Ronald Reagan and Gerald R. Ford at the 1976 Republican National Convention
Gerald R. Ford Presidential Library and Museum

An Extra Special Birthday: Warren G. Harding was the only President to be elected on his birthday. He was elected on November 2, 1920, his fifty-fifth birthday.

Warren G. Harding
Library of Congress

135

Ephemeral Republican Gains: Voters were disillusioned by the economic conditions of the country under President Harry S. Truman in 1946. Republicans won control of both Houses of the U.S. Congress by running on the slogan: "Had Enough?" Two years later the Republicans lost both Houses and Truman won a full term as President.

Harry S. Truman
Harry S. Truman Library and Museum

Curing the Rival Syndrome: Prior to ratification of the Twelfth Amendment to the *U.S. Constitution* in 1804, Presidents and Vice Presidents were not elected on the same ticket. The candidate who garnered the most electoral votes would become President and the candidate who received the second most votes would become Vice President. The U.S. House of Representatives was required to determine the President in case of a tie. This happened in 1804, when Thomas Jefferson and Aaron Burr, both members of the Democratic-Republican Party, tied and the Federalist controlled House selected Jefferson.

Not the Most Popular Endorsement: The Communist Party USA has not nominated a Presidential candidate since 1984. Its default position is to support the Democratic Presidential nominee.

Partisanship Gone Wild: During the 1976 Vice Presidential Debate, Republican Robert J. Dole asserted that all major wars in the twentieth century were started by Democratic Presidents: "I figured it up the other day: If we added up the killed and wounded in Democrat wars in this century, it would be about 1.6 million Americans — enough to fill the city of Detroit." Dole later said he regretted making this remark.

Robert J. Dole Debating Walter Mondale
Gerald R. Ford Library and Museum

Two Jobs, But No Pay: In 1968, former Postmaster General Larry O'Brien served as both Chairman of Democratic Presidential nominee Hubert Humphrey's Presidential Campaign Committee and as Chairman of the Democratic National Committee. He performed both jobs pro bono.

Larry O'Brien
Official Photograph as Post Master General

The Revenge of William McKinley: In 1889, U.S. Representative and future President William McKinley (R-OH) lost a bid to become Speaker of the U.S. House of Representatives to U.S. Representative Thomas Bracket Reed (R-ME) on the third ballot. In 1896, just seven years later, the two competed for the Republican Presidential nomination and McKinley defeated Reed.

William McKinley
Library of Congress

What About Electoral University or Electoral State College: The term "Electoral College" is not mentioned in the *U.S. Constitution*. The provision of the Constitution establishing our electoral system, Article 11 Section 1 Clause 11 states: "Each State shall appoint, in such Manner as the Legislature thereof may direct, a Number of Electors, equal to the whole Number of Senators and Representatives to which the State may be entitled in the Congress: but no Senator or Representative, or Person holding an Office of Trust or Profit under the United States, shall be appointed an Elector." The phrase "Electoral College" was not enshrined into a federal statute until 1845.

Bryan stumps for Himself: In 1896, Democratic Presidential nominee William Jennings Bryan broke precedent by barnstorming the nation, campaigning for himself. He delivered over 600 speeches in 27 states. Prior to this, candidates used surrogates to campaign for them, and only spoke to voters who came to their hometowns to visit them.

William Jennings Bryan
Library of Congress

A Conflicted Electorate: In 1956, President Dwight D. Eisenhower became the first Republican Presidential nominee since Rutherford B. Hayes (in 1876) to be elected or to be re-elected with a Democratic U.S. Congress.

Dwight D. Eisenhower
Harry S. Truman Library and Museum

MacArthur Fades Away: In 1952, U.S. Senator Robert A. Taft (R-OH) persuaded General Douglas MacArthur to be his running mate should he garner the Republican Presidential nomination. This ticket never came to fruition because Dwight D. Eisenhower mustered the nomination, after a hard fought battle.

Robert A. Taft
Official Portrait

The Out-Migration of the African-American Republicans: In 1956, Republican President Dwight D. Eisenhower garnered 39% of the African-American vote in his re-election bid. In 1960, Republican Presidential Nominee Richard M. Nixon mustered 32% of the African-American vote. In 1964, Republican Presidential Nominee Barry Goldwater, who as a U.S. Senator had voted against the Civil Rights Act of 1964, garnered just 6% of the African-American vote.

Young Man With Big Dream: In 1896, The Democratic Party nominated 36-year old William Jennings Bryan for President. He remains the youngest Presidential nominee of a major party in history.

William Jennings Bryan
Library of Congress

America was Watching: At least 120 million Americans viewed some of the four 1960 Presidential debates between Democrat John F. Kennedy and Republican Richard M. Nixon.

John F. Kennedy and Richard M. Nixon
Richard M. Nixon Foundation

Ventura goes his own Way: In 2008, Minnesota Governor Jesse Ventura bucked pleas to endorse a Presidential candidate from either the Democratic or Republican Parties. Instead, he endorsed Natural Law Party candidate John Hagelin, a quantum physicist and an advocate of transcendental meditation.

First To Vote: Under a New Hampshire statute, municipalities and townships with less than 100 citizens are permitted to open their polls on election days at midnight and close them once every vote has been cast. During the New Hampshire primary and in the Presidential election, the first votes are cast in Harts Location, New Hampshire (with a population of under 40) and Dixville Notch (with a population of under 80). By tradition, Dixville Notch's most famous resident, Republican Neil Tillotson, who invented latex gloves and latex balloons, cast the first vote in both the primary and in the general election. After his death at 102 in 2001, the first voter is now selected by lottery.

When the Loan Star State was Political Ground Zero: In 1992, all three major Presidential candidates made campaign stops in Texas the day before the general election. Republican nominee George H.W. Bush won the state with 40.56% of the vote. Democratic nominee Bill Clinton came in second with 37.08% of the vote, and Independent H. Ross Perot came in third with 22.01% of the vote.

Bill Clinton, George H.W. Bush, and H. Ross Perot
George Bush Presidential Library

Making History without Even Trying: In 1872, the Equal Rights Party nominated Civil Rights Leader Frederick Douglass as its Vice Presidential nominee without even consulting Douglass. Douglass did not campaign or actively do anything to support the party's Presidential nominee, Victoria Woodhull. Nonetheless, Douglass made history becoming the first African-American to be nominated to a national ticket.

Frederick Douglass
National Archives and Records Administration

Circumventing the *U.S. Constitution*: Electors are barred in the *U.S. Constitution* from voting for both a Presidential and Vice Presidential candidate from their home state. The Twelfth Amendment reads: "The Electors shall meet in their respective states, and vote by ballot for President and Vice President, one of whom, at least, shall not be an inhabitant of the same state with themselves. . . ." In 2000, the Republican nominee-apparent George W. Bush was set to select Halliburton CEO Dick Cheney as his Vice- Presidential running-mate. There was one problem. Both Bush and Cheney were residents of Texas. Bush lived in Austin where he was serving as Texas Governor. Cheney was living in Highland Park, Texas. Accordingly, Cheney changed his voter registration to his native state of Wyoming, where he also owned a residence. The Bush/Cheney team won Texas in the general election and the 32 Bush electors were free to vote for both men.

Dick Cheney and George W. Bush
White House Photograph by David Bohrer

Ralph Nader Performs well with the Lebanese Americans: In 2000, Green Party Presidential Nominee Ralph Nader (who is of Lebanese descent) garnered 13% of the Arab-American vote. Nationally, Nader garnered just 2.74% of the vote.

Truman Disses Kennedy: Former U.S. President Harry S. Truman supported U.S. Senator Stuart Symington (D-MO) in his bid for the Democratic Presidential nomination in 1960. Truman urged U.S. Senator John F. Kennedy (D-MA) to reconsider his bid for the nomination. Truman stated publicly about Kennedy: "I have no doubt about the political heights that you are destined to rise, but I am deeply troubled about the situation we are up against in the world now and in the immediate future. That is why I hope someone with the greatest possible maturity and experience may be available at this time. May I urge you to be patient?" Truman maintained that the Democratic National Convention was manipulated so that Kennedy would muster the nomination. In protest Truman refused to attend the convention as a delegate. When asked whom he would support if Symington lost the nomination, Truman deadpanned: "I have no second choice." Once Kennedy secured the nomination, Truman became a loyal foot soldier, barnstorming the country campaigning for Kennedy.

John F. Kennedy and Harry S. Truman
Harry S. Truman Library and Museum

The Plumed Knight: Former Illinois Attorney General Robert F. Ingersoll delivered the Presidential nominating speech in 1876 for former Speaker of the U.S. House of Representatives James G. Blaine (R-ME 1869-1875) at the Republican National Convention. Ingersoll dubbed Blaine: "The Plumed Knight" (Blaine was like a medieval knight who fought against adversity and his political opponents' rhetoric). Blaine lost the nomination to Ohio Governor Rutherford B. Hayes, but the nickname "the plumed knight" stuck throughout his political career.

James G. Blaine
Library of Congress

Public Humiliation: The Vice President is responsible for presiding over the U.S. Senate when the Electoral College returns are officially announced. Losing Presidential candidates Richard M. Nixon in 1960, Hubert Humphrey in 1968, and Al Gore in 2000, in their capacity as Vice President, had to make the official announcement of their own defeats.

No Opposition: There have been only three times in American history when a Presidential candidate faced no electoral opposition. In 1789 and 1792 George Washington had no opposition, and in 1820, President James Monroe faced no opposition

Garfield by a Whisker: In the 1880 Presidential election, Republican James Garfield defeated Democrat Winfield S. Hancock by just 7,368 popular votes. In the Electoral College the margin was much wider with Garfield garnering 214 votes and Hancock mustering just 155 votes.

James Garfield
Library of Congress

One Big Step for African-American Women: In 1976 U.S. Representative Barbara Jordan (D-TX) delivered the Keynote Address at the Democratic National Convention. She was the first African-American female to give a keynote address at a major party's political convention.

Barbara Jordan Speaking at the 1976 Democratic National Convention.
Library of Congress

Kansans to Landon: You're OK as our Governor, but not as our President: In 1934, during the first mid-term election of Franklin Roosevelt's Presidency, only one Republican Governor, Kansas's Alfred Landon was re-elected. Landon won the Republican Presidential nomination two years later, but he only garnered eight electoral votes. Landon even lost his home state of Kansas to Roosevelt.

Alfred Landon
Official Photograph

Anatomy of a Landslide Victory: In the 1972 49-state landslide by Republican President Richard M. Nixon over Democratic Presidential nominee George McGovern, Nixon garnered 94% of Republican voters, 66% of Independents, and an astounding 42% of Democratic voters.

Richard M. Nixon
Richard M. Nixon Library and Museum

Now "This" is Embarrassing: Although Jimmy Carter garnered momentum from finishing above all Democratic Candidates in the 1976 Iowa Caucuses (garnering 29% of the vote), he finished ten points behind the winner, which was none other than: "None of the above."

Jimmy Carter
Library of Congress

But Who's Counting? There have been Fifty-Six Presidential elections.

Reagan's Coattails Extend to U.S. Senate: In the 1980 election, Republican Presidential Nominee Ronald Reagan cruised to a 44-state landslide victory. In addition to this victory, his Republican Party captured control of the U.S. Senate for the first time since 1952.

Ronald Reagan
The Ronald Reagan Presidential Foundation and Library

Another Happy Warrior: In his 1964 Presidential campaign, Democratic Vice Presidential nominee Hubert Humphrey flew in an Electra aircraft with the name "Happy Warrior" painted on it. Minnesota Governor Karl Rovagg called Humphrey "The Happy Warrior of our Generation." The term "Happy Warrior" had entered the American Political lexicon in 1924 when former Assistant U.S. Secretary of the Navy Franklin D. Roosevelt used the term "Happy Warrior" in his speech nominating New York Governor Al Smith for President at the Democratic National Convention.

Hubert Humphrey
Lyndon Baines Johnson Library and Museum

Ted K Asserts, "No Way:" In 1968, Democratic Presidential Nominee Hubert Humphrey tried to persuade U.S. Senator Edward M. Kennedy, just 36 years old, to become his Vice Presidential running-mate. Kennedy turned him down because he disagreed with Humphrey's support of the U.S. involvement in the Vietnam War. Kennedy also had family concerns.

Edward M. Kennedy
Library of Congress

Lopsided Election: The most electoral votes ever allocated to a Presidential candidate were given to Ronald Reagan in 1984. Reagan garnered 525 electoral votes. His Democratic opponent, Walter Mondale, mustered just 13 electoral votes.

Ronald Reagan and Walter Mondale
Ronald Reagan Presidential Library and Museum

Tippecanoe and Tyler Too: William Henry Harrison was the first Presidential candidate to have a campaign slogan. The slogan was: "Tippecanoe and Tyler Too." Harrison was nicknamed "Old Tippecanoe" for his role as Governor of the Indiana Territory in squelching an Indian insurrection at the Tippecanoe River. John Tyler was the Vice Presidential nominee. Harrison and Tyler won the election. The campaign slogan was eventually abbreviated to "Tip & Ty."

Campaign Sign for Tip & Ty
Ross County Historical Society, Chillicothe, Ohio

Young Roosevelt Deserts Democrats: After his fathers' death, John Roosevelt, the son of Franklin D. Roosevelt, became an active Republican, campaigning for the Party's Presidential nominee Dwight D. Eisenhower in 1952. His mother Eleanor and his four siblings backed Democratic nominee Adlai Stevenson.

John and Eleanor Roosevelt
Franklin D. Roosevelt Presidential Library and Museum

When Maine was a Republican Citadel: Between 1856 and 1960, Maine voted for the Republican Presidential nominee every year with the exception of 1912, when it voted for Democrat Woodrow Wilson.

Maine Official State Seal

A Long Time Coming: In 1960, Richard M. Nixon became the first incumbent Vice President to win the nomination of his political party for President since Martin Van Buren in 1836.

Richard M. Nixon
Library of Congress

Jimmy Who? In 1974, two years before winning the Presidency, *Harris Interactive* released a poll of potential Democratic Presidential candidates in 1976. Thirty-five potential Democratic candidates showed up in the poll. Georgia Governor Jimmy Carter's name did not even show up on the list. Carter went on to win the 1976 Democratic Presidential nomination and was elected President.

Jimmy Carter
Jimmy Carter Library and Museum

On the Electoral Sidelines: In the 2008 General election, 35 states received no appearances by the major Presidential candidates. When campaigning for President, candidates show great deference to electorally competitive states.

The College of Hard Knocks: In the 2000 Presidential election, Independent H. Ross Perot garnered almost 20 million votes (18.9% of the popular vote), yet did not win a single electoral vote.

H. Ross Perot
U.S. Department of Veteran's Affairs

Dole Rocks Around the Clock: In 1996, Republican Presidential nominee Robert J. Dole spent the last 96 hours of the campaign on a non-stop tour of the country. He ended the trip in Independence, Missouri, the hometown of Harry S. Truman. This was symbolic because Dole used Truman as the archetype of an underdog who won in a major upset. Unlike Truman, Dole could not pull-off a come-from-behind victory. But some credit his effort with galvanizing the Republican base and keeping the U.S. Congress in Republican hands.

Robert J. Dole
Library of Congress

144

Supporter Inadvertently May Have Cost Candidate the Presidency: A few days before the 1884 Presidential election, Republican Presidential nominee James G. Blaine made a campaign appearance in New York, where Presbyterian Minister Samuel Burchard, a Blaine supporter, excoriated the Democrats as the Party of "Rum, Romanticism, and Rebellion." Blaine sat silently during this tirade and made no effort to disassociate himself from these volatile remarks. Unfortunately for the unsuspecting Blaine, many Irish voters took umbrage by the use of the word "rum," believing that the Minister was perpetuating a stereotype that Irish-Americans, who were mostly Democrats, were alcoholics. This galvanized the Irish vote against Blaine in the swing state of New York, where Democrat Grover Cleveland eked out a razor-thin victory, defeating Blaine by just 1,047 votes. New York proved to be the state that made the electoral difference in a very close Presidential election.

James G. Blaine
Library of Congress

The Battle of the Southpaws: In both the 1992, and 2008, general elections, all major Presidential candidates were left-handed. In 1992, Democrat Bill Clinton, Republican George H.W. Bush, and Independent H. Ross Perot were lefties, as were Democrat Barack Obama and Republican John McCain in 2008.

Impavid Mayor Divides Democrats: Minneapolis Mayor Hubert Humphrey delivered an impassioned speech at the 1948 Democratic National Convention in Philadelphia, urging the adoption of a "minority plank" which would commit the party to oppose racial segregation. The plank was narrowly ratified by the Convention. Consequently, thirty-five Southern Convention delegates left the Convention in protest. These delegates subsequently supported the candidacy of Strom Thurmond, the nominee of the States Rights Democratic Party over the Democratic Party's nominee, President Harry S. Truman. Truman went on to win the 1948 election.

Hubert Humphrey addresses the 1948 Democratic National Convention
Library of Congress

Keeping a Dull-Witted Pledge can cost you at the Polls: In 1960, Richard M. Nixon, the Republican Presidential candidate, made a public pledge that he would campaign in all 50 states. This proved an electoral hindrance because he spent too much time campaigning in non-competitive states. The weekend before the election Nixon campaigned in electoral meager Alaska, while his Democratic opponent, John F. Kennedy, campaigned in showdown states. Kennedy eked out a close victory.

Bush Sr's Electoral Setback: In the 1988 Republican Iowa Caucuses, Vice President George H.W. Bush was embarrassed by finishing third behind U.S. Senate Minority Leader Robert Dole (R-KS) and televangelist Pat Robertson. This was an especially embarrassing defeat because Bush had won the Iowa Caucuses in his unsuccessful 1980 run. Nevertheless, Bush recovered and won the nomination and the Presidency.

George H.W. Bush campaigning for President in 1988
George Bush Presidential Library and Museum

The Origins of the American Political Convention: The first national political convention in America was held in 1831 by the American Party, a.k.a. The Know Nothing Party. The party nominated former U.S. Attorney General William Wirt as its Presidential nominee in the 1832 election. Wirt garnered 7.8% of the popular vote, winning just one state, Vermont.

William Wirt
Library of Congress

Obama Garners the Muslim Vote: According to a survey taken by the American Muslim Taskforce on Civil Rights and Elections, 88.9% of Muslim voters in the 2008 Presidential election supported the Democratic Presidential Nominee, Barack Obama.

Barack Obama
White House Photograph by Pete Souza

Getting Your Name to Appear on the Presidential Primary Ballot in New Hampshire: Not as Hard as You Might Think: To appear on the ballot as a candidate for President in the New Hampshire Primary, the requirements are less onerous than one might think. All that is required is that a candidate be Constitutionally eligible to become President and pay a $1,000 fee. In 2008 23 names appeared on the Republican ballot while 21 names appeared on the Democratic Ballot.

Keep the Ball Rolling: During William Henry Harrison's 1840 Presidential campaign, supporters pushed a giant ball from town to town as supporters chanted: "Keep the Ball Rolling." Hence the expression.

William Henry Harrison
Library of Congress

146

It's all in the Spin: Although Bill Clinton dubbed himself "The Comeback Kid" after his strong showing in the New Hampshire Presidential Primary, he actually came in second to former U.S. Senator Paul Tsongas (D-MA). Tsongas garnered 33.2% of the vote while Clinton mustered just 24.8% of the vote. However, Clinton stole much of the media attention from Mr. Tsongas because Clinton had finished better than expected and because Tsongas had been expected to finish strongly in New Hampshire, a neighboring state of Massachusetts.

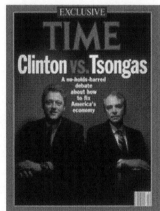

Bill Clinton and Paul Tsongas on cover of *Time Magazine*

"Soccer Mom:" The Origins of a Term: The term "soccer mom" was first seen in print in an article by *Washington Post* Political Columnist E.J. Dionne during the 1996 Presidential election. Dionne quoted Alex Castellenos, a senior media advisor to Republican Presidential Nominee Robert J. Dole, as saying that Dole's Democratic opponent, President Bill Clinton, was appealing to this demographic. A Soccer mom was defined in the article as: "the overburdened middle income working mother who ferries her kids from soccer practice to scouts to school."

Eagleton's Secret Statements: In 1972, as liberal insurgent U.S. Senator George McGovern (D-SD) was winning vital Democratic Presidential Primaries, many establishment Democrats were worried that if McGovern were to garner the nomination his liberal views would lead to an electoral landslide for Republican President Richard M. Nixon. This would bring other Democrats down with him. One of McGovern's Senate Colleagues, Thomas Eagleton, revealed to Columnist Robert Novak, as an undisclosed source: "The people don't know McGovern is for amnesty, abortion and legalization of pot. Once Middle America - Catholic middle America, in particular - finds this out, he's dead. Amnesty, Acid, and Abortion." Once McGovern mustered the nomination, his opponents called McGovern the candidate of "Amnesty, Acid, and Abortion." Without knowing that Eagleton was the originator of that quote, McGovern selected Eagleton to be his running mate. After just 18 days on the ticket, McGovern bowed to public pressure to "Dump Eagleton" when it was revealed that Eagleton had gone through electroshock therapy to cure a bout of clinical depression. Nixon would go on to trounce McGovern in the General Election. Novak did not reveal the source of the quote until 2008, after Eagleton's death.

Campaign Button for the short-lived George McGovern-Thomas Eagleton Campaign

Latinos Vote for Obama: In the 2008 Presidential election, Democrat Barack Obama garnered 67% of the Latino vote. Republican John McCain mustered just 32%.

Barack Obama
White House Photograph

Whistling Dixie: Running for re-election in 1936, Democratic President Franklin D. Roosevelt eviscerated Republican Presidential nominee Alfred Landon in the Solid South. Roosevelt garnered 87.10% of the vote in Georgia, 87.08% of the vote in Texas, 97.06% of the vote in Mississippi, and 98.57% of the vote in South Carolina.

Franklin D. Roosevelt
Franklin D. Roosevelt Presidential Library and Museum

First Results: The earliest states to close their polls on Presidential Election days are Kentucky and Indiana. Both states close them at 6:00 p.m.

Golden State Not Golden for Native Son: In the 1992 Democratic Presidential Primaries, Arkansas Governor Bill Clinton defeated Jerry Brown in California. Brown had served two terms as the state's Governor.

Jerry Brown
Official Photograph, California Attorney General

Rick Perry Once Supported Al Gore: Future Governor Rick Perry (R-TX) was the Texas Chairman for Democrat Al Gore's 1988 campaign for the Democratic Presidential nomination. Perry was a Democrat at the time.

Rick Perry
Official Photograph

Presidential Coattails Don't Always Extend to the U.S. Senate: In the 1972 election and in the 1984 election, the Republican Presidents Richard M. Nixon and Ronald Reagan, respectively, were re-elected, scoring 49-state landslide victories over their Democratic opponents. Yet, in both cases the Democrats actually gained two seats in the U.S. Senate.

When Republicans Called Themselves Liberals: The term "liberal" was not always a term of derision. In fact even Republicans called themselves liberals. In 1940, the Republican Presidential Nominee Wendell Willkie asserted: "The doctrinaires of the opposition have attempted to picture me as an opponent of liberalism, but I was a liberal before many of those men heard the word."

Wendell Willkie
Library of Congress

Most Votes Doesn't Always Guarantee Victory: There were four times in American history when the Presidential candidate who garnered the most votes lost the election because his opponent won more votes in the Electoral College. In 1824, Andrew Jackson defeated John Quincy Adams in the popular vote, but lost the Electoral vote. Likewise in 1876 Samuel Tilden won the popular vote but Rutherford B. Hayes won in the Electoral College. In 1888, Grover Cleveland won the popular vote but lost in the Electoral College to Benjamin Harrison, and in 2000, Al Gore won in the popular vote but lost to George W. Bush in the Electoral College.

The Palin Factor: According to a 2008 exit poll taken by *CNN,* of those who said that Republican Presidential nominee John McCain's decision to select then Alaska Governor Sarah Palin as his Vice Presidential running mate would factor into their vote, 56% voted for the Republican ticket and 43% voted for the Democratic ticket.

Sarah Palin on the Cover of *Time Magazine*

Palmetto State Resists Harding Wave, Big Time: In the 1920 Presidential election, Republican nominee Warren G. Harding won by over 25 percentage points nationally. However, in South Carolina, he garnered a paltry 3.91% of the vote.

Warren G. Harding
Library of Congress

Energizer Alf: Alfred Landon, the 1936 Republican Presidential nominee, lived until 100. He died in 1987.

Alfred Landon
Official Photograph

Richard J. Daley on the Record: While defending the Chicago Police Force against charges of overzealous behavior toward demonstrators during the 1968 Democratic National Convention in Chicago, Mayor Richard J. Daley told members of the media: "Gentleman – get this thing straight once and for all – the policeman is not there to create disorder, the policeman is there to preserve disorder."

Richard J. Daley
Los Angeles Times

GOP First for Asian-American: In 1964, U.S. Senator Hiram Fong (R-HI 1959-1977) became the first Asian-American to seek the Republican Party's nomination for the Presidency and the first to receive votes at that party's convention. He won the votes of the delegations of Hawaii and Alaska. U.S. Senator Barry Goldwater (R-AZ) garnered the party's nomination.

Hiram Fong
Official Photograph

How Quickly they Fall: In 1976, U.S. Senator Robert J. Dole (R-KS) was the Vice Presidential nominee of the Republican Party with President Gerald R. Ford. Four years later, as a candidate for the GOP Presidential nomination, Dole garnered less than 1% of the vote in the New Hampshire Primary. He egressed from the race.

Robert J. Dole with wife Elizabeth and President Gerald R. Ford in 1976
Gerald R. Ford Library and Museum

Part III: The U.S. Congress

U.S. House of Representatives

Mavericks Sure Can Coin a Phrase: U.S. Representative Maury Maverick (D-TX 1935-1939) was the only southern Democratic member of Congress who voted for federal anti-lynching legislation in the 1930's. The Congressman also coined the word "gobbledygook." Maverick is the grandson of Texas cattle rancher Samuel Maverick, who, because of his independent behavior, led Texans to label anyone who was Independent-Minded a "maverick."

Maury Maverick
Library of Congress

Congressman Killed by Wild Animals: In 1916, wild animals killed former U.S. Representative Jeremiah Haralson (R-AL 1875-1877) while he was on a hunting expedition in Colorado.

Jeremiah Haralson
Library of Congress

Getting Elected to Congress without Campaigning: In 1864, Major General and future President Rutherford B. Hayes was elected to represent the Second Congressional District of Ohio in the U.S. House of Representatives. He did not campaign for the office.

Rutherford B. Hayes
Library of Congress

Bloody Shirt Waves on House Floor: The phrase: "Waiving the bloody shirt" was popularized by U.S. Representative Benjamin Franklin Butler (R-MA 1867-1875 and 1877-1879). Butler was an ardent opponent of the Ku Klux Klan. He waved a shirt worn by A.P. Huggins (a Mississippi Superintendent of Schools who was beaten by members of the Klan), on the House Floor while excoriating the actions of the Klan.

Benjamin Butler
Library of Congress

Independent Republican Voice: U.S. Representative Connie Morella (R-MD 1987-2003) is the only Congressional Republican who voted against the use of force in both the Persian Gulf War in 1991 and in the Iraq War in 2002.

Connie Morella
Official Photograph

Perilous Day in the House: In 1954, four members of the National Party of Puerto Rico literally opened fire on the U.S. House floor. Though no one died, five House members were wounded. The casualties included Alvin M. Bentley (R-MN), Clifford Davis (D-TN), George Hyde Fallon (D-MD) Ben F. Jensen (R-Iowa), and Kenneth A. Roberts (D-Alabama).

Lone Dissenter: The only member of the U.S. Congress to vote against the *Authorization of Use of Force* in the wake of the September 11th hijackings was U.S. Representative Barbara Lee (D-CA).

Barbara Lee
Official Photograph

Don't You Mess with Gene: U.S. Representative Gene Taylor (D-MS 1989-2011) earned a black belt in Taekwondo.

Gene Taylor
Official Photograph

Sheriff Manages to Beat the Rap: U.S. Representative James Traficant (D-OH 1985-2002) is the only person ever to win a case under the *Racketeer Influenced and Corrupt Organizations Act* (RICO) representing himself. In 1983, while serving as Sheriff of Mahoning County, the future Congressman was acquitted on charges of racketeering and accepting bribes.

James Traficant
Official Photograph

Very Strange Bedfellows: Conservative Political Strategist Dick Morris and liberal U.S. Representative Jerrold Nadler (D-NY) were roommates at Columbia University.

Arizona Institution: Carl Hayden was elected to the at-large seat in the U.S. House of Representatives from Arizona in 1911 in a special election. This was shortly before the state was awarded statehood. He was the first House member to represent the Grand Canyon state. He served in the House from 1912-1927 and represented the state in the U.S. Senate from 1927-1969. Carl Hayden served in the U.S. Congress for over 56 years.

Carl Hayden
Library of Congress

Congressional Muslim: In 2006, Keith Ellison (D-MN) became the first Muslim elected to the U.S. Congress. He was sworn in on a *Qur'an*. During a later oath reenactment, Ellison used a *Qur'an* once owned by Thomas Jefferson.

Keith Ellison
Official Photograph

Cajun Diversity: In 2008, Anh "Joseph" Cao (R-LA) became the only American of Vietnamese descent ever elected to the U.S. Congress He was elected to the House of Representatives by voters in Louisiana's First Congressional District centered in New Orleans. The district is 64% African-American.

Anh "Joseph" Cao
Official Photograph

Former Student is "Takin' to School" by his Professor: In 1978, future U.S. Representative Chet Edwards (D-TX) lost by 115 votes in the Democratic Congressional primary to Phil Gramm. Gramm had once been Edward's Economics professor at Texas A&M University.

Chet Edwards
Official Photograph

"Show Me" State is Prepared: The Missouri Congressional delegation boasts two eagle scouts: Democrat Russ Carnahan and Republican Sam Graves.

155

A First for the Old Line State: U.S. Representative Stenny Hoyer (D-MD) is the only Marylander to serve as House Majority Leader. Hoyer served from 2007-2011.

Stenny Hoyer
Official Photograph

Madison v. Monroe: In 1788, future Presidents James Madison and James Monroe were political opponents in a race to represent the First Congressional District of Virginia. Madison won the election in a landslide victory. The two men then became allies. Monroe served as Secretary of War and as Secretary of Defense in Madison's Presidential administration.

The Inventor Congressman: U.S. Representative Roscoe Bartlett (R-MD) holds twenty patents.

Roscoe Bartlett
Official Photograph

The Assyrian Congresswoman: U.S. Representative Anna Georges Eshoo (D-CA) is the only member of the U.S. Congress of Assyrian descent.

Anna Georges Eshoo
Official Photograph

Texas Six-Pack: In 1984, Ronald Reagan's landslide win brought in six freshmen Republican members of the U.S. House of Representatives in Texas, four of whom became potent members. The six new members included; Dick Armey, Joe Barton, Beau Boulter, Larry Combast, Tom Delay, and Mac Sweeney. Both Armey and Delay later became House Majority Leader. Barton and Combast later became chairmen of powerful committees; Barton chaired the House Energy and Commerce Committee, while Combast chaired both the House Permanent Select Committee on Intelligence and the House Agricultural Committee.

The Congressional Knitter: U.S. Representative Chellie Pingree (D-ME) has authored five books on knitting.

Chellie Pingree
Official Photograph

Lone Republican From the Lone Star State: U.S. Representative Bruce Reynolds Alger was the only Republican member of the Texas U.S. House delegation from 1955-1963. He was also the first Republican to represent Dallas in the House since Reconstruction.

Bruce Reynolds Alger
Library of Congress

Have You Driven a Ford Lately? House Majority Leader Richard Gephardt (D-MO 1989-1995) is a member of the Board of Directors of Ford Motor Company.

Richard Gephardt
Official Photograph

Double Mike Rogers: The U.S. House of Representatives consists of two members named Mike Rogers. One represents the Third Congressional District of Alabama. The other represents the Eighth Congressional District of Michigan.

Congressman Who Likes to Hit: U.S. Representative Norm Dicks (D-WA) was a linebacker on the University of Washington football team.

Norm Dicks as a Member of the University of Washington Football Team

The "McGovern Name" Coincidence: U.S. Representative Jim McGovern (D-MA) once worked for U.S. Senator George McGovern (D-SD 1961-1981). The two men are unrelated.

Jim McGovern
Official Photograph

Keeping Tabs on Finances: All members of the U.S. House of Representatives are required to submit annual financial disclosure forms to the House Clerk.

Northern Marianna Islands and the Democratic Party: The National Democratic Party does not recognize the Commonwealth of the Northern Marianna Democratic Party as an affiliate. Gregorio Kilili Camacho Sablan, the Delegate to the U.S. House of Representatives, ran as an Independent but Caucuses with the Democrats.

Gregorio Kilili Camacho Sablan
Official Photograph

9-1-1 Alabama Style: The first ever "9-1-1" telephone call was made in 1968 at Haleyville City Hall in Haleyville, Alabama. Rankin Fite, Speaker of the Alabama House of Representatives, made the call to U.S. Representative Tom Bevill (D-AL). Bevill was waiting to take the call at the Haleyville Police Station.

Tom Bevill
Official Photograph

Long-Timer: U.S. Representative Marcy Kaptur (D-OH) is currently the longest serving female member of the U.S. House of Representatives. She has been in office since 1983.

Marcy Kaptur
Official Photograph

I Beat Your Daddy Too: In 1980, U.S. Representative Don Young (R-AK) defeated his Democratic challenger Pat Parnell in the general election. In 2006, Young defeated Parnell's' son, Lt. Governor Sean Parnell, in the Republican Primary.

Don Young
Official Photograph

The Dean of the House: The longest serving member of the U.S. House of Representatives is called "The Dean." The Dean is charged with the duty of swearing in the Speaker of the House. The Speaker then swears in all other members.

Easy Re-Election: Between 1998 and 2010, U.S. Representative Bob Goodlate (R-VA) faced no Democratic challenger in his re-election bids.

Bob Goodlate
Official Photograph

Impeach Nixon: U.S. Representative Jerome Waldie (D-CA 1966-1975) was the first member of the U.S. House Judiciary Committee to publicly call for the impeachment of President Richard M. Nixon.

The Congressional Sisters: California Democrats Loretta and Linda Sanchez are the only sisters ever to serve concomitantly in the U.S. House of Representatives.

Arkansas Anomaly: In 2000, State Senator Mike Ross was the only Democrat to defeat an incumbent Republican member of the U.S. House of Representatives outside of California. He beat U.S. Representative Jay Dickey (R-AR).

Mike Ross
Official Photograph

Blazing the Way: In 2007 voters in the Fifth District of Oklahoma elected Mary Fallin to represent them in the U.S. Congress. She became the first woman member of the Oklahoma Congressional Delegation since 1923.

Mary Fallin
Official Photograph

Secular Representatives: A *New York Sun* survey from 2007 found seven members of the U.S. House of Representatives not affiliated with a religion. The seven included then U.S. Representative Neil Abercrombie (D-HI, now Governor of Hawaii), Tammy Baldwin (D-WI), Earl Blumenauer (D-OR), John Olver (D-MA), John Tierney (D-MA), and Mark Udall (D-CO) who is now a U.S. Senator representing Colorado. U.S. Representative Peter Stark (D-CA) is a Unitarian Atheist. All seven come from safe Democratic Congressional Districts

Democratic House Freshmen Decline: The One Hundred Twelfth session of the U.S. House of Representatives (2011-2112) includes just nine freshmen House Democrats. This is the lowest number of freshmen House members of any party since 1915. By contrast, this session includes eighty-two freshmen Republican House members.

Finally a CPA with Charisma: In 1984, New York Republican Joe DioGuardi became the first Certified Public Accountant elected to the U.S. Congress. He represented the Empire State's Twentieth Congressional District in the U.S. House of Representatives until 1989.

Joe DioGuardi
Official Photograph

A Good Springboard to the White House: Eight future Presidents and eight future Vice Presidents were alumni of the U.S. House Committee on Ways and Means.

Lights, Camera, Action: All committees of the U.S. House of Representatives have video cameras in their hearing rooms, except the Permanent Select Committee on Intelligence, the Committee on Rules, and the Committee on Standards of Official Conduct.

Alabama GOP Job Security: No Democrat has dislodged an incumbent member of the Alabama Congressional Delegation since 1982, when Democrat County Commissioner Benjamin Erdeich ousted U.S. Representative Albert Smith, a Republican.

Only in the House: Under the *U.S. Constitution*, all revenue bills must start in the U.S. House of Representatives before going to the U.S. Senate.

No Lone Star Love: In 2002, U.S. Representative Lloyd Dogget (D-TX) supported U.S. Representative Nancy Pelosi (D-CA) over his fellow Texan Martin Frost in the race for U.S. House Minority Leader.

Lloyd Doggett
Official Photograph

From U.S. House to the Big House: In 2009, U.S. Representative William Jefferson (D-LA) was sentenced to 13 years in jail on charges of bribery and racketeering. No Congressperson has ever been sentenced to such a long incarceration.

William Jefferson
Official Photograph

Conservative Democrats Pay Dearly: Four Democratic members of the U.S. House of Representatives voted against President Obama's Stimulus Plan, the Cap-and-Trade legislation, and the Health Care Reform package. They were: Walt Minnick (ID), Bobby Bright (AL), Gene Taylor (MS), and Parker Griffith (now a Republican). All lost in their 2011 re-election bids.

U.S. Congress

Black Caucus Non-Conformist: U.S. Representative Artur Davis (D-AL 2003-2111) was the only member of the Congressional Black Caucus to vote against the Patient Protection and Affordability Act, a.k.a. the Democrats Health Care Plan in 2009.

Artur Davis
Official Photograph

He's Got the Whole World In His Hands: U.S. Representative John Kline (R-MN) carried the "Nuclear Football" while serving as an army officer stationed at the White House. The Nuclear Football is a black briefcase that goes with the President while away from the White House. It provides him with the capability of authorizing a nuclear response while away from Washington, D.C.

John Kline
Official Photograph

Congressman Called to Serve in Persian Gulf War: U.S. Representative Greg Laughlin (D-TX 1989-1995 and R-TX 1995-1997), a colonel in the Army Reserves, was the only member of the U.S. House of Representatives to serve on active duty during the Persian Gulf War.

Greg Laughlin
Official Photograph

Staff Puts Party Over Boss: In 2009 U.S. Representative Parker Griffith (D-AL) defected to the Republican Party. All but one of his Capital Hill Staffers resigned.

Parker Griffith
Official Photograph

Congressional Institutions: Only three members of the U.S. House of Representatives have served for at least 50 years: James L. Whitten, (D-MS) 1941-1995, Carl Vinson (D-GA) 1914-1965, and John Dingell Jr. (D-MI) 1955-present.

Vietnam Veteran Goes to Congress:
U.S. Representative John Murtha (D-PA
1974-2010) was the first Vietnam Veteran
to be elected to the U.S. Congress.

John Murtha
Official Photograph

Football Player and Congresswoman:
Sidney Williams, the husband of U.S.
Representative Maxine Waters (D-CA),
was a linebacker in the National Football
League from 1964-1969. He played for
the Baltimore Colts, the Cleveland
Browns, the Pittsburgh Steelers, and the
Washington Redskins.

Not Everyone Pays Attention: A poll
taken by *The Pew Research Center* two
weeks after the 2010 mid-term elections
found that only 46% of Americans knew
that the Republicans won control of the
U.S. House of Representatives.

Constitutional Loophole: While the *U.S.
Constitution* requires all elected members
of the U.S. House of Representatives to
"be an inhabitant of that State in which he
shall be chosen," there is no requirement
that the Congressperson must have a
residence in the Congressional District.

**Hispanic Influence in the Lone Star
State:** Seven Texas Congressional
Districts have an Hispanic majority
population.

Only Bailout Holdout from Oklahoma:
In 2008, U.S. Representative Frank Lucas,
a Republican, was the only member of the
Oklahoma U.S. House delegation to vote
against the Bailout of financial markets.

Frank Lucas
Official Photograph

First Jewish Congresswoman: Florence
Kahn was the first Jewish Woman to serve
in the U.S. Congress. The Democrat
represented San Francisco in the U.S.
House of Representatives from 1925-
1937.

Florence Kahn
Library of Congress

First Jewish Congressman: In 1845,
Lewis Charles Levin became the first
Jewish American to serve in the U.S.
Congress. The U.S. House member
represented Pennsylvania's First
Congressional District. Levin was a
member of the Nativist American Party
(a.k.a. Know Nothing Party.) He was
defeated for re-election in 1850.

Chinese-American Congresswoman: U.S. Representative Judy Chu (D-CA), elected in a Special election in 2009, is the only Chinese-American ever to serve in the U.S. Congress.

Judy Chu
Official Photograph

May I Say Madam Chairwoman? U.S. Representative Mae Ella Nolan (R-CA 1923-1925) was the first female to chair a Congressional Committee. She chaired the House Committee on Expenditures in the Post Office Department. She represented the same Congressional District later represented by Nancy Pelosi, the first female House Speaker.

Mae Ella Nolan
Official Photograph

GOP Rules the House: The 1998 Congressional elections marked the first time since 1928 that a Republican majority was re-elected for a second consecutive time in the U.S. House of Representatives.

Arizona Congressional Pioneer: U.S. Representative J.D. Hayworth (1995-2007) is the only Arizonan to serve on The House Committee on Ways And Means.

J.D. Hayworth
Official Photograph

Pencil Him In for the Long Haul: John Murtha was the longest serving U.S. Representative in Pennsylvania history. He served from 1974 until his death in 2010.

John Murtha
Official Photograph

Southern GOP Stronghold: A Republican has represented the First Congressional District of Tennessee in the U.S. House of Representatives (which encompasses the eastern part of the Volunteer State) since 1881.

Members of the U.S. House: The number of voting members of the U.S. House of Representatives is 435. This is a result not of the *U.S. Constitution*, but of The Permanent Apportionment Act of 1929.

Socialist and Proud of it: In 1910, voters from the Fifth Congressional District of Wisconsin elected Victor L. Berger of the Socialist Party of America to represent them in the U.S. House of Representatives, making him the first Socialist elected to the U.S. Congress.

Victor L. Berger
Library of Congress

Early Obama Supporter: In 2007, U.S. Representative Artur Davis (D-AL) became the first Member of Congress outside of Illinois to endorse Barack Obama for President.

Virginia Duo: The only two Republicans to sign the Southern Manifesto (opposing the U.S. Supreme Court's decision requiring desegregation of schools) were U.S. Representatives Jim Broyhill and Richard Poff of Virginia.

Bringing Sunshine to the GOP: In 1954 William C. Cramer became the first Republican elected to the U.S. House of Representatives from Florida since Reconstruction. Voters in the First Congressional District of the Sunshine state elected him. This district encompasses the extreme western part of the Florida panhandle.

Georgia GOP Makes Slow Strides: In 1964, Howard Hollis "Bo" Callaway became the first Republican elected to the U.S. House of Representatives from Georgia. He served one term. In 1966, he became the first Republican Nominee for Governor of Georgia since Reconstruction.

Howard Hollis
Official Portrait

Bill Clinton Does Not Play Well in Mississippi: U.S. Representative Gene Taylor (D-MS) was the only Democratic member of the U.S. House to vote "Aye" on all four articles of impeachment against President Bill Clinton, in 1998.

Gene Taylor
Official Photograph

The Power of Incumbency: The Median tenure for a member of the U.S. House of Representatives is 20 years.

Virtual Congressman Makes his Mark: U.S. Representative Edward Markey (D-MA) was the first American politician to use Second Life, a computerized 3D virtual world.

Edward Markey
Official Photograph

Status Quo in the Golden State: In the 2010 Congressional elections, the Republicans picked up 63 seats in the U.S. House of Representatives. None of these pickups occurred in the largest populated state, California, where all 34 seats held by the Democrats prior to the election remained in Democratic hands.

Korean-American First: In 1992, Chang-jun "Jay" Kim became the first Korean-born American elected to the U.S. Congress. He represented the Forty-First Congressional District of California until losing a bid for re-election in 1998.

Chang-jun "Jay" Kim
Official Photograph

Proud First: In 1989, Donald Payne became the first African-American to assume a seat in the New Jersey Congressional Delegation. He represents the Newark-based Tenth Congressional District in the U.S. House of Representatives.

Donald Payne
Official Photograph

Prestigious Award for a Southern Maverick: U.S. Representative Carl Elliot (D-AL 1949-1965) was the first recipient of the John F. Kennedy Profile in Courage Award for his opposition to racial segregation and for his support of public education.

Carl Elliot
Official Photograph

Few Constituents, Big Territory: The U.S House seat with the smallest number of constituents is the at-large seat in Wyoming. This seat's representative has less than 565,000 constituents in a state almost 100,000 square miles long.

Widow Gets the Call: In a 1973 special election to succeed the deceased U.S. Representative George W. Collins, voters in the Chicago-based Seventh Congressional District of Illinois elected his widower Cardiss Collins. She was the first African-American female elected to Congress representing a Mid-West congressional district.

Cardiss Collins
Official Photograph

Rare GOP losers in Republican Year: The only Republican members of the U.S. House of Representatives to lose their seats in 2010 were Joseph Cao of the New Orleans-centered Second Congressional District of Louisiana and Charles Djou of the Honolulu-based First Congressional District of Hawaii. Both were freshman legislators. Cao lost the election to State Representative Cedrick Richmond, and Djou was defeated by State Senate President Colleen Hanabusa.

Republican Rebel: In 1967, U.S. Representative Tim Lee Carter (R-KY) was the first Republican House member to call for a complete withdrawal of U.S. troops from Vietnam.

Caucus Power: Committee Chairpersons in the U.S. House of Representatives are decided by the caucus of the majority party, not be the amount of time a member has been on the committee.

Direct Democracy at Work: U.S. Representative Berkley W. Bedell (D-IA 1975-1987) had a distinct way of legislating. At town meetings he would allow his constituents to vote on which issues he would propose and work on in Congress.

Berkley W. Bedell
Official Photograph

Irish Citadel: The Tenth Congressional District of Massachusetts has the largest Irish-American population in the U.S.A.

Whip it Good: U.S. Representative Leslie C. Arends (R-IL) was the longest serving House Whip. He served as the Republican Whip from 1943-1974. He was both the Minority and the Majority Whip, depending on which party held the majority in the House.

Leslie C. Arends
Official Photograph

Bicyclists' Hero: U.S. Representative Earl Blumenauer (D-OR) is chairman of the Congressional Bike Caucus. He owns seven bicycles. He bicycles to work and wears a bicycle lapel pin on the House Floor.

Earl Blumenauer
Official Photograph

GOP Shows Vital Signs in the Magnolia State: In 1962, Prentiss Lafayette Walker became the first Republican elected to the U.S. Congress from Mississippi since 1882. He was elected to a U.S. House Seat representing the Fourth Congressional District, which is centered in the state's Gulf Coast region.

Marian Berry gets Personal: During a budget debate in 2005, U.S. Representative Marian Berry (D-AR) referred to his 30-year-old Republican colleague, U.S. Representative Adam Putnam (R-FL) as a "Howdy Doody looking nimrod" during a budget debate.

Adam Putnam
Official Photograph

Dingell Country: A Dingell has represented the Fifteenth Congressional District of Michigan in the U.S. House of Representatives since 1935. John Dingell Sr. served from 1935 until his death in 1955. His son, John Dingell Jr., succeeded him and has represented the District ever since.

John Dingell Jr.
Official Photograph

What a Memory: U.S. Representative Guy Vander Jagt (R-MI) delivered the entire 37-minute Keynote Address at the 1980 Republican National Convention, with no notes.

Guy Vander Jagt
Library of Congress

One-term Wolverine Wonders: In 1966, five freshmen Democratic members of the U.S. House of Representatives from Michigan were defeated in their bids for re-election. They were Raymond Clevenger, Billie Farnum, John Mackie, Paul Todd, and Wes Vivian.

Finds College Life Most Agreeable: U.S. Representative William D. Burlison (D-MO 1969-1980) has seven academic degrees.

William D. Burilson
Official Photograph

Like Father, Un-Like Son: Howard Buffett, the father of Berkshire Hathaway Inc. CEO Warren Buffett, was a Republican U.S. Representative from Nebraska from 1943-1949. Warren Buffett is a Democrat.

Howard Buffet
Library of Congress

Electoral Stunner: When Gerald R. Ford resigned his Grand Rapids, Michigan-based Congressional seat in 1973 to assume the Vice Presidency, Democrat Richard Vander Veen scored a shocking upset by winning the profoundly Republican Congressional seat. Republicans had held the seat since 1912. This proved to be a pre-curser to the post-Watergate 1974 Congressional elections in which the Republican Party lost 48 seats in the House.

Republican Resurgence in the House: In the 2010 Mid-term Congressional elections, the Republicans picked up 63 seats in the U.S. House of Representatives. No party has picked up that many House seats since 1938, when the Republicans gained 81 seats in the U.S. House during the Presidency of Democrat Franklin D. Roosevelt.

Franklin D. Roosevelt
Franklin D. Roosevelt Presidential Library and Museum

No Need to Rush into Things: U.S. Representative Edward Boland (D-MA 1953-1989) did not get married until he was 62 years old. However, he and his bride Mary Eagan had four children.

Edward Boland
Official Photograph

Anatomy of Republican Victory: In the 2010 mid-term elections for the U.S. House of Representatives, the Republican Party garnered 60% of the white vote, 40% of the Asian-American vote, 38% of the Hispanic vote, and 9% of the African-American vote.

The Smoking Gun: The term "smoking gun" was coined in 1974 by U.S. Representative Barber Conable Jr. (R-NY). The phrase was used to describe a tape he heard in which President Richard M. Nixon told his Chief of Staff, H.R. Haldeman, to tell the FBI not to investigate the Watergate Burglary any further.

Barber Conable Jr.
Library of Congress

The Birth of Two Committees: The Constitutionally delegated power given to the U.S. House of Representatives to appropriate money was originally held by the House Committee on Ways and Means. This changed in 1865, when the House Committee on Appropriations was created to appropriate expenditures, and the House Committee on Banking and Currency (Now referred to as the House Committee on Financial Services) was effectuated to regulate banking. The Ways and Means Committee still maintains the responsibility to write tax legislation.

House Powerhouses Lose Power: In the 2010 Congressional elections, three chairmen of full committees in the U.S. House of Representatives lost their House seats. They were: James Oberstar of Minnesota, who chaired the House Committee on Transportation and Infrastructure, Ike Skelton of Missouri, who chaired the House Committee on Armed Services, and John Spratt of South Carolina, who chaired the House Committee on the Budget.

First Puerto Rican Congressman: In 1972, voters in New York's Twenty-First Congressional District, (comprising the South Bronx) made Democrat Herman Badillo the first Puerto Rican elected to the U.S. Congress. Later in life Badillo abandoned the Democratic Party and ran for Mayor of New York in the Republican Primary, losing to Media Mogul Michael Bloomberg in 2001.

Herman Badillo
Official Photograph

Historic Lady in the Garden State: Mary Norton was the first Democratic woman elected to the U.S. House of Representatives. In 1924 she was elected to represent New Jersey's Twelfth Congressional District, which included her home in Jersey City. She served from 1925-1951.

Mary Norton
Official Portrait

Giant Killer: In 1972, Attorney Elizabeth Holtzman defeated U.S. Representative Emanuel Celler (D-NY) in the Democratic primary in the Sixteenth Congressional District of New York. Celler had maintained the seat since 1923. No member of Congress with that long a tenure in Congress has ever lost a primary election. Holtzman made Emanuel's opposition to the proposed Equal Rights Amendment to the *U.S. Constitution* her flagship campaign issue.

Elizabeth Holtzman
Library of Congress

Dems Defy Their Leadership: The only Democratic U.S. Representatives to vote for at least one Article of Impeachment against Bill Clinton in 1999 were: Virgil Goode of Virginia, Ralph Hall of Texas, Paul McHale of Pennsylvania, Charlie Stenholm of Texas, and Gene Taylor of Mississippi. Goode and Hall later switched their political affiliation to the Republican Party.

A Man of the Earth Goes to Congress: In 1968, Wyoming voters made Republican John S. Wold the first geologist elected to the U.S Congress. He served as the at-large member of the U.S. House of Representatives for one term.

Money Don't Vote: In the 2010 Republican Primary, Fifth Congressional District U.S. Representative Parker Griffith spent about $50 per vote. Challenger Mo Brooks spent about $10 per vote. Brooks won with 35,712 votes. Griffith received just 23,494 votes.

Mo Brooks
Official Photograph

Four-year Representative: The only elected official to the U.S. House of Representatives who serves a four-year term is the Resident Commissioner of Puerto Rico. However, he/she does not have the authority to vote on legislation.

Official Flag of Puerto Rico

African-American Stronghold: The First Congressional District of Illinois, which encompasses much of Chicago's Southside, has more African Americans (about 65%) than any other Congressional district in the country.

The Birth of the New Orleans Saints: In 1966, U.S. House Majority Whip Hale Boggs (D-LA) was in a tough re-election contest in his New Orleans based Congressional District. During this time, the National Football League wanted an anti-trust exemption allowing it to merge with the American Football League (AFL). Boggs and U.S. Senator Russell B. Long (D-LA) were credited with brokering a deal with the League, in which the exemption would be granted in return for New Orleans being awarded a National Football Team. The merger passed as an amendment to unrelated tax legislation and was signed by President Lyndon B. Johnson. Boggs won re-election.

Hale Boggs
Official Photograph

"Cooter" Goes Political: Ben Jones, known as Cooter Davenport on the 1970's television series *Dukes of Hazard*, was a Democratic U.S. Representative from Georgia from 1989-1993.

Men of God in the "House of Satan": Two Catholic Priests have served in the U.S. Congress. They were U.S. Representative Robert Drinan (D-MA, 1973-1981), and Robert Cornell (D-WA, 1975-1981). In 1980, Pope John Paul II decreed that priests not serve in elective office.

Ignominious Distinction: In 2008, Republican Bill Sali became the first freshman U.S Representative to lose his re-election bid from Idaho. Democrat Walter Minnick defeated him.

Bill Sali
Official Photograph

Conan O'Brien and Barney Frank: Talk Show Host Conan O'Brien was interested in politics while a high school student at Brookline High School in Brookline, Massachusetts. He interned for then State Representative Barney Frank during his 1980 Campaign to represent the Fourth Congressional District of Massachusetts in the U.S. Congress. Frank won that election.

Endorsing a Third-party Presidential Candidate: In the 2008 Presidential Election, U.S. Representative Ron Paul (R-TX) was the only member of the U.S. Congress to endorse a third party candidate. He endorsed Constitution Party Candidate Chuck Baldwin.

Ron Paul
Official Photograph

171

Republican African-American from Chicago's South Side: In 1929, voters from South Chicago Illinois' First Congressional District elected Republican Oscar Stanton De Priest to represent them in the U.S. House of Representatives. De Priest was the first African-American elected to the U.S. Congress in the twentieth century. He is also the last Republican to represent this congressional district. No other African-American Republican was elected to the U.S. Congress until 1966, when Massachusetts voters elected Attorney General Edward W. Brooke to the U.S. Senate.

Oscar Stanton De Priest
Official Photograph

At Least He Ran: Ali Mohamed, the Republican nominee in New York's 16th Congressional District, mustered just 3% of the vote in 2008 against incumbent Democratic U.S. Representative Jose Serrano.

Jose Serrano
Official Photograph

Too Ironic: U.S. Representative Gary Ackerman (D-NY) lives on a houseboat when in Washington, D.C. The vessel has the ironic name: *Unsinkable II*. His first *Unsinkable* sank.

Gary Ackerman
Official Photograph

Kay Wins: In 1996, Kay Granger became the first female Republican elected to the U.S. House of Representatives from Texas. She was elected to represent the district once held by House Speaker Jim Wright, a Democrat.

Kay Granger
Official Photograph

Democratic Dominance in Bay State: In the 2008 Congressional elections, six of the ten members of the all-Democratic Massachusetts Delegation to the U.S. House of Representatives faced no Republican opposition in their re-election bids.

George W. "Not a Real Texan:" George W. Bush's first political campaign was in 1978. Bush, the Republican nominee, was running against Democrat Kent Hance for an open seat in the U.S. House of Representatives, representing the West Texas-based Nineteenth Congressional District. Hance taunted Bush for being born in Connecticut and educated at Phillips Academy in Andover, Massachusetts, and graduating from Yale University and the Harvard Business School. Hance called Bush: "Not a real Texan," and asserted that: "Yale and Harvard don't prepare you as well for running for the 19th Congressional District as Texas Tech (Hance's *alma mater*) does." Hance won the race. After his Congressional career, Hance left the Democratic Party becoming a Republican and supporting Bush in his runs for Governor of Texas and for President.

Kent Hance
Texas Tech University System

Democratic Entrenchment: The Third Congressional District of Maryland (which includes portions of Annapolis, and Baltimore) has not had a Republican U.S. Representative since 1927.

The Committees: The U.S. House of Representatives has 20 standing (permanent) committees.

Not so "Young" anymore: The Dean of the Republican Congressional Delegation is U.S. Representative C.W. Bill Young (R-FL.). He was first elected to represent the state's Tenth Congressional District in 1968.

C.W. Bill Young
Official Photograph

Playing on the Gridiron on Wedding Day: U.S. Representative Emilio Daddario (R-CT 1959-1971) was a semipro football player in his younger days. In fact, he played a game on his wedding day and used the paycheck from playing in that game to pay for his honeymoon.

Emilio Daddario
Library of Congress

Perfect Attendance: During the 110th Congress, lasting from 2007-2009, only two Members of the U.S. House of Representatives are on record for all 1,876 roll call votes. They were Jason Altmire (D-PA) and Jesse Jackson Jr. (D-IL).

173

Montana's Maverick Trailblazer: The first woman elected to the U.S. Congress was Republican Jeannette Rankin. She served as the at-large representative for Montana in the U.S. House of Representatives from 1917-1919. During that term Rankin, a devout pacifist, voted against U.S. involvement in WWI. Rankin did not run for re-election, choosing instead to run for the U.S. Senate. She lost. After a two-decade congressional hiatus, Rankin won back her House seat in 1940. In 1941, she was the only member of the U.S. Congress to vote against a declaration of War on Japan following the Pearl Harbor invasion. Rankin questioned if President Franklin D. Roosevelt had provoked the attack.

Jeannette Rankin
Library of Congress

They All Want Their Say: The largest committee in the U.S. House of Representatives is the Committee on Transportation and Infrastructure. It maintains 75 members.

No Purses in the House: Purses are disallowed on the floor of the U.S. House of Representatives.

Securing the Border: Ten U.S. House Districts border Mexico.

Is Honesty Really the best Policy? In 2010, U.S. Representative Paul Kanjorski (D-PA) told a local radio station that he would supplant traditional town hall meetings with teleconferences. Kanjorski asserted: "We're going to do everything we can to get opinions from people, to meet with people, but I'm not going to set myself up for, you know, nuts to hit me with a camera and ask stupid questions."

Paul Kanjorski
Official Photograph

California Landslides: In 2008, 50 of the 53 winners in California's U.S. House Congressional Elections garnered at least 60% of the vote.

The Ethical Way of Doing It: The only standing committee in the U.S. Congress which has an equal number of Democrat and Republican members, no matter which party holds the majority, is the House Committee on Official Standards and Conduct, more commonly known as "The House Ethics Committee."

Hail to The Clerk: When legislation is passed in the U.S. House of Representatives, it is certified and processed by the House Clerk.

The Epitome of Bluntness and the Sealing of One's Fate: After losing a re-election bid in 1834, U.S. Representative Davy Crocket (Whig-TN) exclaimed: "I told the people of my district that I would serve them as faithfully as I had done; but if not ... you may all go to hell, and I will go to Texas." He did go to Texas and died at the Battle of the Alamo on March 6, 1836.

Davy Crockett
Library of Congress

Kasich Swims Against Democratic Tide: In 1982, during the first mid-term election of the Ronald Reagan Presidency, only one Republican defeated an incumbent Democrat in the U.S. House of Representatives. Thirty-year-old John Kasich dislodged Freshman U.S. Representative Democrat Robert Norton Shamansky in the Twelfth Congressional District of Ohio.

John Kasich
Official Photograph

Big Benefactors for a Young Bush: Among the donors to George W. Bush's 1978 failed Congressional campaign in Texas were Gene MacArthur, the wife of the late General Douglas MacArthur, Baseball Commissioner Bowie Kuhn, and the Chairman of the Bank of America, A.W. Clausen.

George and Laura Bush on the Campaign Trail in 1978
George Bush Presidential Library and Museum

First and so far Only: The only female Republican to represent Pennsylvania in the U.S. Congress was Melissa Hart. She represented the Fourth Congressional District of Pennsylvania from 2001-2007.

Melissa Hart
Official Photograph

The Medicare District: Florida's Fifth Congressional District, located in Central West Florida, has more Medicare beneficiaries than any other District in the country.

Ralph is in it for the Long "Hall:" U.S. Representative Ralph Hall, (R-TX) born in 1923, is the oldest member of the U.S. Congress. He represents the Fourth Congressional District of Texas and has been in the House since 1981. He was first elected to political office in 1950, when the voters in Rockwell County, Texas elected him as County Judge.

Ralph Hall
Official Photograph

Congressman Marches On: U.S. Representative Ken Hechler (D-WV 1959-1977) was the only member of the U.S. Congress to march with Reverend Martin Luther King Jr. from Selma to Montgomery, Alabama in 1965 in support of Voting Rights for African-Americans.

Ken Hechler
Library of Congress

Discharging: In the U.S. House of Representatives, if more than half of the members sign a discharge petition to get a stalled bill out of a committee, it goes to the House Floor for a full vote.

Dad Played for the Red Skins when they Represented Boston: James Moran Sr., the father of U.S. Representative James Moran Jr. (D-VA), played the position of guard for the Boston Redskins football team, the predecessor of the Washington Redskins. He played in 1935 and in 1936.

James Moran Jr.
Official Photograph

Let's Go to "The Hopper:" When members of the U.S. House of Representatives introduce proposed legislation, they literally place it in a box called "The Hopper."

Lucky Five: There were five Republican challengers who dislodged incumbent Democratic members of the U.S. House of Representatives in 2008. They were: Tom Rooney (who defeated Tim Mahoney in Florida's Sixteenth Congressional District), "Ahn" Joseph Coa (who ousted William Jefferson in Louisiana's Second Congressional District), Lynne Jenkins (who beat Nancy Boyda in the Second District of Kansas), and Pete Olson (who bested Nick Lampson in the Twenty-Second Congressional District of Texas).

Employers: Each voting member of the U.S. House of Representatives represents about 700,000 constituents.

Langevin Earns his Place in History: U.S. Representative James Langevin (D-RI) is the only person to preside over the House of Representatives in a wheelchair. Langevin, who is paralyzed from the chest down, presided in 2010 on the twentieth anniversary of the Americans with Disabilities Act.

James Langevin
Official Photograph

Show Some Respect to His Excellency, The Congressman: U.S. Representative Michael Myers (D-PA 1976-1980) engaged in a fistfight with a waiter in a Washington, D.C. restaurant. Myers alleged the waiter was not showing the proper deference to a Congressman.

The Caucus of One: U.S. Representative Dennis Kucinich (D-OH) is the only vegan in the U.S. Congress.

Dennis Kucinich
Official Photograph

Counting Everyone in the House: The U.S. House is comprised of 435 voting members plus five non-voting delegates and one Resident Commissioner.

Reagan Disses "W": When George W. Bush ran for an open U.S. House seat, representing the Ninetieth Congressional District of Texas, Ronald Reagan (former California Governor and prospective Republican Presidential candidate) supported Bush's Republican primary opponent, former Odessa, Texas Mayor Jim Reese. Reagan spoke on his behalf in a television advertisement. In fact, Reagan's Political Action Committee (PAC) donated to Reese's campaign. Bush's father, George H.W. Bush, a prospective rival for the Republican Presidential nomination in 1978, was offended by Reagan's endorsement of his son's opponent. He said, "I am surprised about what he is doing here in my state." Bush defeated Reese 55.77% - 44.3%, but lost the general election to Democrat Kent Hance.

George W. Bush and Jim Reese
Midland Reporter-Telegram

House Expenses: All members of the U.S. House of Representatives receive "Representational Allowances" to pay for staff, travel, and other amenities. The allocation to members varies from about $1.4 million to about $1.7 million, depending on the distance a member must travel to reach the nation's capital, and the cost of renting an office back in the district.

A Politician who does Not Mince Words: After Americans for Tax Reform alleged that U.S. Representative Gene Taylor (D-MS 1989-2011) had changed his position on Health Insurance Reform, Taylor issued a press release branding the organization: " . . . Lying sacks of scum."

Gene Taylor
Official Photograph

First to File Repeal: U.S. Representative Michelle Bachmann (R-MN) was the first member of the U.S. Congress to file proposed legislation to repeal the Patient Protection and Affordability Act of 2010 (a.k.a. the Obama Health Care Insurance Legislation).

Michelle Bachmann
Official Photograph

435 Seats: 1914 was the first mid-term election after the U.S. House of Representatives was expanded to 435 seats.

But Where are the Checks and Balances in "this" Relationship? U.S. Representative Michael E. McMahon (D-NY 2007-2011) is married to New York State Supreme Court Justice Judith Novellino McMahon.

Michael E. McMahon
Official Photograph

Defense Industry Likes Ike: The U.S. Defense Industry donated $24 million to political campaigns during the 2008 election cycle. U.S. Representative Ike Skelton (D-MO), who served as the Chairman of the House Committee on Armed Services, received the most contributions at $348,511.

Ike Skelton
Official Photograph

Money Isn't Everything: In the 1998 Congressional Elections, the Republicans out-raised the Democrats by over $100 million, but lost 5 seats in the U.S. House of Representatives.

An Indian-American First: In 1956, Democrat Dalip Singh Saund became the first Indian-American elected to the U.S. Congress. Saund won a seat in the U.S. House of Representatives by voters in the Twenty-Ninth Congressional District of California, which included Riverside and Imperial Counties. He served until 1963.

Dalip Singh Saund
Official Portrait

Incumbent Protection: Between 1968 and 2008, no incumbent member of the U.S. House of Representatives from Tennessee lost a re-election bid.

Where There is a Means, there is a Way: The House Committee on Ways and Means is the oldest continuously serving committee in the U.S. House of Representatives. It began as a Select (not permanent) Committee in 1789 and became a Standing Committee (permanent) in 1797.

A Very Big Congressional District: The First Congressional District of Michigan, which includes the Upper Peninsula area as well as parts of the rest of the state, comprises 44% of the state's land. Yet it is only one of 15 Congressional districts in Michigan.

First Hispanic House Member: The first Hispanic American to serve in the U.S. House of Representatives was Joseph Marion Hernandez (Whig-Florida.) He entered office in 1822.

Joseph Marion Hernandez
Library of Congress

Tom Delay Provides "Very" Creative Defense for Dan Quayle and Himself: In 1988, while defending Republican Vice Presidential nominee Dan Quayle's lack of military service during the Vietnam War, as well as his own lack of military service during that time period, U.S. Representative Tom Delay (R-TX) told the Houston media: "So many minority youths had volunteered for the well-paying military positions to escape poverty and the ghetto that there was literally no room for patriotic folks like himself."

Tom Delay
Official Photograph

U.S. Congress

She's in the Money: U.S. Representative Jane Harman (D-CA 1993-1999 and 2001-2011) is the wife of Sidney Harman, the publisher of *Newsweek Magazine.* The couple has over $160 million in assets.

Jane Harman
Official Photograph

Democrats for Bush Surge Strategy in Iraq: The only Democratic members of the U.S. House of Representatives who voted for George W. Bush's Troop Surge Strategy in Iraq in 2007 were Jim Marshall (D-GA), and Gene Taylor (D-MS.)

There are Some Things Money Can't Buy: Businessman Chris Gabrieli spent more than five million dollars in an unsuccessful bid to win the Democratic Primary for an open seat representing the Massachusetts Eighth Congressional District in 1998. He finished in sixth place, garnering just 5,740 votes out of 88,145 cast.

The Non-Voting House Members: The House of Representatives includes five non-voting delegates: one each from America Samoa, Guam, The District of Columbia, The Northern Mariana Islands, and the U.S. Virgin Islands. (Puerto Rico elects a Resident Commissioner rather than a delegate.)

Former Congressman Shows Some Love for his Alma Mater: In 2002, U.S. Representative John S. Wold (R-WY 1969-1971) and his wife Jane donated $20 million to John's alma mater Union College of Schenectady, NY. Wold graduated from the institution in 1938. He made a fortune in the oil industry after leaving the House. This is the largest donation the school has ever received.

Jane and John S. Wold
Union College

Giuliani's War: As a District Attorney from the Southern District of New York, future New York City Mayor Rudolph Giuliani led a criminal investigation of U.S. Representative Charles Wilson (D-TX), who was the feature character in the movie *Charlie Wilson's War*, for alleged cocaine use in 1980. The case never went to trial because of lack of evidence.

Charlie Wilson
Official Photograph

Teflon Ronnie: The term "Teflon President" was used to refer to President Ronald Reagan. The term was derived from a quote by U.S. Representative Patricia Schroeder (D-CO 1973-1997): "He has been perfecting the Teflon-coated presidency. He sees to it that nothing sticks to him."

Patricia Schroeder
Official Photograph

The "Show Me" State: In 1899, U.S. Representative (D-MO) William Duncan Vandiver, in a 1899 speech at the Five O' Clock Club in Pennsylvania, remarked: "I come from a state that raises corn and cotton, and cockleburs, and Democrats, and frothy eloquence neither convinces nor satisfies me. I am from Missouri. You have got to show me." The phrase "show me" had became synonymous with Missouri, and the Vandiver address solidified it. Consequently, the state's unofficial nickname became: "The Show Me State."

Missouri Official State Seal

It's Rogers in a Photo-Finish: U.S. Representative Mike Rogers (R-MI) was first elected to his seat in 2000 by just 111 votes.

Mike Rogers
Official Photograph

Gramm's Unique Political Move: The only member of the U.S. Congress to resign his seat and run for re-election as a member of another political party in the twentieth century was U.S. Representative Phil Gramm of Texas. House Speaker Tip O'Neal dislodged Gramm, a conservative Democrat, from his membership of the coveted House Budget Committee for his role in being the lead Democrat sponsor of the Gramm-Latta Omnibus Reconciliation Bill, which effectuated Ronald Reagan's economic program. Subsequently, Gramm resigned his seat and ran "as a Republican" for an open seat in the Special Election and won.

Unlucky Republicans: In the 2002 mid-term elections, only two Republican members of the U.S. House of Representatives lost their re-election bids. They were Felix Grucci of the Second Congressional District of New York, who lost to Democrat Timothy Bishop, a college administrator, and Connie Morella of the Eighth Congressional District of Maryland who lost to Democrat Chris Van Hollen, a State Senator.

Asian-American First: The only Asian American ever to preside over a state legislative body in U.S. history was Colleen Hanabusa. Her colleagues elected the Hawaii State Senator as President of the State Senate in 2006. In that capacity, she wielded the gavel and presided over the State Senate. Hanabusa was elected to the U.S. House of Representatives in 2010.

Colleen Hanabusa
Official Photograph

African-Americans Run and Win as Republicans in Dixie: In 2010, two African-American Republicans were elected to the U.S. House of Representatives. They were the first two African-Americans to win a Congressional election as Republicans since J.C. Watts of Oklahoma was re-elected in 2000. They were businessman Tim Scott, elected in the coastally situated First Congressional District of South Carolina, and former Army Lieutenant Colonel Allen B. West, elected by voters in the Twenty-second Congressional District of Florida, which includes much of the Florida South Coast. Scott was elected to a district with just over 20% African-American population, while West was elected to represent a district with less than a 4% African-American population.

Most Constituents: The U.S House seat with the most constituents is the at-large seat representing all of Montana. The holder of this seat represents close to 1,000,000 constituents.

Breaking a Congressional Barrier: In 1972, Barbara Jordan became the first African-American female from the South to be elected to the U.S. House of Representatives. As a Congresswoman, Jordan represented the Eighteenth Congressional District of Texas from 1973-1979.

Barbara Jordan
Lyndon Baines Johnson Library and Museum

Out of The Closet: The first openly Gay person to be elected as a freshman to the U.S. Congress was Jared Polis in 2008. He was elected to represent the Boulder-based Second Congressional District of Colorado.

Jared Polis
Official Photograph

Political Mosh Pit: U.S. Representative Gary Condit (D-CA 1989-2003) and U.S. Representative John Kasich (R-OH 1983-2001) shared an affinity for rock-and-roll concerts, and once jumped into a mosh pit at a performance of the rock band Pearl Jam.

U.S. Congress

Gore Makes History: When C-SPAN began televising proceedings in the U.S. House of Representatives in 1979, the first speaker was U.S. Representative Al Gore (D-TN). Gore predicted that: "Television will change this institution, Mr. Speaker, just as it has changed the executive branch, but the good will far outweigh the bad. From this day forward, every member of this body must ask himself or herself how many Americans are listening to the debates which are made."

Al Gore
Official Photograph

Baseball Pedigree: U.S. Representative Ben Chandler (D-KY) is the grandson of Albert Benjamin "Happy" Chandler, who served as the Commissioner of Major League Baseball from 1945-1951.

Ben Chandler
Official Photograph

Bishop Wins by a Nose: In 2010, U.S. Representative Timothy Bishop (D-NY) was re-elected to represent the Long Island-based First Congressional District of New York by just 263 votes out of almost 195,000 votes cast.

Timothy Bishop
Official Photograph

A Lucky Guy: U.S. Representative James Sensenbrenner (R-WI) won $250,000 in the District of Columbia lottery in 1997. In 2007, he twice won $1,000 in the Wisconsin Lottery. Sensenbrenner comes from a patrician background, and is an heir to the Kimberly-Clark Corporation paper products fortune.

James Sensenbrenner
Official Photograph

The Garfield Theorem: While a member of the U.S. House of Representatives, future President James Garfield developed his own mathematical proof to the Pythagorean Theorem $(a^2 + b^2 = c^2)$. Garfield's Proof was published in the *Journal of Education* in 1876.

James Garfield
Library of Congress

The Man Who Beat Obama: U.S. Representative Bobby Rush (D-IL) is the only person ever to beat Barack Obama in an election. Rush trounced Obama by 31 percentage points in 2000, when Obama challenged the incumbent for the House seat in the First Congressional District of Illinois in the Democratic Primary.

Bobby Rush
Official Photograph

"In the Navy:" U.S. Representative Joe Sestak (D-PA 2007-2111) is the highest-ranking military officer to serve in the U.S. Congress. He retired as a Three-Star Admiral in the U.S. Navy before being elected to the Congress.

Joe Sestak
Official Photograph

Bill Clinton's Former Chauffer: U.S. Representative Mike Ross (D-AR) began his political career as a travel aid for Bill Clinton. He did this during Clinton's successful bid to re-capture the Arkansas Governor's Office in 1982.

Mike Ross
Official Photograph

Launching Pad to the White House: During their tenure as members of the U.S. House of Representatives, three future Presidents served as chairmen of the powerful Committee on Ways and Means. They were James K. Polk, Millard Fillmore, and William McKinley.

Speakers of the House

First to Speak: The first Speaker of the U.S. House of Representatives was Frederick Muhlenberg. Muhlenberg represented Pennsylvania's Second Congressional District. He served as Speaker from 1789-1791 and from 1793-1795.

Frederic Muhlenberg
Official Portrait

Actresses Roots: Actress Kyra Sedgwick is a descendent of Theodore Sedgwick, a U.S. Representative from Massachusetts who served as Speaker of the U.S. House of Representatives from 1799-1801.

Theodore Sedgwick
Library of Congress

Speakers House: 53 members of the U.S. House of Representatives have been elected by their colleagues to the position of House Speaker.

I am The Congress: A constituent sent a letter to his Congressman, the autocratic House Speaker Thomas Bracket Reed (R-ME), nicknamed "Czar Reed," asking for him to explain how Congress works. Reed sent the constituent a photograph of himself.

Thomas Bracket Reed
Library of Congress

Speaking from America's Heartland: Republican David B. Henderson was the first Speaker of the U.S. House of Representatives to hail from a district west of the Mississippi River. He represented the Third Congressional District of Iowa. He served as the Speaker from 1899-1903.

David B, Henderson
Official Portrait

An Unwritten Rule: There is no provision in the *U.S. Constitution* mandating that the Speaker of the U.S. House of Representatives be a member of the body.

All Politics is Local: U.S. House Speaker Thomas P. Tip O'Neil Jr. (D-MA 1977-1987) is credited with coining the phrase, "All Politics is Local." This axiom was actually coined by his father Thomas P. O'Neil Sr. Tip had lost a campaign for City Council in Cambridge, Massachusetts. His father told him he should have campaigned more in his own neighborhood, where surprisingly he had underperformed. Tip finished ninth out of sixty candidates in a race where the top eight finishers were elected. The Senior O'Neil told Tip to remember, "All Politics is Local."

Thomas P. "Tip" O'Neil Jr.
Official Portrait

Speaker Finally Spreads his Wings: U.S. House Speaker John McCormack (D-MA 1962-1971) boarded an airplane for the first time at age 71.

John C. McCormack
Lyndon Baines Johnson Library and Museum

Bipartisan Friendship: Although they were political rivals, Sam Rayburn (D-TX) and Joe Martin (R-MA) were close personal friends. Both served as Speaker of the U.S. House of Representatives and as House Minority Leader (depending on which party was in power). Some Democratic members of the U.S. Congress wanted Rayburn to campaign against Martin in his Massachusetts Congressional District. Sam Rayburn responded: "Speak against Joe? Hell, if I lived up there, I'd vote for him."

Sam Rayburn left and Joe Martin Right
Library of Congress

Bay State Rules the House: In the twentieth century, four Speakers of the U.S. House of Representatives hailed from the state of Massachusetts: Republican Frederick Gillette was Speaker from 1919-1925; Republican Joe Martin was Speaker from 1947-1949 and from 1953-1955; Democrat John McCormick was Speaker from 1962-1971; and Democrat Thomas P. Tip O'Neil Jr. was Speaker from 1977-1987.

What the Speaker Does Not Do: The Speaker of the U.S. House of Representatives does not serve on committees and rarely votes on legislation. However, the Speaker is required by the House rules to vote when there is a tied vote in the House Chamber.

Speaker Loses Coveted Post but remains in Congress: In 2007, the Democrats took control of the U.S. House of Representatives. The Republicans no longer held the Speakership, resulting in Speaker J. Dennis Hastert (R-IL) becoming a rank-and-file member of the House. Hastert became the first former Speaker of the House to maintain his House seat since Joe Martin (R-MA) in 1955. Martin maintained his House seat for six terms. He served as House Minority Leader until 1959 when Charles A. Halleck (R-IN) dislodged him from that post. Hastert resigned his seat less than a year into his term.

J. Dennis Hastert
Official Photograph

Republicans' Long Congressional Nightmare: Between 1931 until 1995, the Republicans held control over the U.S. House of Representative only twice, from 1947-1949 and from 1953-1955. The Speaker of the House during both terms was Joe Martin (R-MA).

Joseph Martin
Official Portrait

Speaker Visits Hiroshima: In 2008, U.S. House Speaker Nancy Pelosi, while on an official trip in Hiroshima, Japan, placed a bouquet of flowers at the memorial to the victims of the Atomic Bomb, which ended WWII. She is the highest-ranking U.S. official to do so.

Nancy Pelosi
Official Photograph

The Speaker of the House is not required to represent the Fifth Congressional District of Washington: When House Speaker Tom Foley was running for re-election to his Washington Congressional seat against Republican George Nethercutt, a poll showed that about 25 percent of Foley's constituents believed that whomever won the seat would automatically become Speaker of the House. Nethercutt won the race by just one point and became a Freshmen Representative, not Speaker of the House.

George Nethercutt
Official Photograph

187

U.S. Congress

Constituents to Newt: "Come Home:" In 1990, U.S. Representative and future House Speaker Newt Gingrich defeated his Democratic challenger, David Worley by just 983 votes in Georgia's Sixth Congressional District. Worley could have won the race, but the national Democrats did not fund his campaign. Gingrich who was seen by many constituents as raising his national political profile while ignoring his Congressional District told the *New York Times* the next day that he got the message: "They want me to come home more often, to pay more attention to local issues, and I'm going to do it."

Newt Gingrich
Official Portrait

Speaking from Afar: Speaker of the House Tom Foley (D-WA 1989-1995) was the first Speaker who represented a Congressional District west of the Rocky Mountains.

Tom Foley
Official Portrait

A San Francisco Institution: U.S. Representative and former U.S. House Speaker Nancy Pelosi was re-elected by her San Francisco constituents with more than 80% of the vote all but two times between 1992 and 2010.

Nancy Pelosi
Official Photograph

Speakers Blog: House Speaker J. Dennis Hastert (R-IL 1999-2007) was the first Speaker of the U.S. House of Representatives to publish a blog. The blog was first published on October 27, 2005, and was called: *Speakers Journal.*

J. Dennis Hastert
Official Photograph

When the Speaker Does Not Speak: The only time the Speaker of the U.S. House of Representatives does not preside over a Joint Session of the House and Senate is when the Electoral College votes are officially counted. In that case, the Vice President (The Senate President) presides.

I Quit: In 1889, U.S. House Speaker Thomas Bracket Reed (R-ME) resigned the Speakership and his House seat in the middle of his term. He did this in protest of the activist-interventionist policy his party was supporting under the stewardship of President William McKinley. Reed could not persuade them to change course, so he resigned.

Thomas Bracket Reed
Library of Congress

Three Times a Charm for Newt: Future House Speaker Newt Gingrich lost his first two races to the U.S. House of Representatives to Democrat Jack Flynt in 1974 and in 1976. In 1978, Flynt decided not to seek re-election and Gingrich won the seat, defeating Democratic State Senator Virginia Shappard.

Newt Breaks Long Drought: In 1997, Newt Gingrich became the first Republican Speaker of the U.S. House of Representatives to be elected to two consecutive terms in that post since Nicholas Longworth in 1927.

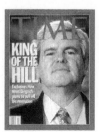

Newt Gingrich on the Cover of *Time Magazine*

Tell them how you really feel Mr. Speaker: House Speaker Thomas Bracket Reed (R-ME 1889-1891 and 1895-1899) said of some of his colleagues: "They never open their mouths without subtracting from the sum of human knowledge."

Thomas Bracket Reed
Library of Congress

A First Edition: Former Speaker of the House Joseph Cannon (R-Illinois 1903-1911) was featured on the cover of the first edition of *Time Magazine*, which debuted on March 3, 1923.

Joe Cannon
First Cover of *Time Magazine*

Security, Security: The Speaker of the U.S. House of Representatives, who is third in line for the Presidency, and the President Pro Tempore of the U.S. Senate, who is fourth in line for the Presidency, receive a security detail.

Speaker can't even keep his Seat: In 1994, U.S. House Speaker Tom Foley (D-WA) became the first incumbent Speaker to lose his bid for re-election to his House seat since 1862.

Tom Foley
Official Photograph

Future Speaker Beats Incumbent and former U.S. Representative: In 1990, future U.S. House Speaker John Boehner won a seat representing the Eighth Congressional District of Ohio by defeating incumbent U.S. Representative Donald "Buz" Lukens. Lukens had been convicted of contributing to the delinquency of a minor. He allegedly paid a 16-year-old girl to have sex with him. Also in the race was former U.S. Representative Tom Kindness, who once led Boehner by 60 percentage points.

John Boehner
Official Photograph

Newt Hits Hustings: In 1994, future U.S. House Speaker Newt Gingrich campaigned for 125 Congressional candidates, promoting the Contract with America. The GOP won control of the House for the first time in 40 years.

Newt Excoriates Reagan: When President Ronald Reagan's popularity was waning because of the Iran-Contra scandal, U.S. Representative Newt Gingrich asserted: "He will never again be the same Ronald Reagan he was before he blew it. He is not going to regain our trust or faith easily."

Ronald Reagan with Newt Gingrich
Ronald Reagan Presidential Foundation and Library

Everyone wants to Run Against Nancy, Except in her Congressional District: In the 2010 Congressional elections, $65 million was spent on advertisements against Democratic candidates, linking them to the unpopular Speaker of the House Nancy Pelosi (D-CA). Interestingly, in Pelosi's San Francisco-based Ninth Congressional District of California, she was resoundingly re-elected, mustering 80.1% of the vote.

Nancy Pelosi
Official Photograph

Republican Longtime Iron Helmsman: U.S. Representative Joe Martin (R-MA) served as either Minority Leader or as Speaker of the House every year from 1939-1959. During that tenure he also chaired all five Republican National Conventions.

Joseph Martin
Harry S, Truman Library and Museum

Pelosi's Other First: In 2007, U.S. Representative Nancy Pelosi (D-CA) became the first Italian-American Speaker of the House in U.S. History.

Nancy Pelosi
Official Photograph

Second-In-Line: The Speaker of the U.S. House of Representatives is second-in-line for the Presidency. The Vice President is first-in-line.

Who Put the "Tipp" in the "Tipp" O'Neill? U.S. House Speaker Thomas P. "Tip: O'Neill (D-MA 1977-1987) was nicknamed "Tip" after James Edward "Tip" O'Neill, a Major League Baseball player from 1883-1892.

James Edward "Tip" O'Neill
1886 Old Judge Cigarettes Baseball Card

Newt Slams Republican Icon: In 1985, when it was announced that President Ronald Reagan would meet with Soviet General Secretary Mikhail Gorbachev, U.S. Representative Newt Gingrich (R-GA) warned the meeting would be "The most dangerous summit for the West since Adolph Hitler met with Chamberlain [British Prime Minister Neville Chamberlain, 1937-1940] in 1938 in Munich."

Ronald Reagan and Mikhail Gorbachev
Ronald Reagan Presidential Foundation and Library

The U.S. Senate

U.S. Senator under 30: The youngest U.S. Senator in history was John Henry Eaton. Although under the *U.S. Constitution* a Senator must be at least 30 years old, Eaton supposedly did not know his age and the issue was never challenged. However, based on the birth date on his tombstone, Eaton would have been only 28 years old when he was sworn into the U.S. Senate in 1818.

John Henry Eaton
Official Portrait

Incapacitated Senator: In 1969, U.S. Senator Karl Mundt (R-SD) suffered a stroke. Mundt served out the remainder of his term, which expired in 1973, but was not able to cast a single vote. He was stripped of all his Committee assignments because he could not participate.

Karl Mundt
Library of Congress

That's "Not" What I Said: It was reported first by *Time Magazine* that U.S. Representative George Smathers made the following charge about U.S. Senator Claude Pepper while campaigning to defeat him in the 1950 Democratic Primary in which Smathers won: "Are you aware that the candidate is known all over Washington as a shameless extrovert? Not only that, but this man is reliably reported to have practiced nepotism with his sister-in-law and he has a sister who was once a wicked thespian in New York. He matriculated with co-eds at the University, and it is an established fact that before his marriage he habitually practiced celibacy." Smathers denied making the quote and offered $10,000 to anyone who could prove he made it. No one did.

George Smathers
Library of Congress

Wisconsin Oddity: Although the Jewish population of Wisconsin is less than 1%, the state had two Jewish U.S. Senators from 1991-2011: Herbert Kohl and Russell Feingold.

JFK and Barack Obama Share Rare U.S. Senate Accomplishment: Since 1960, 50 incumbent U.S. Senators have run for President. The only two to win the Presidency were Democrats John F. Kennedy of Massachusetts in 1960 and Barack Obama of Illinois in 2008.

Deep Thoughts with Roman Hruska: During the confirmation hearings for Richard M. Nixon's failed U.S. Supreme Court nominee Harold Carswell, U.S. Senator Roman Hruska (R-NE) defended allegations that Carswell was of mediocre intelligence by stating: "Even if he were mediocre, there are a lot of mediocre judges and people and lawyers. They are entitled to a little representation, aren't they, and a little chance? We can't have all Brandeises, Frankfurters and Cardozos."

Roman Hrusk
Library of Congress

The First Irishman: David I. Walsh was both the first Irish Catholic Governor and the first Irish Catholic U.S. Senator from Massachusetts. He served as Governor from 1914-1916 and as U.S. Senator from 1919-1925 and from 1926-1947.

David I. Walsh
Library of Congress

End of an Era: U.S. Senator Joseph T. Robinson (D-AR) was the last U.S. Senator selected by a state legislature. He was elected by the Arkansas Legislature to fill the term of Democrat Jefferson Davis, who had died before assuming office. Robinson was elected by the Legislature on January 27, 1913, and took office on March 4, 1913. The Seventeenth Amendment to the *U.S. Constitution* mandates the direct election of U.S. Senators. It was ratified on April 8, 1913.

Joseph T. Robinson
Library of Congress

Fenway Park and the Kennedy Clan: Boston Mayor John "Honey Fitz" Fitzgerald threw out the first pitch at the first game ever played at Fenway Park in 1912. In 2009, his grandson, U.S. Senator Edward M. Kennedy (D-MA), threw out the first pitch at the Boston Red Sox season home-opener.

Fenway Park in its Early Days
Library of Congress

Senator for a Day: The first woman to serve in the United States Senate was Georgia Democrat Rebecca Ann Felton (1922). Peach State Governor Thomas Hardwick appointed her to replace Senator Thomas E. Watson, who died in office. Senator Felton was 87 years of age and was a veteran of the Woman's Suffrage Movement. Unfortunately her tenure in the U.S. Senate was short, only lasting one day. A day later the newly elected U.S. Senator, Walter George, was sworn into office.

Rebecca Latimer Felton
Library of Congress

Senate Youth Movement: In 2009, at 91 years of age, U.S. Senator Robert C. Byrd (D-WV) abrogated the Chairmanship of the coveted U.S. Senate Committee on Appropriations. He was succeeded by Hawaii Democrat Daniel Inouye, a mere 84 years of age.

Daniel Inouye
Official Photograph

First African-American U.S. Senator: In 1870, Mississippi Republican Hiram Revels became the first African-American to serve in the U.S. Senate, filling the seat vacated by U.S. Senator Albert G. Brown. Brown resigned when the South succeeded at the beginning of the U.S. Civil War in 1861.

Hiram Revels
Library of Congress

The Times They Are A-changin': In 2001, when U.S. Senator James Jeffords of Vermont left the Republican Party to become an Independent, he broke what was the longest held Republican seat in U.S. history. The seat had been in Republican hands since 1857. Today, the seat is held by self-professed "Democratic Socialist" Bernie Sanders.

James Jeffords
Official Photograph

Nancy Does It Her Way: In 1978 Republican Nancy Kassebaum became the first female elected to the U.S. Senate whose husband had not been a U.S. Senator.

Nancy Kassebaum
Official Photograph

South Carolina's Energizer Senators: The longest tenure for a state having the same two U.S. Senators is South Carolina, which from November 8, 1966 to January 3, 2005 was served by Democrat Ernest "Fritz" Hollings and Republican Strom Thurmond.

Speck of Red in Sea of Blue: In the 2008 U.S. Senate race, incumbent John Kerry carried 350 of Massachusetts' 351 municipalities. The one town where Republican challenger Jeff Beaty won was Boxford. (50%-47%)

John Kerry
Official Photograph

Biden's First: At 66 years old, U.S. Senator Joseph Biden (D-DE) became the youngest U.S. Senator sworn in for a fifth term. Biden was elected in 1972 at age 29. He turned 30 before being sworn in to the U.S. Senate.

Joseph Biden
Official Photograph

Blue Grass Institution: U.S. Senator Mitch McConnell (R-KY), who assumed his Senate seat in 1985, is the longest serving U.S. Senator in Kentucky history.

Mitch McConnell
Official Photograph

Wartime Buddies: U.S. Senator Robert J. Dole (R-KS 1969-1996) and current U.S. Senator Daniel Inouye (D-HI) both recovered from wounds suffered in World War II at Percy Jones Army Hospital in Battle Creek, Michigan.

Sad News: While presiding over the Senate, U.S. Senator Edward M. Kennedy (D-MA) heard that his brother, President John F. Kennedy, had been shot.

Edward M. Kennedy
Official Photograph

New Mexico Institution: U.S. Senator Pete Domenici (R-NM) holds the record for the longest serving Senator in New Mexico history. He served for 36 years, from 1973-2009.

Pete Domenici
Official Photograph

Big Shots From Russell, Kansas: U.S. Senator Robert J. Dole (R-KS 1969-1996) and U.S. Senator Arlen Specter (R-PA and D-PA 1981-2011) both hail from the small Kansas town of Russell. In 1996 the two ran against each other for the GOP Presidential nomination. Dole won.

Marrying Ms. Kansas: Linda Hall, the wife of former U.S. Senate Majority Leader Tom Daschle (D-SD 2001-2003), was Ms. Kansas in 1976.

Tom Daschle
Official Photograph

A Senator's Other Duty: U.S. Senator Orrin Hatch (R-UT) serves on the Board of Directors for the United States Holocaust Memorial Museum.

Orrin Hatch
Official Photograph

Leahy's Legacy: U.S. Senator Patrick Leahy is the only Democratic U.S. Senator in history to represent Vermont. He was first elected in 1974 and still holds office.

Patrick Leahy
Official Photograph

Roger That: Roger Wicker was the first Republican State Senator from Northern Mississippi since Reconstruction. He was elected to that post in 1986 and served until 1994. He is presently representing Mississippi in the U.S. Senate.

Roger Wicker
Official Photograph

Illinois African-American Pride: Out of the six African-Americans to serve in the U.S. Senate, three represented Illinois. They were: Carol Moseley Braun (1993-1999), Barack Obama (2005-2008), and Roland Burris (2009-2011). All three are Democrats.

Coburn and Keyes: In 2000, then U.S. Representative Tom Coburn (R-OK) was the only member of the U.S. Congress to support conservative activist Allan Keyes's Presidential bid in the Republican primary.

Tom Coburn
Official Photograph

Master Whip: U.S. Senator Trent Lott (R-MS 1989-2007) is the only person to have served as Whip in both Chambers of the U.S. Congress.

Trent Lott
Official Photograph

Sweet Revenge: In 1968, Democrat Mike Gravel ousted incumbent U.S. Senator Ernest Gruening (D-AK) in the Democratic primary. In 1980, Gravel lost the Democratic primary to Clark Gruening, the grandson of Ernest Gruening.

Mission Impossible? Louisiana holds the record for the longest streak of a single party holding both U.S. Senate seats. The Democrats held both seats in the Pelican State from 1915-2005. The streak was broken with the swearing-in of Republican David Vitter in 2005.

David Vitter
Official Photograph

Long-Time Chairman: U.S. Senator J. William Fulbright (D-AR 1945-1975) was the longest serving Chairman of the U.S. Senate Committee on Foreign Relations. He served as Chairman from 1959-1974.

J. William Fulbright
Library of Congress

George Washington and Ted Kennedy: U.S. Senator Edward M. Kennedy (D-MA 1963-2009) was born on February 22, 1932. That was the 200th anniversary of the birth of George Washington.

Mail Call: In 1996, Ron Wyden (D-OR) became the first person to win a U.S. Senate seat in a mail-in election. Oregon was experimenting with postal voting at that time. In 1998, Oregon passed a referendum mandating mail-in elections.

Ron Wyden
Official Photograph

Future U.S. Senator Walks Does Moon Walk: U.S. Senator Harrison Schmitt (R-NM 1977-1983) is the only member of the U.S. Congress to walk on the Moon. Prior to entering the political world, Schmitt was an NASA astronaut. He was aboard Apollo 17 when the spacecraft landed on the Moon in 1972.

Harrison Schmitt
Official Photograph

Landslide Landrieu: U.S. Senator Mary Landrieu (D-LA) won her first election to the U.S. Senate in 1996, garnering 5,799 more votes than her Republican opponent, Newspaper Publisher Louis Elwood "Woody" Jenkins. Over 1.7 million total votes were cast. This was the closest U.S. Senate race in Louisiana history.

Mary Landrieu
Official Photograph

Cowboy State System: Under Wyoming Law, when a U.S. Senate vacancy occurs, the Central Committee of the party of the retired or deceased Senator gets to select three possible successors from their party. They then submit the list to the Governor who selects the new Senator.

Transracial Appeal: In 1966, the voters in Massachusetts made state Attorney General Edward W. Brooke the first popularly elected African-American U.S. Senator in American History. At that time, the African-American population of the Commonwealth was just 2%.

Edward W. Brooke
Library of Congress

Lucky Mark Pryor: In his 2008 re-election bid, U.S. Senator Mark Pryor (D-AR) was the only incumbent U.S. Senator not to face opposition by a major party candidate.

Mark Pryor
Official Photograph

This Lady Walks the Walk: 88-year-old Doris "Granny D" Haddock of New Hampshire walked over 3,200 miles across the United States to draw attention to Campaign Finance Reform. She garnered the Democratic Party's nomination for U.S. Senate in 2004. She lost the election to Republican U.S. Senator Judd Gregg.

Breaking Democratic Stranglehold: U.S. Senator Tim Hutchinson (R-AR 1997-2003) has the distinction of being the first Republican to represent Arkansas in the U.S. Senate since 1879.

Tim Hutchinson
Official Photograph

Indiana Institution: U.S. Senator Richard Lugar (R-IN) is the most senior Republican in the U.S. Senate. He has served in the U.S. Senate since 1977.

Dick Lugar
Official Photograph

Basketball Has Been Very Good to Me: U.S. Senator Herb Kohl (D-WI) has owned the Milwaukee Bucks Basketball franchise since 1985.

Herb Kohl
Official Photograph

The Byrd is the Word: In his 1970 re-election bid, U.S. Senator Robert C. Byrd (D-WV) became the first statewide West-Virginia candidate to win all 55 counties. In his re-election bid in 2006, Byrd won 54 of West Virginia's 55 counties.

Robert C. Byrd
Official Photograph

Record-Breaking Evan Bayh: In his 2004 re-election bid, U.S. Senator Evan Bayh (D-IN) garnered the most popular votes of any Indiana Senator in history. He garnered 1,496,976 votes.

Evan Bayh
Official Photograph

Appropriations Bigwigs: In 2008, the two states with the most earmarks per capita were Alaska and Hawaii. Both had U.S. Senators on the powerful Senate Appropriations Committee. They were Ted Stevens (R-AK) and Daniel Inouye (D-HI).

It's a Knockout: U.S. Senator Barbara Boxer (D-CA) holds the record for the most votes won by a candidate in a statewide election. She was re-elected in 2004, garnering 6,955,728 votes

Barbara Boxer
Official Photograph

Teddy Goes to School: Future U.S. Senator Edward M. Kennedy (D-MA) attended 10 different boarding schools in 13 years.

Boren Blowout: In 1990, U.S. Senator David Boren (D-OK) won every Oklahoma precinct, and garnered 83.2% of the vote in his re-election bid against Republican Steve Jones.

David Boren
Official Photograph

We've Got Trouble: U.S. Senator Robert C. Byrd (D-WV 1959-2011) and billionaire Real Estate Mogul Leona Helmsley (1930-2007) both had dogs named: "Trouble."

Razorback Pioneer: In 1998, Arkansas voters made Blanche Lincoln the youngest woman ever elected to the U.S. Senate. She was just 38.

Blanche Lincoln
Official Photograph

Oregon Oddity: In 1996, U.S. Senator Robert Packwood (R-OR) resigned his seat amid allegations of sexual misconduct. In the special election to replace him, Democratic nominee Ronald Wyden defeated Republican Gordon Smith. Later that year, Smith won the other Oregon U.S. Senate seat. This is the first time in U.S. History that two opposing U.S. Senate Candidates were elected to different Senate Seats during the same year.

Aloha Institution: U.S. Senator Daniel Inouye (D-HI) has held elected office in the Aloha State since 1954, five years before Hawaii became a state in 1959. He has served in the U.S. Senate since 1963.

Daniel Inouye
Official Photograph

Lieberman's Early Words Come Back to Haunt Him: Independent-Democrat Joseph Lieberman of Connecticut won his U.S. Senate seat in 1988 partly by blaming his opponent, then Republican U.S. Senator Lowell Weicker Jr., for having " . . . one of the worst attendance records in the United States Senate." Lieberman added, "He's missed votes that could have really helped middle-class taxpayers, could have helped clean up our environment, could have protected jobs." Weicker's attendance rate was a respectable ninety percent. Ironically, during the 108th Congress, from 2003-2004, while running for President, Lieberman missed 39 percent of U.S Senate Votes.

Joe Lieberman
Official Photograph

The Man in Maryland: U.S. Senator Paul Sarbanes (D-MD 1977-2007) served longer than any other Senator in Maryland history. He served for 30 years.

Paul Sarbanes
Official Photograph

A Five-Term Senator: U.S. Senator Thomas Hart Benton (Democratic-Republican and Democrat-MO, 1821-1851) was the first U.S. Senator to serve five full terms.

Thomas Hart Benton
Library of Congress

Talk To Me: U.S. Senator Robert Bennett (R-UT 1993-2011) once headed the firm Microsonics, which produces audio disks for talking toys.

Robert Bennett
Official Photograph

Lone Star Lineage: Charles S. Taylor, the great-great grandfather of U.S. Senator Kay Bailey Hutchinson (R-TX), signed the *Texas Declaration of Independence* in 1836, the year the Alamo fell to Mexican General Antonio Lopez de Santa Anna.

Native Alaskans: The two current U.S. Senators from Alaska are the only U.S. Senators ever to have been born in Alaska. They are Mark Begich and Lisa Murkowski.

Robert Kennedy Works for Republican Anti-Communist Crusader: Future U.S. Attorney General Robert F. Kennedy (1961-1964) worked for six months on the staff of U.S. Senator Joseph McCarthy (R-WI), and also worked on the staff of the Senate Committee on Investigations, chaired by McCarthy during the Army-McCarthy Hearings.

Joseph McCarthy
Library of Congress

Democratic Dissenters: The only three Democratic U.S. Senators to vote for 1995 legislation opening up a portion of the Arctic National Wildlife Refuge to drilling were Mary Landrieu of Louisiana, Daniel Inouye and Daniel Akaka of Hawaii.

All in the Family: U.S. Senator Sam Nunn (D-GA 1973-1997) is the Grand-nephew of U.S. Representative Carl Vinson (D-GA 1914-1965).

Sam Nunn
Official Photograph

New New Yorker: On the day Robert F. Kennedy was elected to the U.S. Senate from New York, he did not meet the residency requirements to vote in the state.

Robert F. Kennedy
Lyndon Baines Johnson Library and Museum

Magnolia State Smackdown: The two candidates for U.S. Senate Majority Leader in 1996 were both from Mississippi. Republican Trent Lott defeated Republican Thad Cochran 44-8.

David Boren and "The Pusher:" U.S. Senator David Boren (D-OK 1971-1994) is a cousin of musician and actor Hoyt Axton. Axton starred in the movie "Gremlins," and wrote the song *The Pusher*, later recorded by the hard rock band *Steppenwolf* for the popular 1969 movie *Easy Rider*.

Money Can't Always Buy An Election: In the 2004 Illinois Democratic Primary for the U.S. Senate in Illinois, businessman Blair Hull outspent State Senator Barack Obama 6-1. However, Hull finished in third place with just 12% of the vote.

Spaced Out: U.S. Senator Jack Garn (R-UT 1974-1993) was the first incumbent U.S. Senator to fly in space. In 1985, he served as a Payload Specialist aboard the Space Shuttle "Discovery."

Jack Garn
Official Photograph

Octogenarian Senators: Both of Hawaii's U.S. Senators are octogenarians (persons in their eighties). They are Democrats Daniel Inouye and Daniel Akaka.

The Baystate's two John F. Kennedys: From 1955-1961, Massachusetts was represented by John Fitzgerald Kennedy in the U.S. Senate while John Francis Kennedy served as State Treasurer. The two men were not related.

The Praying Senator: U.S. Senator Frank Carlson (R-KS 1950-1969) organized the First National Prayer Breakfast in 1953.

Frank Carlson
Library of Congress

Here's Johnny: U.S. Senator John Edwards (D-NC 1998-2005, and 2004 Democratic Vice Presidential nominee) was given the birth name "Johnny."

John Edwards
Official Photograph

Obama and Town halls: In his first year in the U.S. Senate (2005), Barack Obama (D-IL) held 39 town hall meetings across Illinois.

Barack Obama
White House Photograph by Pete Souza

Young Man Wielding Power: William Knowland (R-CA) was the youngest U.S. Senator elected Senate Majority Leader. He was elected to the position in 1953, at age 45.

William Knowland
Library of Congress

Adopt-a-Politician: U.S. Senator Robert C. Byrd (D-WV 1959-2010) did not find out he was adopted until he was 16 years old.

Robert C. Byrd
West Virginia State Archives

Persistence pays Off: U.S. Senator Phil Gramm (R-TX 1985-2002) failed the third, seventh and ninth grades. He later was awarded a Ph.D. in economics from the University of Georgia.

Phil Gramm
Official Photograph

Legacy Still Stands: Henderson, Nevada is named after Charles B. Henderson, who represented the Silver State in the U.S. Senate from 1918-1921.

Charles B. Henderson
Library of Congress

Strom's Moment: In 1957, U.S. Senator Strom Thurmond (D-SC) filibustered in the U.S. Senate for 24 hours and 18 minutes against the Civil Rights Act of 1957. This is the all-time filibuster record.

Strom Thurmond
Library of Congress

Brave Stand: The only southern U.S. Senators who did not sign the Southern Manifesto of 1956 (which opposed desegregation efforts) were Democrats: Albert Gore Sr. and Estes Kefauver of Tennessee, and Senate Majority Leader Lyndon B. Johnson of Texas.

Nepotism Alabama Style: U.S. Senator (D-AL) Hugo Black resigned his seat in 1937 to assume a seat on the U.S. Supreme Court. Alabama Governor Bibb Graves appointed his wife, Democrat Dixie Bibb Graves, to the vacant Senate seat. Mrs. Graves became the first married woman U.S. Senator in U.S. history. She served for less than one month and then resigned from the Senate.

Dixie Bibb Graves
Library of Congress

Voters give it a lot of thought: In 1952, U.S. Senator Kenneth McKellar (D-TN) ran for re-election on the slogan: "Thinking Feller? Vote McKellar." His Democratic primary opponent, U.S. Representative Albert Gore Sr. (D-TN), replied with the slogan: "Think Some More – Vote for Gore." Gore won.

Kenneth McKellar
Library of Congress

Bi-Coastal Power-Roommates: While students at the University of Virginia Law School, Edward M. Kennedy and John V. Tunney were roommates. Both later became U.S. Senators. Tunney represented California from 1971-1979. Kennedy represented Massachusetts from 1963-2009.

Ranger Ted Kennedy: U.S. Senator Edward M. Kennedy (D-MA 1963-2009) worked as a forest ranger in California one summer.

Edward M. Kennedy
U.S. Navy Photograph

Congressional Longevity: U.S. Senator Robert C. Byrd (D-WV 1959-2010) was the longest serving member of the U.S. Congress in history. He served in the U.S. House of Representatives from 1953-1959 and in the U.S. Senate from 1959-2010. Byrd served during the administrations of eleven Presidents, from Harry S. Truman to Barack Obama.

Robert C. Byrd
West Virginia State Archives

Very Few Original Americans: There have been only two Americans with Native American-lineage who have served in the U.S. Senate. The first was Charles Curtis (R-KS 1907-1913 and 1915-1929). The second was Ben Nighthorse Campbell (D-CO and R-CO 1993-2005).

Ben Nighthorse Campbell
Official Photograph

Senate Tenure: The average tenure for a member of the U.S. Senate is 14 years.

Walking Lawton: In 1970, Florida State Senator Lawton Chiles campaigned for the U.S. Senate, embarking on a 1,003-mile walk of the state from Pensacola to Key West. The 91-day journey earned him the moniker of "Walking Lawton." Chiles won the election.

Lawton Chiles
Official Portrait

To the Victor Goes the Spoils: The term "Spoils System" was originated by a statement from U.S. Senator William Marcy (D-NY) in 1832. He was defending President Andrew Jackson's nomination of former Secretary of State Martin Van Buren (a Jackson political supporter) as the Ambassador to the Court of St. James (England) by saying: "To the victor goes the spoils."

William Marcy
Library of Congress

Inimitable Political Move: After leaving the U.S. Senate in 1943, Wall Doxey (D-MS) served as Sergeant-at-Arms of the U.S. Senate. No other Senator has done this.

Wall Doxey
Library of Congress

Dean Leahy: U.S. Senator Patrick Leahy (D-VT) is the Dean of the New England Congressional delegation. He has served the Green Mountain state in the U.S. Senate since 1975.

Patrick Leahy
Official Photograph

From the Priesthood to the GOP: John McLaughlin, founder and host of the public affairs television program *The McLaughlin Group,* is a former Catholic priest. McLaughlin left the priesthood in 1970 and won the Republican nomination to challenge U.S. Senator John O. Pastore (D-RI). McLaughlin lost the race but became an advisor to President Richard M. Nixon.

Female Senator in the Rough Rider State: Democrat Jocelyn Birch Burdick is the only female ever to represent North Dakota in the U.S. Congress. She was appointed by Governor George Sinner to the U.S. Senate in 1992. She served as a placeholder until a successor was elected to the seat of her late husband, Quentin Burdick.

Jocelyn Birch Burdick
Official Photograph

He Didn't Give Up the Ship: U.S. Senator William Proximire (D-WI 1957-1989), a steadfast supporter of the *United Nations Convention on the Prevention and Punishment of the Crime of Genocide Treaty,* delivered a speech every day the Senate was in session for almost twenty years. He did this until the U.S. Senate ratified the convention in 1986. He gave a total of 3,211 speeches on the subject.

William Proximire
Official Photograph

207

Peacenik Republican: During his 30-year tenure in the U.S. Senate, Mark Hatfield (R-OR 1967-1997), known for his aversion to military interventions, voted against every single military appropriations bill.

Mark Hatfield
Official Photograph

Obama Wins the Cities: In the 2004 Illinois Democratic Primary for the U.S. Senate, State Comptroller Dan Hynes won 80 of the state's 102 counties. However, Barack Obama garnered the nomination with a strong showing in the Chicago area.

Barack Obama
White House Photograph by Pete Souza

GOP Stronghold: Kansas voters have not elected a Democrat to the U.S. Senate since 1932.

Magic 67: For a treaty to be ratified by the U.S. Senate, it needs 67 votes.

Arab-American Wins in the Mount Rushmore State: In 1972, South Dakota residents made James G. Abourezk the first Arab-American elected to the U.S. Senate. He is of Lebanese ancestry.

James G. Abourezk
Official Photograph

Cornhusker-ette: Nebraska has had only one female in its Congressional delegation. U.S. Representative Virginia Smith (R-NE 1975-1991) represented the state's largely rural Third Congressional District, which includes the majority of the state.

Virginia Smith
Official Photograph

Graham v. Gramm: During the 103rd Congress, which lasted from 1993-1994, the Chairman of the Democratic Senatorial Campaign Committee (DSCC) was U.S. Senator Bob Graham (D-FL). The Chairman of the Republican Senatorial Campaign Committee (RSCC) was U.S. Senator Phil Gramm (R-TX).

The Model Senator: As a 22-year-old Boston College Law student, future U.S. Senator Scott Brown (R-MA) was named *Cosmopolitan*'s Sexiest Man. He posed nude for the magazine.

Scott Brown
Official Photograph

Finally a Little Quiet Time: U.S. Senator Richard Russell (D-GA 1933-1971) had 14 siblings. Ironically, he never married or fathered children.

Richard Russell
Library of Congress

Cheesehead Stands Alone: Russell Feingold (D-WI 1993-2011) was the only U.S. Senator to vote against the U.S.A. Patriot Act in 2001.

Russell Feingold
Official Photograph

Get your Own Damn Dam: U.S. Senator Frank Church (D-ID 1957-1981), a stalwart supporter of President Lyndon B. Johnson on most issues, broke from the President on his handling of the Vietnam War. He told the President he was persuaded by nationally syndicated columnist Walter Lippman that the U.S. should negotiate with the North Vietnamese Government. Johnson responded: "The next time you want a dam in Idaho, go talk to Walter Lippman."

Frank Church
Official Photograph

GOP breaks Senate Lock in Arkansas: In 1996, Republican Tim Hutchinson was elected to the U.S. Senate. He became the first Republican U.S. Senator from Arkansas. No other state had gone that long without electing a Republican to the U.S. Senate seat. He was dislodged from office in 2004, losing his re-election bid to Democrat Mark Pryor.

Tim Hutchinson
Official Photograph

Carpetbagger Sets Record: James Shields is the only U.S. Senator to serve three states. He was elected to the U.S. Senate from Illinois. His election was subsequently nullified when it became known he had not lived the requisite nine years in the state prior to his election. He won the Special Election (by that time he had met the requirement) to replace himself. After losing a re-election battle, Shields moved to Minnesota and in 1858 was elected as one of the state's first Senators. Long after losing his re-election bid, Shields was a resident of Wisconsin and won an 1877 Special Election to fill the remainder of the late Lewis Boggs' term. Shields did not seek re-election.

James Shields
Library of Congress

It Took More Than a Century: In 1981, Mack Mattingly became the first Republican to represent Georgia in the U.S. Senate since 1873.

Mack Mattingly
Official Photograph

The Power of Incumbency: No incumbent U.S. Senator from South Carolina has lost a re-election bid since 1930, when former U.S. Representative James Byrnes dislodged Coleman Livingston Blease in the Democratic Primary.

Coleman Livingston Blease
Library of Congress

Goldwater Recommends all Good Christians Kick Ass: Reverend Jerry Falwell was a vociferous opponent of Ronald Reagan's nomination of Sandra Day O'Connor to the U.S. Supreme Court. He urged "All Good Christians to oppose the nomination of Sandra Day O'Connor to the U.S. Supreme Court." U.S. Senator Barry Goldwater (R-AZ) deadpanned: "All Good Christians should kick Jerry Falwell's ass."

Barry Goldwater
Library of Congress

Missing Votes: During the 110th U.S Congress (2007-2008), U.S. Senator John McCain (R-AZ) missed 63.9% of his Senate votes while running for President. This was on the heels of his unsuccessful 2000 Presidential bid for the GOP Presidential nomination, when McCain missed 30% of his Senate Votes while on the campaign Hustings.

John McCain
Official Photograph

Fifteen-year-old Go Getter: In 1912, at just 15 years of age, future U.S. Senator George Bender (R-OH 1954-1957) accumulated 10,000 signatures on a petition urging former President Theodore Roosevelt to run again for President. Roosevelt did, and notified the young George Bender.

Pretty Evenly Divided: Former U.S. Senator and 1972 Democratic Presidential nominee George McGovern (D-SD) was elected to the U.S. Senate in 1962 by just 597 votes. In 1978, future Senate Majority leader Tom Daschle won his first race, the at-large U.S. House seat in South Dakota, by just 139 votes. In 2002, South Dakota Democrat Tim Johnson was re-elected by just 524 votes.

Little Time for Day Job: During the 110th Congress (2007-2008), U.S. Senator Barack Obama (D-IL) missed 46% or 303 of the 657 Senate votes. At the time, Barack Obama was running for President.

Barack Obama
White House Photograph by Pete Souza

Now That is Dumb: In 1974, the liberal publication *New Times Magazine* named U.S. Senator William Lloyd Scott (R-VA) the "dumbest Congressman." Scott responded by calling a press conference to deny the charges.

William Lloyd Scott
Library of Congress

Breaking Democrats Hammerlock in the Old Dominion State: In 1972, Virginia voters elected U.S. Representative William Lloyd Scott to the U.S. Senate. He would become the first Republican to serve in the U.S. Senate representing Virginia since 1889.

Joe's Way: U.S. Senator Joseph Lieberman's (I-CT) favorite song is: *My Way* by Frank Sinatra.

Joseph Lieberman
Official Photograph

The Press Knows Dole: U.S. Senator Robert J. Dole (R-KS 1969-1996) holds the record for appearances on the national public affairs program *Meet the Press*. He appeared 64 times.

Robert J. Dole
Library of Congress

Dem Elected by Defecting Republican: In 1994, U.S. Senator Thomas Daschle (D-SD) defeated U.S. Senator Christopher Dodd (D-CT) by one vote in the election for Senate Minority Leader. The last vote to come in was an absentee vote by U.S. Senator Ben Nighthorse Campbell (D-CO). Campbell broke the 23-23 tie, handing the election to Mr. Daschle. Shortly thereafter, Campbell defected from the Democratic Party and became a Republican.

"And This 'Byrd' You Cannot Change:" Between 1933 and 1983, a member of the Byrd family held a U.S. Senate seat from Virginia. Democrat Harry Byrd Sr. served from 1933-1965. His son, Harry Byrd Jr. succeeded him in the Senate and served from 1965-1983. In 1970, Harry Byrd Jr. became an Independent, but he continued to caucus with the Democratic Party. (The Byrd's are not related to U.S. Senator Robert C. Byrd (D-WV).

Harry Byrd Sr.
Official Photograph

Town of Senators: U.S. Senator Lindsey Graham (R-SC) lives in the same town that former U.S. Senator and Vice Presidential candidate John Edwards was born in, Seneca, South Carolina. The city has a population of less than 8,000 people.

Lindsey Graham
Official Photograph

Political Trash Talking: In 1919, U.S. Senate Majority Leader Henry Cabot Lodge Sr. (R-MA) called Democratic President Woodrow Wilson "the most sinister figure that ever crossed the country's path."

Henry Cabot Lodge Sr.
Library of Congress

A lot of votes: U.S. Senator Robert C. Byrd (D-WV 1959-2010) cast a record 18,689 roll-call votes during his 51-year U.S. Senate career.

Robert C. Byrd
Official Portrait

The Kerry-Heinz Fortune: According to financial disclosure forms, John Kerry's net worth was $188.6 million in 2009. Much of that fortune is from his wife, Teresa Heinz Kerry, who is the widow of the late U.S. Senator John Heinz, heir to the H.J. Heinz Company (food manufacturing) fortune.

Gerald the Giant Killer: As a result of an investigation by U.S. Senator Gerald Nye (R-ND), corruption was spotlighted during the administration of President Warren G. Harding, who had recently died. Nye discovered that former Interior Secretary Albert B. Fall did not follow competitive bidding practices. Land was leased to the Mammoth Oil Company in reciprocation for campaign contributions being given to the Republican National Committee. For Senator Nye's role in unearthing this scandal, he received the moniker: "Gerald the Giant Killer."

Gerald Nye
Library of Congress

Arkansan Takes on Agriculture: In 2009, Democrat Blanche Lincoln became the first Arkansan to chair the Senate Agriculture, Nutrition, and Forestry Committee.

Blanche Lincoln
Official Photograph

Kerry Saves Life of a Republican Senator: In 1988, while attending a Republican Senate luncheon, U.S. Senator Chic Hecht (R-NV) almost choked to death on an apple. He left the room thinking he would throw up. As he left the room, U.S. Senator John Kerry (D-MA) spotted Hecht in the hallway and noticed that he was in distress. Kerry proceeded to perform the Heimlich maneuver four times. The apple was safely dislodged, saving Hecht's life. Ironically, Senator Kerry was Chairman of the Democratic Senatorial Campaign Committee that year and was targeting Hecht for defeat in Nevada.

Chic Hecht
Official Photograph

Photo Finishes in Nevada: In 1964, U.S. Senator Howard Cannon (D-NV) was re-elected, defeating Republican Paul Laxalt, the state's Lieutenant Governor, by just 48 votes out of 137,378 votes cast. Laxalt asked for and received a state recount, which determined that Cannon had actually won by 84 votes. This was the first time a recount was ordered in Nevada at a state level. In 1974, Laxalt was on the other end of a photo finish, defeating Lieutenant Governor Harry Reid for an open U.S. Senate seat by just 624 votes. In 1998, Harry Reid, who was elected to the U.S. Senate in 1986, was re-elected, defeating U.S. Representative John Ensign by just 429 votes.

Warner v. Warner: In the 1996 U.S. Senate race in Virginia, the Democrats nominated Mark Warner to challenge Republican U.S. Senator John Warner. Mark Warner's slogan was "Mark not John." He was once asked if that was a biblical reference? John Warner won the election.

John Warner
Official Photograph

West Virginia Honors State "Byrd:" In 2000, the West Virginia Legislature voted U.S. Senator Robert C. Byrd as "West Virginian of the Twentieth Century." As the Chairman of the Senate Committee on Appropriations, Byrd earmarked billions of dollars for federal projects in West Virginia.

Robert C. Byrd
U.S. Department of Transportation
Photograph

Maverick Miller: U.S. Senator Zell Miller (D-GA 1999-2009) was the only incumbent Democratic member of the U.S Congress to endorse President George W. Bush in his 2004 re-election campaign.

214

Landslide Frankin: In 2008, Democrat Al Frankin, a former comedian and radio talk show host, defeated incumbent Republican U.S. Senator Norm Coleman. He won by just 312 votes out of the almost 3 million votes cast.

Al Frankin
Official Photograph

Rare Democrat in Idaho: Frank Church is the only Democratic U.S. Senator from Idaho to be re-elected. Elected in 1962, Church was re-elected in 1968 and again in 1974. He lost his bid for a fourth term in 1980 to Republican Steve Symms.

Frank Church
Library of Congress

Breaking Down Barriers: In 1954, future U.S. Senator Edward W. Brooke (R-MA 1967-1979) became the first African-American Commander of American Veterans (AMVETS), an advocacy organization for American Veterans.

Miller Switches Allegiances: In 1992, Georgia Governor Zell Miller was the keynote speaker at the Democratic National Convention, which nominated Arkansas Governor Bill Clinton for President. In 2004, Miller, at the time a U.S. Senator, was the Keynote Speaker at the Republican National Convention, which nominated President George W. Bush for re-election.

Zell Miller
Official Photograph

Extravagant Expenditure: U.S. Senator John F. Kerry (D-MA) owns a $7 million, 76-foot yacht. The yacht is named Isabel, which is the middle-name of his late mother.

Son of Senator was a Rocker: Jeff Gramm, the son of U.S. Senator Phil Gramm (R-TX 1985-2003) was a vocalist and guitarist for the Indie pop band "Aden" from 1995-2002.

Lieberman reprimands a prominent Volunteer to his first State Senate Campaign: As a student at Yale University Law School in 1970, Bill Clinton was a volunteer for insurgent State Senate Candidate Joe Lieberman. Lieberman defeated State Senate Majority Leader Edward Marcus in a New Haven based District. In 1998, as a U.S. Senator, Lieberman was the first Democrat to verbally reprimand President Bill Clinton for his conduct during the Clinton-Lewinsky affair.

Now Starting for the Green Bay Packers, Tight End Ted Kennedy: U.S. Senator Edward M. Kennedy (D-MA) played tight end for the Harvard University Crimson Football team and was recruited by Green Bay Packers coach, Lisle Blackbourn. Kennedy turned down the offer, telling Blackbourn that he: "intended to go into another contact sport, politics."

Edward M. Kennedy (right) with Harvard Crimson Teammates
John F. Kennedy Presidential Library and Museum

Fueling the Partisan Fire: In the 2004 U.S. Senate race, Senate Majority Leader Bill Frist (R-TN) broke precedent by campaigning directly against his counterpart in the Senate, the Minority Leader Tom Daschle (D-SD). There had been an unwritten rule that Senate party leaders don't directly campaign against their Senate counterparts. Bucking tradition, Frist traveled to South Dakota and campaigned for Republican John Thune in his successful effort to dislodge Senate Minority Leader Tom Daschle from his U.S. Senate seat.

Venture Capitalists in Lopsided Duel: In the 1994 Massachusetts Republican U.S. Senate Primary, John Lakien outspent fellow venture capitalist Mitt Romney, but only garnered 18% of the vote.

Electioneering Begins at Home: In 1952, U.S. Senator Henry Cabot Lodge, Jr. (R-MA) took his re-election bid largely for granted and became Chairman of Dwight D. Eisenhower's Presidential campaign. He spent an inordinate amount of time barnstorming the nation for Eisenhower rather than campaigning for himself in Massachusetts. The result was that Eisenhower was elected in a landslide victory. Unfortunately for Lodge, Democrat John F. Kennedy upset Lodge by less than three percentage points.

Henry Cabot Lodge Jr.
Official Photograph

Future Leader Defeats Present Leader: In 1950, Republican Everett Dirkson defeated U.S. Senator Scott Lukas (D-IL). Lukas was the U.S. Senate Majority Leader. Ten years later, Dirkson became U.S. Senate Minority leader.

Everett Dirkson
Library of Congress

The Eponym heard Around the World: The term "McCarthyism," refers to U.S. Senator Joseph McCarthy's (R-WI) escapades in searching for domestic Communists. *Washington Post* Political cartoonist Herbert Block coined the term "McCarthyism." McCarthy compared *The Washington Post* to the *Daily Worker* (A now defunct Communist newspaper published in New York City).

Joseph McCarthy
Library of Congress

Even as a senior citizen, Thurmond attracted young women: At age 66, U.S. Senator Strom Thurmond (R-SC 1955-2003) married Nancy Moore, the 22-year-old Miss South Carolina.

Strom Thurmond with Wife Nancy and Immediate Family
Strom Thurmond Institute

"No" on Hillary: The only two U.S. Senators to vote against Hillary Clinton's confirmation as Secretary of State in 2009, were Jim DeMint (R-SC) and David Vitter (R-LA).

Hillary Clinton
William J. Clinton Presidential Library and Museum

Unpopular Vote: The *Gulf of Tonkin Resolution*, giving President Lyndon B. Johnson carte blanche to use military force in South East Asia, passed the U.S. House of Representatives 416-0 and passed the U.S. Senate 98-2. The two dissenting U.S. Senators were Ernest Gruening (D-AK) and Wayne Morse (D-OR). Both senators were defeated for re-election in 1968.

Lyndon B. Johnson Signs the Gulf of Tonkin Resolution
Lyndon Baines Johnson Library and Museum

Senator Tom-Tom: U.S. Senator James Thomas Heflin (D-AL 1920-1931) was nicknamed "Tom-Tom" because he had the habit of beating his chest like a drum when speaking.

James Thomas Heflin
Library of Congress

Relatives of Democratic Leaders Go Head to Head: In 1962, the brother of President John F. Kennedy, Edward M. Kennedy, faced the nephew of House Speaker John McCormick, Edward J. McCormick Jr., in the Massachusetts Democratic Senatorial primary. Kennedy won the primary and the General Election.

Edward M. Kennedy in 1962
John F. Kennedy Library and Museum

Republican Senators Forge a Very Close Relationship: Republican U.S. Senators Nancy Kassebaum of Kansas (1978-1997) and Howard Baker of Tennessee (1967-1985) got married in 1996.

Union All The Way: U.S. Senator and future President Andrew Johnson (D-TN) was the only Southern Senator who did not leave the Union and join the Confederacy.

Andrew Johnson
Library of Congress

Bucking the Party Line: The only five Republican U.S. Senators to vote for the confirmation of Elana Kagan to the U.S. Supreme Court in 2010 were: Susan Collins and Olympia Snowe of Maine, Lindsey Graham of South Carolina, Judd Gregg of New Hampshire, and Richard Lugar of Indiana. The only Democrat to vote against her confirmation was Ben Nelson of Nebraska.

Elana Kagan
Official Photograph

Republican Renegades: The only two Republican U.S. Senators to oppose George W. Bush's $1.35 trillion tax cut package in 2001, were John McCain of Arizona and Lincoln Chaffee of Rhode Island.

Senator gets Diploma from President: In 1963, President John F. Kennedy, the Commencement Speaker at American University's College of Law in Washington, D.C., handed a diploma to U.S. Senator Robert C. Byrd (D-WV). Byrd earned his Law Degree attending night school while serving in the U.S. Senate. Byrd remains the only sitting member of the U.S. Congress to earn a Law Degree while in office.

Robert C. Byrd
West Virginia State Archives

After 40 years, the Last Frontier Switches Horses: In 2008, Democratic Senatorial nominee Mark Begich defeated U.S. Senator Ted Stevens (R-AK). Stevens, who served in the Senate since 1968, became the longest-serving member of the U.S. Senate to lose a re-election bid.

Mark Begich
Official Photograph

Mountaineer Office Holder: Matthew Mansfield Neely has the distinction of being the only West Virginian to serve as Governor and to serve in both the U.S. House of Representatives and the U.S. Senate.

Mathew Mansfield Neely
Library of Congress

"Wayne's World:" During his tenure in the U.S. Senate, Wayne Morse was a Republican (1945-1952), an Independent, (1952-1955) and a Democrat (1955-1969).

Wayne Morse
Lyndon Baines Johnson Library and Museum

It was meant to be: The longest ever serving U.S. Senator was Robert C. Byrd of West Virginia (1959-2010), and the longest ever serving Republican U.S. Senator was Ted Stevens of Alaska (1968-2009). Both men died less than two months apart. During their Senate tenures, both served as President pro tempore and both Chaired the Appropriations Committee.

Harry Reid Defeats "God Almighty:" In 1992, the name "God Almighty" appeared on the primary ballot for U.S. Senate in Nevada. This was the name used by Emil Tolliti Jr., an anti-tax crusader. "God Almighty" garnered just 1.52% of the vote. Incumbent U.S. Senator Harry Reid won the primary and went on to win re-election as well.

Harry Reid
Official Photograph

Worth Every Penny: Before being elected to the U.S. Senate, Democrat Edward M. Kennedy served as the Assistant to the District Attorney for Middlesex County in Massachusetts. He was paid one dollar a year.

Edward M. Kennedy
Library of Congress

In the Minority: The only two U.S. Senators to oppose the candidacy of segregationist Democrat James Eastland (D-MS) for the Chairmanship of the Judiciary Committee in 1956, were Herbert Henry Lehman (D-NY) and Wayne Morse (R-OR). Eastland would wield the gavel as Chairman for over 22 years.

James Eastland
Official Photograph

Yada-Yada-Yada: U.S. Senator John Thune (R-SD) is a voracious watcher of *Seinfeld* reruns.

John Thune
Official Photograph

Moving on Up: Sixteen former U.S. Senators became Presidents at some point in their lives.

Senator Campaigns rather than Votes: As a Presidential candidate, U.S. Senator John Kerry (D-MA) missed 72% of Congressional votes during the 108th Congress from 2003-2004.

John Kerry
Official Photograph

Not Exactly a Model Student: U.S. Senator John McCain (R-AZ) finished fifth from the bottom of his class at the United States Naval Academy at Annapolis in 1958.

John McCain as a student at Annapolis
U.S. Navy Photograph

An Earmarker's Paradise: The largest committee in the U.S. Senate is the *Committee on Appropriations*, which consists of 29 members.

From the Latin: The term "President pro tempore" is Latin for "President for a time."

Republican Scott Brown Shatters Democrat Hammerlock: Between 1997 and 2010 there were no Republican members of the Massachusetts Congressional Delegation. This changed when Scott Brown won a Special Election to assume the U.S. Senate seat formally held by Edward M. Kennedy.

Scott Brown
Official Photograph

Another Humphrey in the Senate: In January of 1978, after the death of U.S. Senator and former Vice President Hubert Humphrey (D-MN), Minnesota Governor Rudy Perpich appointed his widow, Muriel Humphrey to succeed Hubert Humphrey in the U.S. Senate. She served until a Special Election was held in November of 1978 to fill the remaining three years of the term. She is the only wife of a Vice President to hold an elective office.

Muriel Humphrey
Official Photograph

Write-In Rarity: In 2010, U.S. Senator Lisa Murkowski (R-AK), after losing the Republican nomination for re-election to Attorney Joe Miller, won a write-in campaign in the General Election as an Independent. This made her the first candidate to win a U.S. Senate seat as a write-in candidate since Strom Thurmond won a write-in campaign for the U.S. Senate in South Carolina in 1954.

Lisa Murkowski
Official Photograph

First Elected Female Senator: In 1932, Hattie Caraway became the first female elected to the U.S. Senate. Arkansas Governor Harvey Parnell had appointed her to a vacant U.S. Senate seat representing Arkansas the year before. Her late husband, Thaddeus H. Caraway, formerly occupied the seat. Hattie Caraway subsequently won a Special Election to fill the remaining year of her late husband's term. She then won two full six-year terms before being defeated for re-election in 1944.

Hattie Caraway
Library of Congress

Empire State Senators Quit in Protest: In 1881, both U.S. Senators from New York resigned their office in protest of President James Garfield's appointment of William H. Robertson as the Collector of Customs of the Port of New York (The Collector of Customs is responsible for collecting import duties on products from overseas). Republicans Roscoe Conkling and Thomas E. Platt resigned their seats because President Garfield had failed to consult the two Senators beforehand concerning the appointment of Robertson, a proponent of Civil Service Reform. Conkling and Platt were steadfast supporters of the patronage system and opposed any changes to it.

William H. Robertson
Engraving by George Edward Perine

Late Voter: U.S. Senate Majority Leader Bill Frist (R-TN 2003-2007) had no record of having voted until he was 36 years old. He was elected to the U.S. Senate in 1994, at age 42.

Bill Frist
Official Photograph

Burr Breaks the "Cursed Seat:" In 2010, U.S. Senator Richard Burr (R-NC) was the first person "re-elected" to North Carolina's "Cursed Senate Seat." This seat was known as the Cursed Seat because no one had been reelected to the seat since 1975. Democrat Robert Burren Morgan, who won the seat in 1974, was defeated for re-election in 1980 by Republican John Porter East. East did not run for re-election in 1986. He committed suicide that year most likely because he suffered from Hypothyroidism. After the Senator's suicide, Governor Jim Martin appointed Republican Jim Broyhill to fill the position to serve out the remaining months of the unexpired term. Broyhill then lost his bid to serve a full term that year to Democrat Terry Stanford. Stanford served for just one term, losing his re-election bid to Republican Lauch Faircloth. Faircloth served just one term, losing a re-election bid in 1998 to Democrat John Edwards. Edwards did not seek re-election to the seat in 2004, opting instead to run for President. (He later became the unsuccessful Democratic nominee for Vice President.) Republican Richard Burr won the seat in 2004. In 2010, he broke the "Re-election Curse" by winning re-election.

A Centenarian in the Senate: South Carolina Republican Strom Thurmond was the oldest incumbent U.S. Senator in history. He was 100 years old when he left office in 2003.

Strom Thurmond receives a cake for his 100th birthday from Army Chief of Staff Eric Shinseki
U.S. Army Photograph by Jerome Howard

Equivocating on "Unequivocal:" The day after being elected to the U.S. Senate from Illinois in November of 2004, Barack Obama said: "I can unequivocally say I will not be running for national office in four years, and my entire focus is making sure that I'm the best possible senator on behalf of the people of Illinois." In February of 2007, he announced his candidacy for the Presidency of the United States.

Richard Burr
Official Photograph

Barack Obama
Official Photograph

Democrats for Robert Bork: U.S. Senators Ernest Hollings (D-SC) and David Boren (D-OK) were the only U.S. Senate Democrats to vote in favor of the nomination by Ronald Reagan of conservative jurist Robert Bork to the U.S. Supreme Court in 1987. Mr. Bork's nomination failed, 58-42.

Robert Bork on the Cover of *Time Magazine*

JFK and JFK: Future U.S. Senator John F. Kerry (D-MA) once dated the half-sister of First Lady Jacqueline Kennedy, Janet Auchincloss. He once joined the Kennedy family, including President John F. Kennedy, to watch the America's Cup Race.

**John F. Kerry & John F. Kennedy
Watching America's Cup Race**
John F. Kennedy Presidential Library and Museum

Landslide O'Daniel: The only person ever to beat Lyndon B. Johnson in a general election was Wilbert Lee O'Daniel. He defeated Johnson in a 1941 special U.S. Senate election to succeed the late U.S. Senator Morris Sheppard (D-TX). O'Daniel won the election by just 1,306 votes. O'Daniel did not seek re-election in 1948. Johnson ran for the seat that year and won it.

Wilbert Lee O'Daniel
Official Photograph

Ford Garners Support from an Unlikely Source on Nixon Pardon: Many Democrats and some Republicans excoriated President Gerald R. Ford in 1974 when he pardoned his predecessor. Richard M. Nixon for all crimes committed during his Presidency. One of very few Democrats to support the pardon was U.S. Senator Hubert Humphrey (D-MN), the former Vice President who ran against Nixon in the 1968 Presidential race. Humphrey shocked the political establishment by asserting: "The Pardon is right, "It's the only decision President Ford could make."

Hubert Humphrey
Official Photograph

Pertaining to the Congress

The Email Tax Hoax: In 1999, a Canadian trickster circulated an email warning that there was legislation in the U.S. Congress to impose a five-cent tax on all emails. This enraged some recipients of the email and calls came in to offices of Congress demanding members to oppose the proposed legislation. Many members posted on their websites the fact that this was a hoax and that they would not support any legislation to tax emails. During a U.S. Senate debate in 2000 between Democratic nominee Hillary Clinton and Republican nominee Rick Lazio, the moderator of the debate read a question from a viewer asking where the candidates stand on this proposed legislation. Both candidates voiced vociferous opposition to the idea of taxing emails.

Influential Lobby: The Financial Lobby has five lobbyists for every member of the U.S. Congress.

Do as the Romans Do: The archetype for the U.S. Capitol Rotunda is the Pantheon in Rome.

Living Comfortably in The Congress: In 2008, the "median" net worth of a member of the U.S. House of Representatives was $622,254.00. For members of the U.S. Senate, the median net worth was $1.79 million.

Free Mailing: All members of the U.S. Congress are granted "franking" privileges, which allow them to send official correspondence to their constituents without paying the postage.

Failed Effort: In 2004, U.S. Senator Barbara Boxer (D-CA) and U.S. Representative Stephanie Tubbs Jones (D-OH) filed an objection to the certification of Ohio's 20 electoral votes, which went to President George W. Bush. They charged voting irregularities. The objection was rejected 74-1 in the Senate and 267-31 in the House.

Long Weekends: When in session, the U.S. Congress usually meets for just three days per week.

Washington is a Lobbyist Kind of Town: There are 30 registered lobbyists for every incumbent member of the U.S. Congress.

Republican Year, Big Time: In the 1994 mid-term elections, no incumbent Republican Governor, U.S. Senator, or U.S. Representative lost his or her seat.

Great Year to be a Democrat: No incumbent Democratic U.S. Representative, U.S. Senator, or Governor lost his or her seat in the 2006 mid-term elections.

Nuclear Option: The *U.S. Constitution* gives the authority to both houses of the U.S. Congress to expel a member: "for disorderly behavior" if two-thirds of the body vote to do so. Expulsion is a rare form of punishment. In fact, the U.S. Senate has expelled just fifteen members and the U.S. House of Representatives has expelled just five members.

A Two-Part Process: The U.S. House of Representatives has the Constitutional power to impeach a civil officer, while the U.S. Senate has the power to convict that official. A civil officer must be impeached before being convicted.

Just an Opinion: The U.S. Congress can render an official opinion on an issue by voting for a "Sense of Congress" resolution. It is not binding, and does not require a Presidential Signature.

Lobbyists Need Not Apply: Former members of the U.S. Congress enjoy the same free parking privileges as current members, so long as they are not registered lobbyists.

Friendship has its Perks: Members of the U.S. Congress are allowed to accept meals and gifts worth less than $50.00 from individuals. However, those individuals who are given the status of "personal friend" can give up to $250.00 in meals and gifts.

Through the Years, But Who's Counting? Since its inaugural session in 1789, there have been about 10,000 members of the U.S. Congress.

Bi-Cameral Achievement: Less than 650 Americans have served in both the U.S. House of Representative and the U.S. Senate.

This Brief is Well Supported: In 2009, U.S. Senators Kay Bailey Hutchinson (R-TX), John Tester (D-MT), U.S. Representatives Mike Ross (D-AR) and Mark Souder (R-IN) wrote an Amicus Curie (friend of the court) brief in the case of *McDonald v. Chicago*. They supported the notion that the Second Amendment's protection of the right to bear arms applies to the states through the *Selected Incorporation Doctrine*. Fifty-Eight U.S. Senators and 251 U.S. Representatives signed the brief. No other *Amicus Curie* brief in American history has been signed by that many members of the U.S. Congress.

No Work, No Pay: A statute from 1856, (Title 2, Section 39) states: "The Secretary of the Senate and the Sergeant-at-Arms of the House, respectively, shall deduct from the monthly payments of each member the amount of his salary for each day that he has been absent from the Senate or House, respectively, unless such member assigns as the reason for such absence the sickness of himself or of some member of his family." However, the statute has never been enforced. In 2005, after being on the books for nearly 150 years, the Senate exempted itself from this law. Interestingly, the act still applies to the U.S. House of Representative, but again, it has never been enforced.

GOP Congress Stays Seated: The 1996 Congressional Elections marked the first time since 1928 in which a Republican majority in both houses of the U.S. Congress was re-elected.

Cornhusker Hospitality: In Nebraska, every Wednesday when Congress is in session, the Congressional Delegation holds a bi-partisan breakfast where any Nebraskan can attend.

Unions Flex Political Muscle: During the 2010 midterm elections, public sector unions spent $91 million, supporting mostly Democratic Congressional candidates.

Cowboy State Democratic Drought: No Democrat has served in the Wyoming Congressional delegation since 1979.

The Year the U.S. Congress Began: The First U.S. Congress convened in 1789. It consisted of 59 members of the U.S. House of Representatives and 20 members of the U.S. Senate.

Part IV: The U.S. Judiciary

Defining a Mission: There is no language in the *U.S. Constitution* mandating that U.S. Supreme Court Justices must decide their cases based on Constitutional Permissibility. The U.S. Supreme Court established its role as arbiter of the Constitution (Judicial Review) in the landmark 1803 case *Marbury v. Madison,* written by Chief Justice of the United States, John Marshall.

John Marshall
Library of Congress

Tall Order for a Young Man: At age 32, Joseph Story became the youngest U.S. Supreme Court Justice. He was nominated by President James Madison and confirmed by the U.S. Senate in 1811. He served on the High Court until his death in 1845.

Joseph Story
Library of Congress

"Three Generations of Imbeciles is Enough:" In 1927, the U.S. Supreme Court ruled in *Buck v. Bell* that states are permitted to pass laws to forbid: "feebleminded and socially inadequate" individuals from procreating using compulsory sterilization. Justice Oliver Wendell Holmes, in writing for the Majority, declared: "Three Generations of imbeciles is enough." This ruling remains on the books.

Oliver Wendell Holmes
Library of Congress

The Wisdom of Age: In 1909, the U.S. Senate confirmed President William Howard Taft's nomination of Horace Lurton to the U.S. Supreme Court. At 65 years of age, Lurton became the oldest person confirmed to the Supreme Court. He served less than five years, dying in 1914.

Horace Lurton
Official Portrait

John Paul Stevens and "The Babe:" U.S. Supreme Court Justice John Paul Stevens (1975-2010) attended the World Series game at Wrigley Field in 1932, where New York Yankees slugger Babe Ruth allegedly pointed to Centerfield before hitting a home run to Centerfield.

John Paul Stevens
Official Photograph

Hole-in-one: In 2000, U.S. Supreme Court Justice Sandra Day O'Connor scored a hole-in-one at the Paradise Valley Country Club in Scottsdale, Arizona.

Sandra Day O'Connor
Official Photograph

Seniority "Does" have its Privileges: When the U.S. Supreme Court deliberates in private, the most junior justice is responsible for opening the door when someone knocks on it.

Nonagenarian Leaves the Supreme Court: Oliver Wendell Holmes was the oldest sitting Supreme Court Justice in U.S. History. He resigned from the Court in 1932, at age 91.

Oliver Wendell Holmes
Library of Congress

Judicial Energizer Bunny: The Longest serving Supreme Court Justice in U.S. history was William O. Douglas. He served from 1939-1973, and served with every President from Franklin D, Roosevelt (who nominated him) to Richard M. Nixon.

William O. Douglas
Library of Congress

Here Come the Judges: California hosts the largest judiciary in the United States with 1600 judges. By contrast, the federal judiciary has only 876 judges.

Just Call Him "Chief:" The official title of John Roberts is: "Chief Justice of the United States" not "Chief Justice of the United States Supreme Court."

John Roberts
Official Photograph

Supreme Court Justice Wages War on Horse Thieves: Supreme Court Justice Louis Brandeis was a member of The Society in Dedham (Massachusetts) for Apprehending Horse Thieves.

Louis Brandeis
Library of Congress

Contingency Plans: If a Chief Justice of the United States dies, the most senior Associate Justice takes over the duties of the Chief Justice, until the U.S. Senate confirms a new Chief Justice.

Partisan Nomination of Arbiters: New York is the only state where political parties at partisan conventions nominate state judges.

Supreme Court Testimony: The first U.S. Supreme Court nominee to testify before the U.S. Senate Judiciary Committee was Harlan Fiske Stone in 1925. President Calvin Coolidge nominated him. Stone was confirmed to the U.S. Supreme Court.

Harlan Fiske Stone
Library of Congress

Chief Justice Goes Old School: Chief Justice of the United States John Roberts writes his opinions longhand.

John Roberts
Official Photograph

Americans Keep Priorities Straight: According to a 2006 poll administered by Zogby International, 77% of Americans were able to identify at least two of the seven dwarfs. In contrast, only 24% of Americans could name at least two U.S. Supreme Court Justices.

Clarence Thomas and the State of the Union Address: Supreme Court Justice Clarence Thomas does not attend the President's annual State of the Union Address because he believes the forum is too partisan.

Clarence Thomas
Official Photograph

First Meeting: The U.S. Supreme Court first convened at the Merchants Exchange Building in what was then the nation's capital, New York City, New York.

Female First: In 1989 Associate Justice Sandra Day O'Connor swore in Vice President Dan Quayle. This was the first time a woman swore in a Vice President.

Sandra Day O'Conner
Official Photograph

Inglorious Distinction: The only U.S. Supreme Court Justice to be impeached by the U.S. House of Representatives was Samuel P. Chase. In 1804, the Democratic-Republican controlled House charged Chase with allowing his partisan Federalist philosophy to influence his rulings. The U.S. Senate acquitted him.

Samuel P. Chase
Library of Congress

Rare Occurrence: In its history, the United States Supreme Court has only heard 139 cases on Original Jurisdiction. (Hearing a case for the first time)

Female First: In 1879, American Suffragist Belva Ann Bennett Lockwood became the first female to petition before the U.S. Supreme Court.

Belva Ann Bennett Lockwood
Library of Congress

Sign of Judicial Civility: U.S. Supreme Court Justices shake the hand of every other justice before hearing a case or before deliberating to discuss a case. This is referred to as "The Conference Handshake." The practice was the brainchild of Chief Justice of the United States Melville Fuller (1888-1910).

Melville Fuller
Library of Congress

Ageism in Territorial Judiciary: All Justices on the Supreme Court of Puerto Rico are required to leave the bench at age 70.

Justice in Virginia: The Virginia Judicial system is the oldest judicial system in the nation.

Lucky 13 Strikes Again: The American judicial system consists of thirteen jurisdictions.

Small Court: The U.S. Court of Appeals for the First Circuit, which encompasses Massachusetts, Maine, New Hampshire, Puerto Rico, and Rhode Island, is the smallest of the 13 Appeals Courts. It has just 6 active and 3 senior judges.

This Won't Pay the Bills: Federal Jurors are paid $40 a day for their service.

Luddite on The U.S. Supreme Court: U.S. Supreme Court Justice David Souter (1990-2009) does not own a computer, answering machine, or television set.

David Souter
Official Photograph

Partisan Mavericks: In 1914, President Woodrow Wilson nominated Louis Brandeis to a seat on the U.S. Supreme Court. He was confirmed by the U.S. Senate, making him the first Jewish-American to serve as a U.S. Supreme Court Justice. The only Democrat to vote against the confirmation of Louis Brandies was Francis Newlands of Nevada. The only Republicans to vote for Brandeis's conformation were Robert M. La Follette Sr. of Wisconsin, George Norris of Nebraska, and Miles Poindexter of Washington State.

Louis Brandeis
Library of Congress

Justice Remains: William Cushing was the longest serving of the six original U.S. Supreme Court Justices. He served from 1789-1810.

William Cushing
Library of Congress

Just Stay for as Long as You Want: There have been 17 Chief Justices of the United States.

Words to Live By: The front of the U.S. Supreme Court building in Washington, DC displays the following inscription: "Equal Justice Under the Law."

U.S. Supreme Court Building
U.S. Supreme Court

Good Record: Of the 151 persons nominated by Presidents to be U.S. Supreme Court Justices, the U.S. Senate has confirmed 124.

Sotomayor Steps up to the Plate for Baseball Players: As a District Court Judge, future Supreme Court Justice Sonia Sotomayor drafted a preliminary injunction against Major League Baseball, ordering the League to restore free agency. This ended the Baseball Strike of 1994-1995. She took just fifteen minutes to issue her injunction. The *Second Circuit Court of Appeals* upheld her decision.

Sonia Sotomayor
Official Photograph

It Pays to Be a Federal Judge: The "Rule of 80:" Once a Federal Judge or Justice reaches age 65, any combination of years of age and years of service on the federal bench which total to the number 80, entitle the judge to "senior status." Examples of reaching the 80 number are: 65 years of age with 15 years of service, 70 with 10 years of service, 75 with 5 years of service. When a justice achieves senior status, he/she may retire with full compensation at current salary level.

How Many U.S. Supreme Court Justices Does it Take to Hear a Case? It takes four U.S. Supreme Court Justices to agree to hear a case.

"All Aboard:" Until 1890, U.S. Supreme Court Justices were required to "ride the circuit" in addition to their court work.

Chief Justice Shows his Stripes: Chief Justice of the United States William Rehnquist (1986-2005) wore gold stripes on his robe. He did this as a tribute to Lord Chancellor, a character in the Gilbert and Sullivan Opera *Iolanthe.*

William Rehnquist
Official Portrait by Thomas Loepp

A Silent Thomas: U.S. Supreme Court Justice Clarence Thomas has not questioned an attorney during a Supreme Court hearing since February 22, 2006.

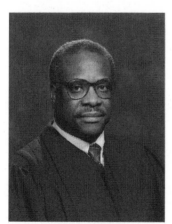

Clarence Thomas
Official Photograph

From Six to Nine: The Original U.S. Supreme Court in 1790 had six justices. Today, the court has nine justices.

It's been a Long Time: The last Chief Justice of the United States nominated by a Democratic President was Fred M. Vinson. He was nominated by President Harry S. Truman and confirmed by the US. Senate in 1946.

Fred M. Vinson (L) with President Truman
Harry S. Truman Library and Museum

The Four Supreme-ettes: Four women have been confirmed by the U.S. Senate to be Supreme Court Justices. They are: Sandra Day O'Conner, nominated by Ronald Reagan in 1981, Ruth Bader Ginsberg, nominated by Bill Clinton in 1993, Sonia Sotamayer, nominated by Barack Obama in 2009, and Elana Kagan, nominated by Barack Obama in 2010.

Counting District Courts: The United States has 94 Federal District Courts.

Court Time: The U.S. Supreme Court usually hands down its decisions on the last day of its term. Each term begins on the first Monday of October and ends in late June or in early July.

Long Orientation: Though the U.S. Supreme Court was established in 1790, it spent its first two years defining its role and establishing its authority. It did not hear its first case until 1792.

Part V: Founding Documents

Obscure Founder: John Dickinson, a representative from Pennsylvania during the Second Continental Congress in 1777, led the committee which wrote the *Articles of Confederation and Perpetual Union*.

John Dickinson
Library of Congress

The Framers Could have used Spell-check: In the original *U.S. Constitution*, the word Pennsylvania is misspelled as "Pensylvania" (sic) directly above the signers of the documents.

The Obscure Figure who Wrote the U.S. Constitution: The Engrosser (letter designer) Jacob Shallas transcribed the original *U.S. Constitution* on parchment paper. He was paid the sum of $30.

Sorry Pot Heads: Though some believe the *Declaration of Independence* was written on hemp paper, it was actually written on parchment paper which is derived from animal skin.

Unicameral Congress: Under the *Articles of Confederation and Perpetual Union*, the U.S. Congress, which was referred to as the Congress of the Confederation, was a unicameral (one house) body.

Productive Young Man: The youngest person to sign the *U.S. Constitution* was Jonathan Dayton, a former army captain who was just 26 years old. Dayton, a member of the Federalist Party, later became Speaker of the U.S. House of Representatives and a U.S. Senator representing New Jersey.

Jonathan Dayton
Library of Congress

Granite State's Pivotal Role: New Hampshire was the ninth state to ratify the *U.S. Constitution*. The approval of nine states was required for the Constitution to take effect.

The First State: On December 7, 1787, Delaware became the first state to ratify the *U.S. Constitution*.

Inimical Series of Words: The *U.S. Constitution* consists of 4,400 words.

Before the Advent of Word Processors: *The Declaration of Independence* and *The U.S. Constitution* were both written with quill pens.

1337 Words that Changed the World: The *Declaration of Independence* is 1,337 words long.

State Legislatures and The Military: Under the *Articles of Confederation and Perpetual Union*, the State Legislatures had the duty of appointing Colonels and lower ranking military officers.

Founding Documents

Oldest Signer of Historic Document: Benjamin Franklin of Pennsylvania was the oldest man to sign the *U.S. Constitution*. He was 81 years old.

Benjamin Franklin
Library of Congress

The Constitution Survives: The *U.S. Constitution* is the oldest written Constitution still in use. It was ratified in 1787.

Interesting Constitutional Loophole: There is no Constitutional requirement for a U.S. Supreme Court Justice to be a lawyer.

The Add-ons: There are 27 Amendments to the *U.S. Constitution*.

War Powers Clause: Despite Article 1, Section 8, Clause 11 of the *U.S. Constitution* which grants the U.S. Congress the power to declare war, the Congress has acted on this clause just five times. These include; The War of 1812, the Mexican-American War, the Spanish-American War, World War I and World War II. The President has sent U.S. troops on military missions 126 times without a formal declaration of war from the U.S. Congress.

Future Presidents Declare Their Support for Independence: The only future Presidents to sign the *Declaration of Independence* were John Adams and Thomas Jefferson.

July 2nd "Not" July 4th - The Pen Proves Mightier than the Spoken Word: The Continental Congress officially declared Independence from England on July 2, 1776. However, the language of the *Declaration of Independence* was not formalized until July 4, 1776. The document was not signed by the delegates of the Constitutional Convention until August 2, 1776. The July 2nd motion to declare independence was made by Delegate Richard Henry Lee of Virginia.

Richard Henry Lee
Library of Congress

Constitutional Requirements: The *U.S. Constitution* requires U.S. Senators to be at least thirty years of age to be a U.S. citizen for at least nine years, and to be a resident of the state served on Election Day.

A Picture That is Worth 1,337 Words: A bargain hunter from Philadelphia bought an old painting for $4.00 because he planned on re-using the frame. When he pulled out the picture, an original copy of the *Declaration of Independence* fell out. The item sold at auction for $2.42 million in 1991. The item was resold in 2000 for over $8 million.

At Least It Does not Say "Made In China:" The back of the original *Declaration of Independence* reads: "Original Declaration of Independence dated 4th July 1776."

The Trilogy: *The Declaration of Independence, The U.S. Constitution,* and the *Bill of Rights* are all domiciled in the National Archives in Washington, D.C.

National Archives
Library of Congress

Constitutional Rebels: Elbridge Gerry, George Mason, and Edmund Randolph were the only delegates present at the signing of the *U.S. Constitution* who refused to sign it.

A Thank You to the Constitution: The original purpose of the Thanksgiving Holiday was for the nation to give thanks for the new *U.S. Constitution.*

When in Rome: The *U.S. Constitution* is based on the system used by the Roman Republic, which lasted from 509 B.C. to 20 B.C.

U.S. Constitution: There are seven Articles in the *U.S. Constitution.*

Signing the U.S. Constitution: Thirty-Nine Delegates to the Constitutional Convention in Philadelphia in the summer of 1787 signed the *U.S. Constitution.*

Pennsylvanian's Enduring Words: The Preamble to the *U.S. Constitution* reads: "We the People of the United States, in Order to form a more perfect Union, establish Justice, insure domestic Tranquility, provide for the common defense, promote the general Welfare, and secure the Blessings of Liberty to ourselves and our Posterity, do ordain and establish this Constitution for the United States of America." These words were written by Gouverneur Morris, a Pennsylvania delegate to the Constitutional Convention of 1787.

Gouverneur Morris
Library of Congress

Direct Democracy: The nation's first governing document was the Mayflower Compact. It created a governing structure for the newly formed Plymouth Colony. The compact set up a Direct Democracy. In 1620, the forty-one surviving passengers of the Mayflower signed the document, agreeing to be public citizens and agreeing to abide by the opinion of the majority of the new colonists.

The Constitution is Silent on Partying: Political Parties are mentioned nowhere in the *U.S. Constitution.*

The Real Document of Limited Government: The purported purpose of the Constitutional Convention of 1787 in Philadelphia was to amend the existing *Articles of Confederation and Perpetual Union.* The conventioneers scrapped the *Articles* in favor of a completely new document, *The U.S. Constitution.* The new Constitution provided the federal government greater authority. Anti-Federalists, those who were opposed to an expanded government and feared an encroachment of civil liberties, attached the *Bill of Rights* to the document. Still, delegates to the Constitutional Convention, including Elbridge Gerry of Massachusetts, George Mason of Virginia, and Edmond Randolph of Virginia, refused to sign the document on the grounds that it would expand the role of the Federal Government. They argued that the President would not merely be an executive officer making sure that the laws were faithfully executed, but a disguised monarch, similar to the one in England, under King George lll, who the colonists broke away from. Anti-Federalist Patrick Henry of Virginia warned: "The Constitution has an awful squinting, it squints in the direction of monarchy."

Constitutional Convention
Painting by Howard Chandler Christy

Americans Confuse Karl Marx with Nation's Founding Fathers: A 2002 survey taken by the Columbia School of Law found that two-thirds of Americans attributed the phrase: "From Each According to his ability, to each according to his needs" to the framers of the *U.S. Constitution.* The phrase was actually written by Communist theorist Karl Marx, appearing in his 1875 publication *Critique of the Gotha Program.*

Karl Marx
Library of Congress

Please Sign Right Here: Robert Morris of Connecticut and Roger Sherman of Pennsylvania were the only two Founding Fathers who signed the *Declaration of Independence*, the *Articles of Confederation and Perpetual Union*, and the *United States Constitution*.

First War Powers Clause: Under the *Articles of Confederation and Perpetual Union,* nine of the thirteen colonies had to agree to declare war.

No Federal Taxes: Under the *Articles of Confederation and Perpetual Union* there was no explicit power for the Federal Government to collect taxes. Federal Revenue had to be collected from state governments.

State and Territorial Government

Part: VI: State and Territorial Government

Governorships

Yankee Ways: Vermont and New Hampshire are the only states in which the Governor is up for re-election every two years, not every four years

Massachusetts Rules: A Massachusetts Governor must have been domiciled in the Commonwealth for at least seven consecutive years prior to assuming office.

Only in Kansas: Under Kansas law, there is no limit as to how many terms a Governor can serve in office, but he/she can only serve two consecutive terms. A Governor who serves two consecutive terms can run again after sitting out one election.

Automatic Lame Duck: In Virginia, the Governor is limited to serving just one four-year term.

Tombstone State Stepping Stone: Five Secretaries of State have succeeded to the Governorship in Arizona. The state has no Lieutenant Governor and under state law the Secretary of State succeeds to the Governorship in the event of a political vacancy.

Idaho Looks to Iowa for Leadership: Five Idaho Governors were born in "Iowa."

Vermont and Gay Marriage: Vermont was the first state to allow gay marriage by an act of the legislature, not by a court order.

No Overrides: Between 1994 and 2008, the Oklahoma Legislature did not override a single veto of a Governor.

Contrasting Governorships: In Texas the Governor's power is limited. With the exception of the Secretary of State, voters elect all Constitutional officers. Accordingly, these executive officials are accountable to the voters and not to the Governor. By contrast, the New Jersey Governor has the power to nominate the entire cabinet. The New Jersey State Senate must then confirm them. The New Jersey Governor, along with the Lieutenant Governor, are the only state-wide (non-federal) officials elected by voters in the state.

No Public Housing for Governors: The only states which fail to provide their governors with an official residence are: Arizona, California, Idaho, Massachusetts, Rhode Island, and Vermont.

Duties of the Governor, But not the Title: In Massachusetts if a Governor leaves office before his/her term expires; the Lieutenant Governor takes over the responsibilities of the Governor. However, the replacement Governor does not assume the title of Governor. He/she holds the title of Lieutenant Governor-Acting Governor.

Utah Anomalies: Despite being one of the most Republican states in the nation, from 1965-1985 Democrats held the Utah Governorship.

Tie Goes to the Legislature: Under the Wisconsin Constitution, if there is a tie between the top two finishers in the race for Governor, the Legislature chooses the new Governor between the top two contenders.

Term Limits for the Governor: Thirty-six states have gubernatorial term limits.

Not Born Here? Not to Worry: Only one of Idaho's first 24 Governors was actually born in the state. Democrat C. Ben Ross 1931-1937 was the first Governor born in Idaho.

Republican Hegemony in the Mount Rushmore State: No Democrat has been elected Governor of South Dakota since 1974. This is the longest current streak of one political party holding a state Governorship.

Seating the Governors: At National Governors Association Conferences, governors are seated by the year their states were admitted into the Union.

Long GOP Hiatus in Georgia: Between 1876 and 1966, the Georgia Republican Party did not field a nominee to run for Governor.

Oklahoma Imports: 11 of the 26 Governors of Oklahoma who served during the first 100 years of statehood were not born in the state. Oklahoma did not become a state until 1907.

No More Automatic Lame Duck Governors: Prior to 1972, West Virginia Governors were permitted to serve just one four-year term.

Governor, My Governor: There have been over 2,300 Governors in the U.S.

Executive Authority: Forty-three states allow their Governors the Line-Item-Veto, which provides them the ability to eliminate certain provisions in a piece of legislation without vetoing the entire bill. The seven states that do not allow this practice are: Indiana, Maryland, Nevada, New Hampshire, North Carolina, Rhode Island, and Vermont.

Massachusetts GOP Governors an Anomaly: Although Massachusetts is known nationally as a citadel of liberalism, where the Democrats have had supermajorities in both houses of the General Court (legislature), from 1991-2007, the Commonwealth had a series of Republican governors including William F. Weld, Paul Cellucci, (acting Governor) Jane Swift, and Mitt Romney.

Why Can't I? In Virginia, although the Governor is disallowed from seeking re-election, the Lieutenant Governor is not.

Cowboy State Oddity: Wyoming, which has not voted for a Democratic Presidential nominee since 1964, and where the Democratic Party has not held a majority in a legislative chamber since 1936, has had Democratic Governors for all but eight years, from 1975 – 2011.

Governors

Governor Pays for Militia with his own Money: New York Governor Daniel D. Tompkins was desperate to borrow money to fund his state's militia in the War of 1812. He used his own personal property to back a loan. In 1824, while Tompkins was serving as Vice President, the U.S. Congress finally reimbursed him.

Daniel D. Tompkins
Library of Congress

Carter Sees UFO Leaving Lion's Club: In 1973, then Georgia Governor Jimmy Carter filed a report with the Center for UFO Studies in Evanston, Illinois, claiming to have seen an unidentified flying object (UFO). Carter says he witnessed the sighting in the sky over Leary, Georgia in 1969 as he was leaving a Lions Club meeting.

Jimmy Carter
Jimmy Carter Library and Museum

Howard Stern for Governor? In 1994, Radio Talk Show Host Howard Stern won the Libertarian nomination for Governor of New York. He dropped out of the race because he would not file a financial disclosure form. Stern argued it was a violation of his privacy.

The North rose again for the Dems: In 1872, Indiana's Thomas A. Hendricks became the first Democrat elected Governor in the North.

Thomas A. Hendricks
Library of Congress

Two-Timing Governor: The only man to be Governor of two separate states was Sam Houston. He served as Governor of Tennessee from 1827–1829 and as Governor of Texas from 1859–1861.

Sam Houston
Library of Congress

Governor Surrounded By Presidents: California Governor Edmund Gerald "Pat" Brown Sr. beat former Vice President and future President Richard M. Nixon in Brown's bid for re-election in 1962. In 1966, while seeking a third term, Brown lost to another future President, Ronald Reagan.

Edmund Gerald "Pat" Brown Sr.
Official Photograph

A Long Time Coming: In 1992, Kurt Fordice became the first Republican Governor of Mississippi since Reconstruction.

Kurt Fordice
Official Photograph

Greek Blood: In 1967, Spiro Agnew (R-MD) became the first American Governor of Greek decent.   In 1975, Michael Dukakis (D-MA) became the second.

There are Democrats in Utah: Democrat Calvin Rampton was the first Governor of Utah to serve three terms. He served from 1965-1977.

Calvin L. Rampton
Official Portrait

Lonestar Ladies: Two females have served as Governor of Texas. Miriam A. Ferguson served from 1925-1927, and Ann Richards served from 1991-1995.

Sooner Republican: Henry L. Bellmon was the first Republican Governor in Oklahoma's history. He served from 1963-1967 and later from 1987-1991.

Henry L. Bellmon
Official Photograph

Born in the U.S.A: New Jersey Governor Chris Christie has attended over 120 Bruce Springsteen Concerts.

Chris Christie
Official Photograph

The Origins of a Famous Name: Delaware Governor Jack Markell, a former Nextel executive, is credited with naming the company "Nextel."

Jack Markell
Official Photograph

State and Territorial Government

Aloha Governor: William Quinn was both the last Governor of the Territory of Hawaii (1957-1959) and the first Governor of the state of Hawaii (1959-1961) He was originally appointed territorial Governor by President Dwight D. Eisenhower. When Hawaii became a state, Quinn was elected Governor.

William Quinn
Official Photograph

Lonestar Justice: In 2011, while on a jog with his dog, Texas Governor Rick Perry encountered a coyote. Fearing the coyote would attack him or his dog, Perry shot the coyote with his pistol.

Rick Perry
Official Photograph

The Name "Mitt:" The Middle name of former Massachusetts Governor Willard "Mitt" Romney came from his father's cousin, Milton Romney, who played Quarterback for the Chicago Bears from 1925 – 1929.

Lone-Star Longevity: In 2008, Texas Governor Rick Perry broke Allan Shiver's record of seven and a half years as Governor of the Loan-Star state.

Rick Perry
Official Photograph

Breaking the Democratic Stronghold: Alabama Governor Guy Hunt (1987-1993) was the first Alabama Republican Governor since Reconstruction.

Guy Hunt
Official Portrait

Bluegrass Female Governor: Democrat Martha Layne Collins was the only female Governor in Kentucky history. She served from 1983-1987.

Martha Layne Collins
Official Portrait

First Baystater to Serve 4-Year Hitch:
John Volpe was the first Massachusetts
Governor to serve a four-year term. Prior
to this date, The Commonwealth had two-
year Gubernatorial terms. Volpe served
from 1961-1963 and from 1965-1969.

John Volpe
Official Portrait

Transpartisan Support: Governor Jim
Douglas (R-VT 2003-2009) garnered the
endorsement of the Democratic and
Republican Parties in his successful 1994
bid to become State Treasurer.

Jim Douglas
Official Photograph

Third Party Governors: California has
elected two Governors from third parties.
John Neely Johnson was elected in 1856
as a member of the American Party (a.k.a.
The Know Nothing Party), and Frederick
Low was elected in 1863 on the National
Unity Ticket.

Popular Okie: In 1982, George Nigh
became the first Oklahoma Governor to
be re-elected.

George Nigh
Official Photograph

It's the Truth: In 1955, West Virginia
Governor-elect Cecil Underwood was the
first guest on the popular television game
show: *To Tell The Truth.*

To Tell the Truth **Official Logo**

Oldest Former Governor: On March
18, 2011, 101-year-old Albert Rosellini
became the oldest former Governor in
American History. The Democrat was
Governor of Washington from 1957-1965.

Albert Rosellini
Official Photograph

Playing Second Fiddle Pays Off: Zell Miller served as Georgia's Lieutenant Governor for 16 years (1975-1991) with three Governors. Finally, in 1991 he became Governor.

Zell Miller
Official Photograph

An Unlikely Civil Rights Crusader: During his short two-year tenure as Governor of Maryland (from 1967 to 1969), future Vice President Spiro Agnew became the first Southern Governor to sign a fair housing act. In addition, he signed legislation repealing an anti-miscegenation law, and was the first Old Line State Governor to appoint an African-American to his senior staff.

Spiro Agnew
Library of Congress

Governor did not beg Pardons: During his four-year term as Governor of Massachusetts, lasting from 2003 to 2007, Governor Mitt Romney issued no pardons.

Governor Drafted by Professional Hockey Team: In 1972, while serving as Governor of Minnesota, Wendell Anderson was drafted by the Minnesota Fighting Saints of the World Hockey Association (a short-lived competitor of the National Hockey League). Anderson, a former Hockey player at the University of Minnesota, refused to sign a contract with the ice franchise.

Wendell Anderson
Official Photograph

Huey Longs Marionette: Louisiana Governor Oscar Allen was a close ally of former Governor Huey Long, who had left the Governorship to assume a seat in the U.S. Senate. Many believed that Long continued to govern the state and that Allen was his puppet. It is thought that Allen was ordered to sign all documents that came to his desk following approval by Senator Long. Some even quipped that a leaf flew in his office window and Allen signed it thinking it was legislation approved by Long.

Oscar Allen
Louisiana State Archives

Barracuda: As a basketball player for the Wasilla (Alaska) High School Basketball team, future Alaska Governor and 2008 Republican Vice Presidential nominee Sarah Palin received the moniker: "Sarah Barracuda" for her playing style.

Sarah Palin
Official Photograph

Lone Star GOP Takes Governorship after a Long Hiatus: In 1979, Republican William P. Clements became the first Republican to assume the Texas Governorship since 1874.

William Clements
Official Portrait

They Still Believe in a Place Called Hope: Former Arkansas Governor and President Bill Clinton, and former Arkansas Governor Mike Huckabee were both born in the town of Hope, Arkansas. The town currently has a population of just over 10,000 inhabitants.

Texas Tea: After Texas Governor Dolph Briscoe left office in 1979, oil and gas was discovered on his land. He sold drilling leases, and eventually became the biggest landowner in the state.

Dolph Driscoe
Texas State Library and Archives Commission

Governor Finds the Stress of the Office Too Much: In 1907, just thirty-eight days into his term, Arkansas Governor John Sebastian Little suffered a nervous breakdown and was forced to resign and enter a rehabilitation facility.

John Sebastian Little
Encyclopedia of Arkansas History and Culture

Working for Governor a Real Bonus: Massachusetts Governor Romney (2003-2007), with a net worth of over a hundred million dollars, gave his salary away as Governor of Massachusetts to his staff in the form of bonuses.

High School Drop Out Ascends to Governorship: Utah Governor Jon Huntsman Jr. (2005-2009) dropped out of High School to play Keyboard in the rock-and-roll Band *Wizard*. Once his rock-and-roll dream died, Huntsman earned a GED and eventually graduated from the University of Pennsylvania.

Jon Huntsman Jr.
Official Photograph

George "The Body" Janos: Minnesota Governor Jesse Ventura's (1999-2003) birth name was James George Janos.

Jesse Ventura
Official Photograph

Mitt's Failed Crusade: In 2004, Massachusetts Governor Mitt Romney launched "Team Reform" in which he helped to recruit 131 Republican candidates to run for legislative seats in the state's overwhelmingly Democratic Legislature. Despite campaigning for many of the recruits and raising a redoubtable $3 million for the effort, no incumbent Democrat lost his/her seat. The Democrats actually picked up two seats in the Massachusetts House of Representatives and two seats in the Massachusetts State Senate.

The Duke of Massachusetts: Michael Dukakis is the longest serving Governor in Massachusetts history. He served three terms in all. His first term spanned from 1975-1979. His second two terms extended from 1983-1991.

Michael Dukakis on the Cover of *Time Magazine*

Historic Cajun: David C. Treen was both the first Republican U.S. Representative and the first Republican Governor of Louisiana since Reconstruction. He represented the First Congressional District of Louisiana in the U.S. House of Representatives from 1973-1980, and was Governor of the Bayou state from 1980-1984.

David C. Treen
Library of Congress

Extreme Commuter: Acting Governor Jane Swift (R-MA 2001-2003) commuted 110 miles to work. She lived in Williamstown, Massachusetts on the New York border, and worked at the opposite end of the Commonwealth, at the State House in Boston.

A Man for All Offices: Don Siegelman is the only Alabaman to serve in the all of the top four Constitutional Offices of his state. From 1979–2003, Siegelman served as Secretary of State, Attorney General, Lieutenant Governor, and Governor.

Don Siegelman
Official Photograph

You Just Can't Go Back: Orval Fabus, who served as Governor of Arkansas from 1955-1967, tried to re-assume the Governorship twice, once in 1974 and again in 1986. However, he could not even win his party's primary, losing to former U.S. Representative David Pryor in 1974 and to Governor Bill Clinton in 1986.

Orval Fabus
Official Photograph

Twenty-Four Year Old Governor: The youngest Governor in American history was Democrat Stevens T. Mason. In 1835, Mason, a former Territorial Governor of the Michigan Territory, was elected as Governor of the newly-established state of Michigan.

Stevens T. Mason
Library of Congress

Taking a Firm Stand: On June 15, 1991, after the U.S. Senate voted to authorize President George H.W. Bush to use military force to repel Iraqi forces from Kuwait, then Arkansas Governor Bill Clinton told members of the media: "I guess I would have voted with the majority if it was a close vote. But I agree with the arguments the Minority made."

Bill Clinton in 1991
Old State House Museum

Resounding Defeat: In 1996, Arkansas Governor Jim "Guy" Tucker supported a referendum to improve the state's highway system by raising taxes. The referendum lost 87%-13%.

Jim "Guy" Tucker
Official Portrait

Ronald Reagan the Gun Controller: As Governor of California, Ronald Reagan signed into law one of the most all-embracing gun control measures in U.S. history. The Mulford Act of 1967 prohibited "the carrying of firearms on one's person or in a vehicle, in any public place or on any public street."

Ronald Reagan
The Ronald Reagan Presidential
Foundation and Library

Arkansas Governor pardons a Rolling Stone: In 2006, Governor Mike Huckabee (R-AR) pardoned lead guitarist Keith Richards of the Rolling Stones. Richards was pulled over for reckless driving in 1975. He paid a $162.50 fine for the offense. When Huckabee was accused of pardoning Richards because of his celebrity status, he replied: "Hey, if you can play guitar like Keith Richards, I'll consider pardoning you too."

Mike Huckabee
Official Portrait

People were heard in Peach State: Georgia Governor Lester Maddox (1967-1971) designated one day per month as "People's Day" allowing Georgia residents to meet with him personally to tell him their concerns.

Lester Maddox
Official Photograph

Prestigious Alumni: Bill Clinton is the only former Chairman of the National Governors Association (NGA) to be elected as President of the United States. Clinton was Chairman of the NGA from 1986-1987.

NGA Chairman Bill Clinton and Arkansas First Lady Hillary Clinton with President Ronald Reagan and First Lady Nancy Reagan at an NGA Dinner
White House Photograph

Former Governor Takes the Ball: After losing re-election as Governor of South Dakota in 1958, Republican Joe Foss became the first Commissioner of the American Football League (AFL), which later merged with the National Football League (NFL).

Joe Foss
Official Photograph

Hispanic Governor in the Golden State: The only Hispanic to serve as Governor of California was Romualdo Pacheco. He was Lieutenant Governor but ascended to the Governorship in 1875 when Governor Newton Booth resigned to serve in the U.S. Senate. Pacheco served for just one year.

Romualdo Pacheco
Library of Congress

Brother "Swears-in" Brother: In 1978, when Henry L. Wollman assumed the Governorship of South Dakota to fill the remaining months of Richard F. Knelps' term (Knelps left to become U.S. Ambassador to Singapore), he was sworn in by the Chief Justice of the State's Supreme Court, Roger L. Wollman, his brother.

Female Tar Heel breaks the Glass Ceiling Twice: North Carolina Governor Beverly Perdue holds the distinction of being both the Tar Heel State's first female Lieutenant Governor and Governor.

Beverly Perdue
Official Photograph

Governor's Mobile Home: In 1998, while the Arkansas Governors Mansion was being renovated, Governor Mike Huckabee and his family lived in a "triple-wide," a large mobile home on the grounds of the mansion.

Mike Huckabee
Official Photograph

84-Year-Old Cheese Head: The oldest Governor in American history was Walter Samuel Goodland. In 1947, the Wisconsin Governor died in office at age 84.

Non-Mormon leads in Utah: In 1916, Utah voters elected former State Senator Simon Bamberger as their Governor. Governor Bamberger, a Jewish-American, became the first non-Mormon Governor in Utah history.

Simon Bamberger
Library off Congress

The Republican Who Saved Bill Clinton's Life: As a young man, future Republican Arizona Governor Fife Symington saved the life of future Democratic President Bill Clinton by swimming out to save him from a riptide. On Clinton's last day in office, he returned the favor by pardoning Symington who had been convicted of bank and wire fraud charges. (All charges were overturned).

Fife Symington
Official Photograph

First Jewish Governor: Washington Bartlett was the first person of Jewish descent elected Governor of a U.S. state. The San Francisco Mayor was elected as Governor of California in 1886. He died less than a year into his term of kidney disease.

Washington Bartlett
Official Photograph

Ex-Governor Joins the Army: After leaving office in 1897 as Governor of South Carolina, John Evans volunteered to serve in the U.S. Army and participated in the Spanish-American War.

John Evans
South Carolina Department of Archives and History

Bolting the GOP and Surviving: Philip Fox La Follette was the only Wisconsin Governor to serve non-consecutive terms. He served from 1931-1933 and from 1935-1939. In 1930, he was elected as a Republican. After losing the Republican primary for re-election, he ran for his old office again in 1934 as the nominee of the newly-formed Wisconsin Progressive Republican Party, and won. He was re-elected in 1936. At the time, Governors were elected to two-year terms.

How Far the Mighty Sometimes Fall: Orval Fabus served a record twelve years as Governor of Arkansas (1955-1967). After leaving office, he ran into financial turmoil and took a job as a bank teller in Huntsville, Arkansas.

Orval Fabus
Official Portrait

Governor Wages a War on Soda: South Carolina Governor Coleman Livingston Blease had an antagonistic relationship with soda. He preached against soda in his State of the State Address in 1911, vehemently warning about: "the evil of the habitual drinking of Coca-Cola, Pepsi-Cola, and such like mixtures, as I fully believe they are injurious. It would be better for our people if they had nice, respectable places where they could go and buy a good, pure glass of cold beer than to drink such concoctions."

Coleman Livingston Blease
Library of Congress

Governor Gives Birth in Office: Massachusetts Acting Governor Jane Swift (2001-2003) was the first Governor to give birth while in office. She gave birth to twins in 2001.

Jane Swift
Official Photograph

Nothing Personal, It's Just Politics: In 1954, South Carolina Democratic Governor James Byrnes supported the "write-in candidate" Strom Thurmond (the state's former Governor) in the Special Election to fill the U.S. Senate seat left vacant upon the death of Burton Maybank. The Democratic Party elites nominated State Senator Edgar Allen Brown for the vacant U.S. Senate seat. Brynes supported Thurmond despite his long-time friendship with Brown. In fact, Brown was Byrne's best man at his wedding. Thurmond won the election.

James Byrnes (left) with Strom Thurmond (right)
Special Collections Clemson University

Lowell Weicker Takes to the Ring: Connecticut Governor Lowell Weicker Jr. (1991-1995) sits on the Board of World Wrestling Entertainment (WWE).

Lowell Weicker Jr.
Official Photograph

How One Politician Circumvented a Gubernatorial Term Limit: Bibb Graves was the first Alabama Governor to serve two 4-year terms. At the time, Alabama barred its Governor from serving two "consecutive" terms. Governor Graves served two non-consecutive terms. His first was from 1927-1931. His second was from 1935-1939.

Bibb Graves
Library of Congress

Grammar Policeman takes over the Governorship: California Governor John Neely Johnson (1856-1858) vetoed a bill because of "bad spelling, improper punctuation and erasures."

John Neely Johnson
Official Photograph

Oops: In 1907, a mental patient from Lynn, Massachusetts shot at a union leader from Lynn, Massachusetts, mistaking him for Massachusetts Governor Curtis Guild Jr.

Curtis Guild, Jr.
Official Photograph

Gopher State Republicans Turn on Former GOP Governor: After his endorsement of Democrat Barack Obama's 2008 Presidential bid and his endorsement of Independence Party nominee Tom Horner for Minnesota Governor in 2010, the Republican Central Committee of Minnesota banned Republican Governor Arne Carlson (1991-1999) from all state Republican Party events for two years.

Arkansans Stick with Clinton: In 1986, Bill Clinton became the first Arkansas Governor elected to a four-year term. Prior to that time, Arkansas Governors served two-year terms.

Bill Clinton
Old State House Museum

Golden in the Golden State: Earl Warren was the only California Governor to win a third term. He served as the Golden State's Chief Executive from 1943-1953, before being confirmed as Chief Justice of the United States.

Earl Warren
Library of Congress

King Sticks it to Teddy: In the 1980 Democratic Presidential Primary, Massachusetts Democratic Governor Ed King endorsed President Jimmy Carter over his home state's Democratic U.S. Senator, Edward M. Kennedy.

Ed King
Official Portrait

The Only Two: In 2007, when David Patterson assumed the Governorship of New York, he joined Massachusetts Governor Deval Patrick as the only two African-American Governors ever to serve concurrently.

Maryland Governor loses Re-election: In 2006, only one Governor, Republican Robert Ehrlich, lost re-election. Democrat Martin O'Malley defeated him.

Robert Ehrlich
U.S. Department of Health and Human Services Photograph

What Was This "Guy" Doing in Lebanon? Arkansas Governor Jim "Guy" Tucker (1992-1996) once taught American History at the University in Beirut, Lebanon.

Jim "Guy" Tucker
From the collection of the Old State House Museum, Arkansas

Sad Day in Alabama: Lurleen Brigham Wallace (D-AL) is the only female Governor of any state to die in office. She died of cancer on May 7, 1968.

Lurleen Wallace
Official Portrait

Governor Gets Booted from Office for not being a Resident of the State. In 1935, just five weeks after assuming office, North Dakota Governor Thomas H. Moodie was forced from office by the State Supreme Court when it became known that he violated North Dakota law that required governors of the state to be domiciled in North Dakota for five consecutive years. It was discovered that Moodie had voted in Minnesota in 1932, just three yeas prior to his gubernatorial inauguration.

Thomas H. Moodie
State Historical Society of North Dakota

Blue Man in a Red State: Democrat Cecil Dale Andrus was elected to four, four-year terms in Republican dominated Idaho. He served from 1971-1977 (he left mid-term to serve as Interior Secretary in the Carter administration) and served from 1987-1995. Andrus served longer than any Governor in Idaho history.

Cecil Dale Andrus
Official Photograph

Cowgirl Governor: Nellie Ross was the first female Governor elected in the United States. She was elected Governor of Wyoming in 1924 and served from 1925-1927.

Nellie Ross
Library of Congress

Bill Clinton's Meager salary: As Governor of Arkansas, Bill Clinton made just $35,000 a year. That was the lowest salary of any Governor in the country.

Bill Clinton as Governor of Arkansas
Arkansas Historical Commission

Strange Duo: After retiring from politics, Georgia Governor Lester Maddox (an arch segregationist) teamed up with African-American Bobby Lee Sears (who once served as a dishwasher in Maddox's restaurant) to perform the comedy: "The Governor and the Dishwasher."

GOP Chairman Becomes Democratic Governor: Mark Parkinson served as Chairman of the Kansas Republican Party from 1999-2003. He became a Democrat in 2006 to be the running mate of Governor Kathleen Sebelious. He succeeded her as Governor when Sebelious was confirmed as the Secretary of Health and Human Services.

Mark Parkinson
Official Photograph

The Governors' Curse: Nine Governors have resigned their offices to be appointed by their successors to a vacated U.S. Senate seat. Albert Benjamin "Happy" Chandler (D-KY) was the only Senator to be elected beyond his interim appointment. He was appointed in 1939. All other appointed Senators were defeated. These Senate appointees were: Governor John Edward Erickson (D-MT) appointed in 1933, Governor Charles Gossett (D-ID) appointed in 1945, Governor Edward Carville (D-NV) appointed in 1945, Governor John Hickey (D-WY) appointed in 1961, Governor Edwin Mechem (R-NM) appointed in 1962, Governor Howard Edmondson (D-OK) appointed in 1963, Governor Donald Russell (D-SC) appointed in 1965, and Governor Wendell Anderson of Minnesota (D-MN) appointed in 1976.

State and Territorial Government

A "Family Feud" in the Governors Mansion: In 1976, Louisiana Governor Edwin Edwards was a staunch supporter of Democratic Presidential nominee Jimmy Carter in his Presidential bid. Governor Edwards's wife, Elaine Edwards, supported the Republican nominee, Gerald R. Ford. Carter carried Louisiana with 51.73% of the popular vote.

Edwin Edwards
Official Photograph

First African-American Governor: The first African-American Governor in U.S. history was Louisiana's Pinckney Benton Stewart Pinchback. Pinchback was the state's Lieutenant Governor and was promoted to Governor when Governor Henry Clay Warmoth was forced to resign for his role in election fraud. Governor Pinchback served the last thirty-five days of Warmoth's unexpired term.

Pinckney Benton Stewart Pinchback
Library of Congress

Youngest and Oldest Governor of West Virginia is the Same Man: In 1957, Cecil Underwood, born in 1922, became the youngest Governor in West Virginia history. He could not run for re-election in 1960 because at the time there were term-limits for Governor. In 1997, after a 37-year hiatus, Underwood again assumed the office. This time he became the oldest governor in West Virginia history.

Cecil Underwood
Official Photograph

Bill Richardson's "World" Record: New Mexico Governor Bill Richardson (2003-2111) holds *The Guinness Book World Records* for the most handshakes in an eight-hour period. In 2002, candidate Bill Richardson shook the hands of 13,392 of his future constituents.

Bill Richardson
Official Photograph

34-Year-Old Ex-Governor: After losing the Arkansas Governorship in 1980, Bill Clinton, age 34, became the youngest Ex-Governor in U.S. history.

Bill Clinton, First Term as Governor of Arkansas
Official Portrait

Sonny Day for Peach State GOP: In 2003, Sonny Perdue became the first Republican Governor of Georgia since 1873.

Sonny Perdue
Official Photograph

Popular Lamar: In 1982, Republican Lamar Alexander became the first Tennessee Governor elected to a second term (prior to 1978, Governors of this state could not succeed themselves).

Lamar Alexander
Official Portrait

Mitt was on the Move: In 2006, Massachusetts Governor Mitt Romney spent at least part of 212 days outside of Massachusetts, mostly campaigning for Republican candidates.

Mitt Romney
Official Photograph

Perpetual Perpich: Rudolph Perpich Sr. was the only Minnesota Governor to serve two non-consecutive terms, making him the longest serving Governor in the state's history. He served from 1976-1979 and from 1983-1991.

Ex-Governor Takes on Mount Everest: After leaving office, New Mexico Governor Gary Johnson (1995-2003) climbed Mount Everest, the world's highest mountain, Mount Everest is located in Nepal, and stands 29,029 feet above sea level.

Gary Johnson
Official Photograph

Carter calls on Nixon to Resign: In 1973, as Governor of Georgia, Jimmy Carter was the first sitting Governor to call for President Richard M. Nixon to resign because of his role in the Watergate affair.

Jimmy Carter
Official Photograph as Governor of Georgia

Clinton Calls for Competency Testing in Schools: In 1983, Arkansas Governor Bill Clinton became the first Governor to sign legislation requiring competency testing for public school teachers.

Bill Clinton being sworn in as Governor of Arkansas
William J. Clinton Presidential Library and Museum

Gubernatorial Elections

Showing up for "The Body" Voter turnout increased by 15% in Minnesota in 1998 when Jesse Ventura won the Governorship of Minnesota.

Jesse Ventura
Library of Congress

Ed King vs. Ed King: In 1978, Edward F. King of Massachusetts lost in his bid for the Republican Gubernatorial nomination. Had he won, he would have faced off against the Democratic nominee whose name ironically was also Edward King. The two men were not related.

GOP Takes Back the Virginia Governorship after a Long Hiatus: In 1969, Virginia voters elected Republican Abner Linwood Holton Jr. Governor. He became the first Republican elected Governor of the Old Dominion State since Reconstruction.

Linwood Holton Jr.
Official Photograph

Coming out of Nowhere: In 1966, Baltimore County Executive Spiro Agnew was elected as Governor of Maryland by just 81,775 votes. Two years later, the obscure first-term Governor was elected Vice President of the United States with Richard M. Nixon.

Spiro Agnew
Official Photograph as Governor of Maryland

Republican Defies Party Registration Deficit in Bay State: In 1994, Republican Massachusetts Governor William F. Weld was re-elected with a record 71% of the vote, despite the fact that Republicans accounted for less than 15% of the Bay State's electorate.

William F. Weld
Official Photograph

New Governors: In the 2010 mid-term elections, twenty-nine non-incumbent Governors were elected. This is a record.

Republican Performs well with Traditional Democratic Constituencies: In his successful 1998 re-election bid as Governor of Arkansas, Mike Huckabee garnered 30% of the vote from self-identified liberals, 48% of the African-American vote, 60% of the female vote, 75% of the vote from voters between 18 and 28 years of age, and 78% of those voters whose median income was below $15,000.

Mike Huckabee
Official Photograph

If you can't beat him: Endorse Him: In 1946, California Governor Earl Warren, a Republican, was nominated for re-election not just by the Republican Party, but also by the Democratic and Progressive Parties. He won, garnering 90% of the vote.

Earl Warren
Library Of Congress

Beebe Bucks GOP Tide in the Natural State: In the 2010 mid-term elections, the Republican Party won three of Arkansas' four seats in the U.S. House of Representatives. In addition, the GOP dislodged Democratic U.S. Senator Blanche Lincoln. Despite these defeats, Democratic Governor Mike Beebe cruised to re-election, garnering 66% of the vote.

Mike Beebe
Official Photograph

Brother Against Brother: In 1888, the two major party Gubernatorial nominees in Tennessee were brothers. The Democrats nominated former U.S. Representative Robert Taylor. The Republicans nominated his older brother, attorney Alfred Taylor. The two brothers remained on good terms and traveled together throughout the campaign. Robert won this election, and would go on to serve for four years. Alfred would eventually win the Tennessee Governorship in 1920.

Two Democrats Get Swept up in Republican Tide: The only two incumbent Democratic Governors to lose their re-election bids in 2010 were Chet Culver, who lost to former Republican Governor Terry Branstad in Iowa, and Ted Strickland, who lost to former U.S. Representative John Kasich (R-OH).

What a Difference Two Years Makes: In 1990, two years before being elected President, Bill Clinton won the Democratic Primary for re-election as Governor of Arkansas with just 54% of the vote. He defeated Tom McCrae, the former President of the Winthrop Rockefeller (charitable) Organization.

Bill Clinton
William J. Jefferson Presidential Library

Democrat Disses long-time Friend to Endorse Bush: In 1998, Texas Lieutenant Governor Bob Bullock, a Democrat, bucked party lines and endorsed Republican Governor George W. Bush for re-election over the Democratic nominee, Gary Mauro, despite Bullock's status as the Godfather of Mauro's two children.

Bob Bullock, left, and George W. Bush
Baylor Library Digital Collections

As Governor, George W. Bush Garnered Widespread Appeal: When running for re-election as Governor of Texas in 1998, George W. Bush garnered 68.24% of the vote. In this landslide victory, Bush garnered 60% of the female vote, 49% of the Latino vote, and 25% of the African-American vote.

George W, Bush
Official Portrait as Governor of Texas

Lingle Picks Democratic Hammerlock in Aloha State: In 2002, Linda Lingle became the first Republican to be elected Governor of Hawaii since 1962.

Linda Lingle
U.S. Navy Photograph

Plurality Governors: No Governor of Minnesota has won a majority of the vote since 1994. This is due to the formidable presence of the Minnesota Independence Party.

Making History in the Nutmeg State: In 1974, Connecticut Democrat Ella Grasso became the first female elected Governor of a state who was not the wife of a previous Governor.

Ella Grasso
Library of Congress

Indian-American leads Deep South State: In 2007, Louisiana voters elected Bobby Jindal as the first Indian-American Governor in history.

Bobby Jindal
Official Photograph

New Mexico Elects Latina Republican to lead them: In 2010, Republican Susana Martinez won the Governorship of New Mexico, becoming the first Latina elected as Governor of a state.

Susana Martinez
Official Photograph

Defeating a Popular Lady in the Lone Star State: Despite having a personal approval rating of 60% (higher than any Texas Governor in over thirty years), George W. Bush defeated Ann Richards in her 1994 re-election bid for the Governorship.

Ann Richards
Ann Richards Texas State Libraries and Archives Commission

Longer Terms in the Gem State: In 1946, Charles Armington Robbins became the first Idaho Governor elected to a four-year term. Prior to his election, Idaho Governors served just two-year terms.

Great Seal of Idaho

Real Bad Timing for Underdog Challenger: The only debate between Massachusetts Democratic Governor Michael Dukakis and his Republican opponent George Kariotis came at the same time as the seventh game of the 1986 World Series between the hometown Boston Red Sox and the New York Mets.

Patience is a Virtue: Butch Otter served as the Lieutenant Governor of Idaho from 1987-2001. No other Idaho Lieutenant Governor has served for this long a time period. In 2006 he was elected as the state's Governor.

Butch Otter
Official Photograph

Transcending Partisanship: In 1952, Allan Shivers garnered the nominations of both the Democrat and the Republican Parties for the Governorship of Texas. His name appeared on the ballot twice. In effect, he ran against himself.

Allan Shivers on the Cover of *Time Magazine*

Not a Partisan Issue in the Place where America's Day Begins: In Guam, all Gubernatorial elections are non-partisan.

Going Where No Man has Gone Before: In 1974, Hawaii voters made George Ariyoshi the first Asian-American elected as Governor of a state. He served as Governor for three four-year terms.

George Ariyoshi
Official Portrait

Political Forgiveness: In 1982, George C. Wallace, after apologizing for his past vociferous opposition to desegregation, was re-elected for an unprecedented fourth term as Governor of Alabama. He carried all ten of the state's African-American majority counties.

George C. Wallace
Lyndon Baines Johnson Library and Museum

Opponents Switch Party Loyalty: In 1978, the Democratic Candidate for Governor of Massachusetts was Conservative Democrat Ed King. King defeated Liberal Republican Frank Hatch. Later in life, King switched to the Republican Party and Hatch became a Democrat.

Don't Gamble on Gibbons: In 2010, scandal-plagued Jim Gibbons became the first incumbent Nevada Governor to lose a primary for re-election. The state's former Attorney General, Brian Sandoval, beat Gibbons 55.5% - 27.2% in the Republican Gubernatorial primary.

Jim Gibbons
Official Photograph

Nixon was Just Having a Bad Day: After losing the California Governorship to incumbent Edmund Gerald "Pat" Brown Sr., former Vice President Richard M. Nixon told reporters: "You won't have Nixon to kick around anymore." Six years later he was elected President of the United States.

Richard M. Nixon
Los Angeles Times

Political Split in Rap Community: In the 2002 Gubernatorial election in New York, Rapper P-Diddy endorsed Democrat Carl McCall while "LL Cool J" backed Republican Governor George Pataki. Pataki won the race.

State and Territorial Government

Sooner Squeaker: In the 1970 Oklahoma Gubernatorial election, Democrat David Hall dislodged incumbent Republican Governor Dewey Bartlett by just 2,181 votes. This was the closest race in Oklahoma Gubernatorial history.

David Hall
Official Photograph

Ending Republican Drought in the Old Line State: In 2002, Robert Ehrlich became the first Republican elected as Governor of Maryland since 1966.

Robert Ehrlich
Official Portrait

Popular Democratic Governor in Republican Territory: Despite the fact that over 60% of Wyoming's registered voters are Republican, Democratic Governor Dave Freudenthal was re-elected with 70% of the vote in 2006.

Dave Freudenthal
Official Photograph

Massachusetts Voters Defy Race and Religion: In 2002, the Massachusetts electorate chose Mitt Romney, a Mormon, as their Governor, despite the fact that Mormons comprise less than one percent of the state's population. In 2006, Massachusetts voters chose Deval Patrick, an African-American, as their Governor, despite the fact that African-American comprise less than 7% of the state's population. Subsequently, in 2010, Patrick became the first African-American Governor in history to be re-elected.

Deval Patrick
Official Photograph

TR's Long Day: In 1898, while running for Governor of New York, Theodore Roosevelt made 19 speeches in just one day.

Theodore Roosevelt
Library of Congress

Lieutenant Governors

Teacher and Student Move up the Political Ladder: In 1970, Nevada State Assemblyman and future U.S. Senate Majority Leader Harry Reid was elected Lieutenant Governor of Nevada at just 30 years of age. He ran with successful Gubernatorial candidate Mike O'Callaghan, who had been Reid's Civics Teacher at Basics High School in Henderson, Nevada.

Harry Reid
Official Photograph

What an Oversight: Despite the fact that in Arkansas the position of Lieutenant Governor was created in 1914, Arkansas had no one serving in that position until 1926. This was the result of an oversight or error on the part of Arkansas state politicians. The measure to add the position of Lieutenant Governor was voted upon in 1914, and the measure won by just over 300 votes (45,567 to 45,206). However, the Arkansas Speaker of the House declared the measure lost because "he thought" there needed to be a majority of the total vote, rather than a majority of those voting on the specific question. A dozen years later it was discovered that the Initiative and Referendum of 1910 had changed the law so that only a majority of those voting on a specific question was enough to pass the measure. So, in 1926 the Initiative of 1914 was declared valid and Harvey Parnell was elected Arkansas' first Lieutenant Governor.

Punk Rock Republican: Massachusetts Republican Lieutenant Governor Kerry Healey (2003-2007) is a fan of the punk rock band "The Ramones."

Kerry Healey
Official Photograph

The Legislature picks Lieutenant Governor: Tennessee and West Virginia are the only states where the state legislatures rather than he voters elect the Lieutenant Governor.

Long-Time #2: John Shelton Wilder served as Tennessee Lt. Governor for 39 years, from 1971 to 2007.

First Female Lieutenant Governor: Consuelo N. Bailey was the first female to serve as Lieutenant Governor in U.S. history. She served as Lieutenant Governor of Vermont from 1955-1959.

No Number Two: Arizona, Maine, New Hampshire, Oregon and Wyoming are the only states with no office of Lieutenant Governor.

No Lieutenant Governor in the Isle of Enchantment: Puerto Rico is the only U.S. territory that has no Lieutenant Governor.

Potentially Rocky Arraignment: In 18 states the Governor and Lieutenant Governor are elected separately, and can be members of different political parties.

Doctor Dean: From 1987-1991, as Vermont's sitting Lieutenant Governor, Democrat Howard Dean continued his medical practice. In fact, he was examining a patient when he heard that Governor Richard A. Snelling had died and that he would become Governor.

Howard Dean
National Governors Association

Razorback Republicans: Arkansas has had only four Republican Lieutenant Governors since Reconstruction: Maurice Britt (1967-1971), Mike Huckabee (1993-1996), Winthrop Paul Rockefeller (1996-2006), and Mark A. Darr (2011-present).

Other Constitutional Officers

A Political Office where Women Dominate: Denise Merrill is the thirteenth female to serve as Secretary of State of Connecticut.

Denise Merrill
Official Photograph

Political Wunderkind: Walter Mondale was the youngest Minnesota Attorney General in history. He assumed office in 1960 at age 32.

Walter Mondale
Library of Congress

He Must really like this Job: Frank J. Kelley (D-MI) served longer than any state Attorney General in American history. He served from 1961-1988. When he was sworn in at age 36 in 1961, he was the youngest Attorney General in Wolverine state history. When he left office in 1988 at age 74, he was the oldest.

Massachusetts is Kennedy Country: Massachusetts Treasurer and Receiver-General John T. Driscoll won his office in 1960 by defeating John B. Kennedy and John M. Kennedy in the Democratic primary. He was re-elected in 1962 by defeating primary opponent John M. Kennedy in a rematch, as well as former State Treasurer John Francis Kennedy.

Wolverine Makes History: In 1970, Richard A. Austin, elected as Michigan Secretary of State, became the first African-American elected to a statewide office in the Wolverine State. He served in that post from 1971-1994.

State Legislators

Barney Frank Fails to Toe Party Line: In the mid-term elections of 1978, Massachusetts State Representative Barney Frank, a liberal Democrat, bucked party loyalty by supporting Republican Gubernatorial candidate Frank Hatch over incumbent Democratic Governor Ed King. He also supported the re-election of Republican U.S. Senator Ed Brooke over Democratic nominee Paul Tsongas.

Barney Frank
Official Photograph

Young man with high hopes: In 1970, 22-year old Chester G. Atkins was elected by voters to a seat in the Massachusetts House of Representatives, making him the youngest individual ever elected to the state's General Court (the Legislature).

Chester G. Atkins
Official Photograph

Legislative "Lifer" From the Golden State: Democrat Ralph C. Dills holds the record for the longest service of any California State Legislator. He served in the California Assembly (House) from 1938-1949 and in the State Senate from 1967-1998: A total of 42 years.

Scott Brown's Political Shadow: When Wrentham, Massachusetts Selectman Scott Brown ran for State Representative, Richard J. Ross succeeded him on the Board of Selectmen. When Brown won a seat in the State Senate, Ross succeeded him as State Representative. When Brown won a seat in the U.S. Senate, Ross succeeded him in the State Senate.

Robert J. Ross
Official Photograph

Small Governing Body in the Pacific: The Guam Legislature consists of just one body, which is made up of only 15 members.

Guam Official Coat of Arms

Combating Political Careerism: Fifteen States have impose term limits on their state legislators.

At Least He is Honest: In 1966, after losing a State Senate Race in California, Democrat Dick Tuck said during his concession speech: "The people have spoken, the bastards."

One Legislator Can Make a Difference: At the end of 2010, State Representative-elect Noble Ellington announced he was leaving the Democratic Party to become a Republican. His defection handed the Louisiana House of Representatives to the Republican Party for the first time since Reconstruction.

Noble Ellington
Official Photograph

They Just Need the right Web Designer: The American Samoa Legislature, called the Fono, is the only state or territorial legislature without a web site.

Young Kennedy Gets Elected: The youngest Kennedy to win elective office was Patrick J. Kennedy, who won a seat in the Rhode Island House of Representatives in 1988 while a student at Providence College. He was just 21 years of age.

Patrick J. Kennedy
Official Photograph

The Law Makers: The U.S. has approximately 14,000 state legislators.

The Duke of the Road: The first no-fault automobile insurance legislation was passed in 1971. State Legislator Michael Dukakis, a future Massachusetts Governor and Democratic Presidential nominee, wrote the legislation.

Michael Dukakis
Official Photograph

Neatness Isn't Everything: In 1974, State Representative Barney Frank, known for his disordered appearance, ran for re-election with the campaign slogan: "Neatness Isn't Everything."

Barney Frank Campaign Poster

Incumbency is Golden in the Golden State: Between 2002 and 2008, 99% of state legislative candidates in California who sought re-election won their races.

Long Time Okie Legislator: Gene Stipe served in the Oklahoma State Senate longer than any other member of that body. Stipe served from 1957-2003.

Part VII: State and Territorial Political Facts

John Hancock's Land: The Massachusetts State House sits on land once owned by John Hancock, the state's first Governor.

John Hancock
Library of Congress

State Senate Districts bigger than Congressional Districts: In California, each State Senator represents about 800,000 constituents. By contrast, U.S. House members represent about 650,000 constituents.

At least its Something: In South Dakota, all state legislators are reimbursed five cents for every mile traveling to and from the State Capitol located in Pierre when the Legislature is in session.

The Union State: New York has the highest rate of union membership, with 25% of private sector employees and 75% of public sector employees being members of unions.

Atheists and Agnostics Need Not Apply: Article 6, section 8 of the *North Carolina State Constitution* disallows any individual who does not believe in God from holding elective office. "The following persons shall be disqualified for office: First, any person who shall deny the being of Almighty God."

Razorbacks in the Big Leagues: Over 430 Arkansans served in the Clinton Administration.

Arkansas State Flag

No Need to Register in the Peace Garden State: North Dakota is the only state without voter registration. A voter needs only to prove at the polls that he/she has been a resident in the state for at least 30 days.

Sunshine State Helmet Provision: In Florida, motorcyclists are required to wear helmets when riding, unless they have purchased at least $10,000 in medical insurance.

Worth Every Penney: New Hampshire State Legislators earn $100 a year.

Going Nuclear: Thirty-one states have nuclear reactors.

A Massachusetts Masterpiece: *The Constitution of the Commonwealth of Massachusetts* is the oldest continuous written and functioning Constitution on earth. John Adams, Samuel Adams, and Samuel Bowdoin wrote the document. It went into effect in 1780.

Old Chamber: The oldest state legislative chamber in continuous use is Representative Hall in Concord, New Hampshire, which houses the New Hampshire Legislature. The body has met there since 1829.

279

Democrats by a Different name in the land of 10,000 lakes: In Minnesota, the official name for the Democratic Party is the "Democratic-Farmer-Labor Party" (DFL). In 1944, the Democratic Party merged with the redoubtable third party called the Farmer-Labor Party.

Democratic-Farmer-Labor Party Official Logo

No Income Tax: The only states without a state income tax are: Alaska, Florida, Nevada, New Hampshire, South Dakota, Tennessee, Texas, Washington, and Wyoming.

Granite State Constitution: The 1776 *New Hampshire Constitution* (Supplanted by The *Constitution of the State of New Hampshire* in 1784) was the first Constitution ratified in the U.S. The Provincial Congress ratified it.

Granite State's Big House: Consisting of 400 members, the New Hampshire House of Representatives is the second largest legislative body in the United States behind the U.S. House of Representatives, which consists of 435 voting members. Each Representative from New Hampshire has approximately 3,000 constituents.

Not Exactly a Stepping Stone to the Governorship: No Lieutenant Governor of Maryland has ever been elected in his own right as Governor. The office of Lieutenant Governor was established in 1864.

No Longer a Secret: Massachusetts was the first state to use the Australian (secret) ballot in elections.

Montana Law: Under Montana Law, when the State Legislature is tied numerically, the party that holds the Governorship determines the majority.

Montana State Flag

Cornhusker Distinction: Nebraska is the only State whose Legislature is composed of just one house (unicameral), and which is non-partisan.

A Quirky Alabama Statute: Under Alabama law, all municipal elections are non-partisan unless a municipality has a population over 300,000. The state's largest city, Birmingham, has a population of only about 230,000.

It's the Law, Massachusetts Style: Under Massachusetts Law, voters are required to receive notice at least ten days prior to an election of a change in polling places.

Judging the Judges: In 33 states, voters elect state trial court judges.

Click it or Ticket: Thirty-one states have primary seatbelt laws, allowing law enforcement officers to ticket any driver for not wearing a seatbelt.

Female State Senate Majority: In 2009, the New Hampshire Senate became the first American legislative body to have a female majority.

Fono's Distinction: The American Samoa Legislature, called the Fono, is the only legislative body in the U.S. that is non-partisan and bi-cameral. (Fono is Polynesian for Councils).

America Samoa Official Flag

Legislative Prerogatives: In Alabama, the state Legislature can override a Gubernatorial veto by a simple majority, rather than by a two-thirds vote.

Federally Owned Frontier: The Federal Government owns 69% of Alaska.

Dual Role: In Kentucky, The Speaker of the House of Representatives is also Chairman of the House Rules Committee.

No Seatbelt Laws: New Hampshire is the only state that does not require adult motorists to wear seatbelts.

Long Constitution: *The Alabama Constitution* is the longest operational Constitution in the world. It contains 357,157 words.

Death Penalty: Capital Punishment is permissible in 36 states, and at the federal level.

Getting a Head Start: Rhode Island declared Independence from Great Britain on May 4, 1776. This was two months before the *Declaration of Independence* was formalized.

The Federal State: The Federal Government owns about 86% of Nevada.

Nevada Official State Seal

The Pinnacle of Irony: New Hampshire prisoners make license plates with the imprimatur: "Live Free or Die."

Oregon Bottle Bill: In 1972, Oregon became the first state to institute container-deposit legislation (The Oregon Bottle Bill mandates certain beverages be returned for a refund).

Lone Star Legislating: Under Texas law, "Special Sessions" of the State Legislature can be called by the Governor, but sessions cannot exceed 30 days.

How Many State Legislators Does it Take? There are approximately 7,000 State Legislators in America.

First State to Legalize Abortion: In 1967, Colorado became the first state to allow abortion. The practice was only allowed in cases of rape, incest, and in cases where the pregnancy could lead to permanent physical disability of the mother.

No Sales Taxes: Alaska, Delaware, Montana, New Hampshire, and Oregon have no Sales Tax.

Green Mountain State Distinction: The only state without a Balanced Budget Amendment enshrined in its Constitution is Vermont.

Vermont Official State Seal

Conservative West Virginia Electorate Likes Democrats in the U.S. Senate: Although West Virginia voted for the Republican Presidential nominee in the last three elections, it has not had a Republican U.S. Senator since 1959.

Utah GOP Rule: In Utah if a Republican Congressional Candidate can garner 60% of the vote at the state Republican Convention, he/she is awarded the Party's nomination without a primary.

When the Golden State was a GOP citadel: In 1925 the Republicans held 37 of the 40 State Senate Seats in California.

Letting the Legislature Decide on a Governor: In Mississippi and Vermont, if no candidate for Governor garners a majority of the vote, the state legislature decides between the top two finishers.

Where American Education Began: The first compulsory education statute in the United States took effect in the Massachusetts Colony in 1647.

We Don't Want "Surplus" Surpluses: In Oregon, the state government is disallowed from maintaining budget surpluses of over 2%.

Temperance in the Magnolia State: In 1918, Mississippi was the first state to ratify the Eighteenth Amendment to the *U.S. Constitution*, prohibiting the sale of alcoholic beverages.

Mississippi Official State Seal

The Tonic Tax: Arkansas and West Virginia are the only two states that tax soft drinks.

Lone Star Legislature Gets Lots of Time Off: The Texas State legislature meets for 140 days every two years.

Holdouts on the Bill of Rights: Georgia, Massachusetts, and Rhode Island did not ratify the *Bill of Rights* to the *U.S. Constitution* until 1939.

66,592 Signatures is simply not enough in Massachusetts: For a state initiative to appear on the ballot in Massachusetts the initiative must receive 66,593 confirmed signatures.

Last Holdouts: Iowa and Mississippi are the only states which have never elected a female as Governor or to the U.S. Congress.

Northern Colonies Unfortunate Legacy: In 1641, Massachusetts Bay Colony became the first colony to legalize slavery. In 1780, the colony outlawed the practice.

From Countries to States: California, Hawaii, Texas, and Vermont were once independent nations.

Massachusetts Knew Nothing: In 1854, the anti-immigrant American Party, a.k.a. the Know Nothing Party, captured all Constitutional Offices and an overwhelming majority in both houses of the General Court (The State Legislature) and the entire state Congressional Delegation.

Massachusetts Official State Seal

Working for Rival campaigns: In 2006, the Brookline, Massachusetts signature-gathering company *Spoonworks* (owned by Harold Hubschman), collected signatures for three competing candidates in the Massachusetts Gubernatorial campaigns: They were Democrat Chris Gabrieli (who lost the Democratic Primary), Republican nominee Kerry Healey, and Independent Christy Mihos.

Government Can be Very Expensive: In California, about eighty cents of every dollar received by the state government goes to compensate state employees.

Green Mountain State Leads the Way: In 1793, Vermont became the first state to disallow slavery.

Small State Capital in Small State: Montpelier, Vermont is the smallest state capital in population. The city has only about 8,000 permanent residents.

Property Tax Disparity: All ten counties with the nation's highest property tax burden are located in New Jersey and New York. Contrawise, four of the five counties with the lowest tax burden are in Alaska.

Beaver State Started the Madness: In 1910, Oregon became the first state to establish a Presidential Preference Primary, requiring the state delegation to support the winner at their respective conventions. 1912 was the first year when the primary system was instituted. Twelve other states followed Oregon and held partisan primaries that year.

Oregon Official State Flag

A Resounding Victory for "None of these Candidates:" In Nevada, voters have the option of voting for *None of these Candidates* instead of the candidates on the ballot. In 1976, this phrase won the Republican primary for the at-large Congressional seat garnering 16,097 votes. Walden Earhart came in second with 9,831 votes. By Nevada law, if *None of these Candidates* wins, the second-place finisher is declared the winner.

Weird Term Limit in the Big Sky State: The Montana Constitution stipulates that a Governor can serve for any eight years during any sixteen-year time period.

No Pyrotechnics Sold Here: Delaware, Massachusetts, New Jersey, and New York are the only states that prohibit the sale of all consumer fireworks.

Bay State Begins a Trend: In 1912, Massachusetts became the first state to enact a minimum wage. It applied to woman and children only.

Oregon Recalls: In 1908, Oregon became the first state to institute recall elections for state officials.

Kentucky Colonel: The Governor of Kentucky can confer upon individuals the honorific title of "Kentucky Colonel." The only two Presidents to receive this prestigious honor were Lyndon B. Johnson and Bill Clinton. Recipients of this award are judged for their service and contributions to Kentucky and to the global community.

Official Emblem of Honorary Order of Kentucky Colonels

Garden State Leads the Way: New Jersey was the first state to ratify the *Bill of Rights* to the *U.S. Constitution* in 1789.

Lone-Star Power Trilogy: From 1955-1961, the President of the United States was Dwight D. Eisenhower, the Speaker of the U.S. House of Representatives was Sam Rayburn, and the U.S. Senate Majority Leader was Lyndon B. Johnson, All three lived in Texas at some point in their lives. Eisenhower and Johnson were born in Texas, and Rayburn moved there as a young child. Both Johnson and Rayburn maintained residence in Texas throughout their lives.

Ocean State Adverse to Change: Rhode Island was the only state not to attend the Constitutional Convention in 1787. Rhode Island officials did not want to alter the existing governing authority, the *Articles of Confederation and Perpetual Union.*

Pardon this Clause: Under the *Ohio Constitution*, a Governor is not allowed to pardon individuals when impeachment or treason is involved.

Ohio Official State Seal

The Landlord Holds the Key: In Massachusetts, a rent receipt from a landlord on his/her letterhead is considered a valid identification to use to register to vote at the polls.

Some Very Odd States: Kentucky, Louisiana, Mississippi, New Jersey, and Virginia are the only states to hold statewide election contests in odd years.

Volunteer State ekes out a Victory for Women's Suffrage: Tennessee was the last state to ratify the *Eighteenth Amendment* to the *U.S. Constitution*, allowing women the right to vote. The Amendment passed by "one" vote. Tennessee Governor Albert H. Roberts put out a "full court press" to get the amendment passed.

Federal Ownership of Utah: The Federal Government owns about 70% of the state of Utah.

Record Setting year in the Gem State: In 2003, the Idaho Legislature held its longest session in the state's history. It lasted 118 days.

The Brits Still Use the Title: Before the current *North Carolina Constitution* took effect in 1868, the state's House of Representatives was called the "House of Commons."

North Carolina Official State Seal

You Can Bank On It: The only state-owned bank in the U.S. is the Bank of North Dakota. The institution has been in operation since 1919 and was started by Socialist Party Activist A.C. Townley.

No Automobile Insurance? Not a Problem: Wisconsin and New Hampshire are the only states that do not require drivers to purchase automobile insurance.

Guns on Campus: Utah is the only state with a statute permitting the carrying of concealed weapons on public college campuses.

Register and Vote: Idaho, Maine, Minnesota, Oregon, and Wisconsin all allow same-day voter registration.

Bay State Property Tax Limits: Under a 1980 ballot initiative, property tax increases in Massachusetts cannot exceed two and a half percent in a municipality without the approval of voters via an override, unless the increase is for new growth, capital exclusion, debt exclusion, and in some cases, expenses related to water and sewer.

Palmetto State Rules: In South Carolina, if a candidate running in a primary does not have an opponent, that candidate's name does not appear on the primary ballot

South Carolina Official State Seal

For the Common Good: Four U.S. States are "Commonwealths." They are Kentucky, Massachusetts, Pennsylvania, and Virginia. The term means that the "government [is] based on the common consent of the people." As a practical matter, the difference between a commonwealth and a state is semantic. However, the term takes on a different meaning when applying to the Commonwealths of Puerto Rico and the Northern Mariana Islands. In this case, the U.S. Department of State defines a Commonwealth as a territory that is "self-governing under a constitution of its adoption and whose right of self-government will not be unilaterally withdrawn by Congress."

No Self-Service: In Oregon and New Jersey it is illegal for customers to pump their own gas.

Concern Over Pronunciation: In 1881 the Arkansas Legislature established the proper pronunciation for their state. The legal pronunciation for the state is "Ar-kan-saw." No other state has a Legislatively-designated pronunciation.

Miscellaneous Governmental Facts

Part VIII: Miscellaneous

The Other Presidents

The Real First President? President George Washington is credited with being the First President of the United States. However, prior to his inauguration in 1781, when the U.S. was governed by the *Articles of Confederation and Perpetual Union*, John Hanson Jr. was elected by the Continental Congress as: "First President of the United States in Congress Assembled." He resigned after one year and had seven successors. George Washington wrote to President Hanson congratulating him on winning "the most important seat in the United States." Some argue that Washington should be referred to as the "Eighth" President of the United States.

John Hanson Jr.
Library of Congress

John Hanson Jr.'s Lasting Legacy: John Hanson Jr., the first President of the Congress Assembled, approved the Great Seal of the United States in 1782.

Official Presidential Seal

More Excitement in the Congressional Trenches: In 1788, Henry Laurens resigned his post as the President of the Continental Congress. He concluded that he could wield more power as a rank-and-file member of the Continental Congress.

Henry Laurens
Library of Congress

Jefferson Davis Says No Thank You to College Presidency: Former Confederate President Jefferson Davis was offered the first Presidency at Texas Agricultural and Mechanical University (Texas A&M). He declined the offer.

Jefferson Davis
Library of Congress

Line-Item-Veto and the Confederacy: While the President of the United States does not have the Line Item Veto (The power to cancel specific provisions without vetoing the entire bill), during the Civil War the *Constitution of the Confederate States of America* granted the President the Line Item Veto.

Six Years and Out for Confederate President: Under the *Constitution of the Confederate States of America*, the President was limited to serve one six-year term.

The White House

White House has Plenty of Places to Go: The White House has thirty-five bathrooms.

The White House
Library of Congress

Looking fore a Room: The White House has 132 rooms.

Just Call it the Peoples House: The original term for the President's house was "The Executive Mansion." In 1901 President Theodore Roosevelt changed the name on the official mansion's stationery to "The White House." That informal title stuck.

From Bowling to Crisis Management: The White House Situation Room was once the White House bowling alley.

George W. Bush with advisors in the White House Situation Room
White House Photograph

I bet it could fetch a fortune on E-Bay: The most famous piece of furniture in the Oval Office is the "Resolute Desk." The desk is made of wood from the British ship, "The Resolute." The Resolute was abandoned when it became wedged in the ice in the Arctic in 1854. The ship was later salvaged by a U.S. ship and was brought to Connecticut. The ship was repaired and given to Queen Victoria of the United Kingdom as a symbol of friendship between the two countries. When the ship was finally retired, Queen Victoria had some of the timbers fashioned into this now famous "Resolute desk." She presented it to President Rutherford B. Hayes in 1880. President Barack Obama now uses the desk in the Oval Office.

Barack Obama sitting at the Resolute Desk
White House Photograph by Pete Souza

"How May I Direct Your Call?" The White House switchboard employs 14 telephone operators. They receive about 4,000 calls every weekday and 2,500 calls during the weekend.

A Ghostly Guest in the White House? The land that houses the White House and much of the nation's capital was sold to the Federal Government by landowner David Burns. Burns sold the U.S. 600 acres of his family-owned land in 1791. His ghost has allegedly been seen in the White House.

White House is not all "Brick and Mortar:" The White House has 147 windows.

The "House of Doors:" There are 412 doors in the White House.

"Up and Down or Side to Side:" The paint color of the exterior of the White House is "Whisper White." It takes about 570 gallons of paint to paint the exterior of the White House.

The Electoral College

Electoral College Rules: If no candidate garners the requisite 270 votes needed to win a Presidential Election, the election is thrown into the U.S. House of Representatives. The House must then choose a President from the three top finishers. The U.S. Senate next chooses the Vice-President from the top two Vice-Presidential finishers.

Small States, Small Say: The 10 smallest populated states in America have a combined 32 votes out of 538 votes in the Electoral College.

Persistence Does Not Always Pay Off: There have been over 700 proposed Amendments introduced in the U.S. Congress to abolish or alter the Electoral College. No other issue has had as many proposed Constitutional Amendments. None has become the law of the land.

Electors with no Faith: Faithless Electors are members of the Electoral College who vote for a candidate who they are not "pledged" to vote for. Of the 22,453 Presidential Electoral College electors in American political history, only eleven have been "faithless." To discourage electors from being faithless, twenty-four states have statutes punishing faithless electors. However, the penalties for digressing from one's pledge are minor. They are usually small fines.

Budget and Taxes

U.S. Defense Expenditures Way Out in Front: According to The Stockholm International Peace Research Institute, between 2008 and 2009, the U.S. spent $607 billion on defense expenditures (41.5% of the world's share). By contrast, China spent just $84.9 billion on Defense, (just 5.8% of the world's Defense Expenditures).

Medicare Recipients: About Forty-seven million Americans are on Medicare.

Intelligence Money: The U.S. spends about $80 billion each year in Intelligence Gathering.

Maxed Out: In fiscal year 2010, forty-two cents out of every dollar the U.S. spent was borrowed money.

Miscellaneous

Skyrocketing Health Care Costs: In 1960, the U.S. spent just 5% of its Gross Domestic Product (GDP) on Health Care. Today, the U.S. spends 18% of its GDP on Health Care.

Federal Income Taxes Enter the Scene: The first Federal Income Tax was established by the Federal Revenue Act of 1861. The act, signed by President Abraham Lincoln to pay for the Civil War, imposed a flat 3% tax on all income above $800. Close to two years later, the U.S. Congress passed, and Lincoln signed, The Revenue Act of 1863, establishing a graduated system in which those earning an annual income of between $600 and $10,000 were required to pay a 3% income tax, and those earning over $10,000 were mandated to pay a 5% income tax. The tax was repealed in 1871. In 1894, Congress passed more income tax legislation, establishing a flat rate tax. It was ruled Constitutionally impermissible by the U.S. Supreme Court because it was not allocated to each state's population. In 1913, the Sixteenth Amendment to the *U.S. Constitution* was ratified, stating: "The Congress shall have power to lay and collect taxes on incomes, from whatever source derived, without apportionment among the several States, and without regard to any census or enumeration."

The Federal Budget: Social Security, Medicare, Medicaid, defense and interest on the debt are the five largest expenditures in the national Budget.

Voluminous Indeed: The Federal Tax Code is over 70,000 pages long. It was just 400 pages long in 1913 after the Sixteenth Amendment to the *U.S. Constitution* was ratified, re-instituting the Income Tax.

Where Our Money is Going: Medicare, Medicaid and Social Security account for over 40% of the U.S. Federal Budget.

Big Revenue Source: About 45% of all federal revenue is produced from the federal income tax.

China to the Rescue: China owns about $900 billion in U.S. debts.

Government Employment: The federal, state, and municipal governments employ approximately 20 million Americans in the aggregate.

Federal Employees: America employs over two million federal employees, excluding the U.S. Postal Service and the U.S. Military.

The Real National Debt: It's Not as Good as the Government claims it is: The American government calculates the National Debt by amalgamating the Social Security Surplus with the General Revenue. This is called "Unified Budgeting." When calculating the National Debt, the Government uses "cash accounting" rather than "accrual accounting." Accordingly, "unfunded liabilities" such as future Social Security obligations and other unfunded entitlement programs, are not factored into the calculation. This results in a National Debt of less than $15 trillion. However, once the obligations of the unfunded liabilities from the entitlements programs are added into the mix, the National Debt increases to almost $60 trillion.

The Mighty U.S. Military Budget: The U.S. spends more on its military budget than the next seventeen countries combined spend on theirs.

Miscellaneous

Taking care of the Veterans: Over 40 million Americans receive Veterans Benefits from the Federal Government.

Defense-a-paluzza: The Department of Defense is the nation's largest employer. Its payroll includes about 1.5 million active duty military personnel, more than a million National Guard and Reservists, and almost 720,000 civilian employees.

A Relatively Small Department: The U.S. Department of Education is the smallest federal cabinet department. It employs only about 5,000 people and its annual budget is less than $70 billion.

Uncle Sam Needs You to Imbibe: In 1910, taxes on alcoholic beverages constituted 30% of all federal revenue.

At Your Discretion: 12% of the federal budget is discretionary (not mandatory).

Running on Foreign Oil: The U.S. imports about 60% of its oil supply.

Made In the USA: The U.S. produces almost 20% of the world's output, making it the largest manufacturer in the world

The Good Old Days: The First record of America incurring a National Debt was in 1791. The debt was $75,463,476.52.

The Black Budget: The U.S. Defense Department has a "black budget" to fund classified projects. This budget was about $50 Billion in 2009.

Per Capita GDP: The Per Capita Gross Domestic Product in the U.S in January of 2011 was $47,400.

Earmarks: Congressional Earmarks constitute about 1% of the federal budget.

A Complete Partisan "Role Reversal:" In 1964, the Democratic Congress passed a $10 billion tax cut proposal first proposed by President John F. Kennedy, then promoted and later signed into law by President Lyndon B. Johnson. The legislation slashed the top marginal tax rate from 91% to 70%. At the time, this was considered a liberal proposal to stimulate the economy. Democrats were more sympathetic to tax cuts as a way to stimulate economic growth, while Republicans argued for fiscal austerity. Republican leaders, including former President Dwight D. Eisenhower and U.S. House Minority Leader Charles Halleck (R-IN), argued that broad-based tax cuts would balloon the deficit. Despite conservative opposition, enough Republicans defied party leadership and voted for the legislation. Ironically, today it is considered conservative orthodoxy to support tax cuts and liberal orthodoxy to oppose them.

Entitlement Expenditures: The U.S. spends three times more on entitlements and interest on the National Debt than it does on the military.

Budget Buster: The U.S. spends over $2.5 trillion annually on health care.

Tax Lawyers At Work: Though General Electric earned $5.1 Billion in the U.S. in 2010, it paid no U.S. taxes.

Go No Lower: The federal minimum wage is $7.25 an hour.

The Fine Print: Article 1, Section 8, Clause 1 of the *U.S. Constitution* says the U.S. Congress: "shall have the power to lay and collect Taxes, Duties, Imposts, and Excises."

Municipal Officials

33-year old Leads Hub: Daniel A. Whelton was the youngest Mayor in Boston history. He took office in 1905 at age 33.

Daniel A. Whelton
Official Photograph

Taking Nothing for Granted: In 2009, New York Mayor Michael Bloomberg spent a record $90 million in his bid to secure a third term, defeating New York City Comptroller William Colridge Thompson Jr. Despite the fact that Bloomberg outspent Thompson 14-1, he beat him by just over four percentage points.

Michael Bloomberg
Official Photograph

19-year-old Mayor in Oklahoma: John Tyler Hammons, the Mayor of Muskogee, Oklahoma, was elected in 2008 at age 19. He defeated Former Mayor Herschel McBride who was 70 years old.

Young Man in a Hurry: In 2006, Suffolk University undergraduate student Ryan Fattman won a seat on the Board of Selectmen in Sutton, Massachusetts. He defeated two incumbents, garnering 70% of the vote. At age 21, Fattman became the youngest Selectman in Massachusetts history.

Ryan Fattman
Official Photograph

Birthday Boy becomes Mayor: Richard M. Daley was sworn is as Mayor of Chicago on April 24, 1989, his 47th birthday.

Richard M. Daley
Official Photograph

GOP was once Formidable in the City by the Bay: Though San Francisco is now considered a citadel for the Democratic Party, it had all Republican Mayors from 1912-1964. Since 1964, all Mayors have been Democrats.

294

Tragic Day in Iowa: In 1986, a gunman entered Mount Pleasant City Hall in Mount Pleasant, Iowa and shot Mayor Ed King and two City Council members. King died from his wounds. Current U.S. Secretary of Agriculture Tom Vilsack was elected to succeed him.

Tom Vilsack
Official Photograph

Massachusetts City Looks Beyond Race: Newton, Massachusetts has an African-American population of less than one percent, yet voters elected an African-American Governor in 2006 (Deval Patrick), an African-American President in 2008 (Barack Obama), and an African-American Mayor in 2009 (Setti Warren).

Providence leads the Way: In 2002, Providence, Rhode Island became the first state capital to elect an openly Gay candidate, David N. Ciciline, as its Mayor. Ciciline was re-elected with a resounding 83% of the vote in 2006.

David N. Ciciline
Official Photograph

Curley's Strange Personal Life: Long-time Boston Mayor and Massachusetts Governor James M. Curley outlived his first wife and seven of his nine children. He died in 1958 at age 66.

James Michael Curley
Library of Congress

Finest City: San Diego Mayor Pete Wilson (1971-1982) coined the city's slogan: "San Diego, Americas finest city."

Pete Wilson
Official Photograph

Jerry! Jerry! Jerry! Talk Show Host Jerry Springer served as Mayor of Cincinnati, Ohio from 1977-1978. As a member of the City Council, his colleagues selected him as Mayor. Springer had been considered a rising star in Ohio politics until it was revealed that he had paid a prostitute with his personal check for her services. His political career came to an end in 1982 when he lost a Democratic Gubernatorial Primary.

Miscellaneous

Odds and Ends

Papal Visit: Pope John Paul II was the only Pontiff to visit Washington, DC while in office. He came to the nation's capital in 1979 and met with President Jimmy Carter.

Jimmy Carter and Pope John Paul II
Jimmy Carter Presidential Library and Museum

First Watergate Casualty: The first person to be convicted in the Watergate affair was Richard M. Nixon's Special Counsel, Charles Colson. He pleaded guilty to charges of Obstruction of Justice.

Just Chad: The plural for "Chad" (holes in paper from voting machines) is not "Chads" but "Chad."

Reserve: The U.S. Dollar is the world's reserve currency.

Low Maintenance: Consumer advocate and perennial Presidential candidate Ralph Nader does not own a car or a color television set.

City Says: Don't Comply with the Feds: In 2003, Arcata, California became the first municipality in the U.S. to pass a law forbidding city employees from complying with the U.S.A. Patriot Act. The penalty for violating this ordinance is a $57 fine.

Special Privilege: Helen Thomas was the only member of the press ever to have her own chair reserved at briefings in the White House Press Room. She covered every President from John F. Kennedy to Barack Obama.

Helen Thomas with Lyndon B. Johnson and his Grandson Nugget
Lyndon Baines Johnson Library and Museum

A lot of Politicians: There are about 511,000 elected offices in the United States. This includes all federal, state and municipal offices.

Ideological Composition of American Voters: A Gallop Poll taken in July of 2010 found that 42% of voters identified themselves as conservative, 35% as moderates, and 20% as liberals.

False Belief: A *Time Magazine/CNN* survey taken almost two years after the 9/11 attacks found that a staggering 70% of Americans believed Iraqi President Saddam Hussein was behind the 9/11 hijackings.

On the Money: All U.S. paper currency printed contains the name of the U.S. Treasury Secretary and the Treasurer of the United States.

John Smoltz Should Stick with Baseball: In 2006, Atlanta Braves pitcher John Smoltz made automated telephone calls supporting former Christian Coalition Executive Director Ralph Reed. Reed was running for the Republican nomination for Lieutenant Governor of Georgia. Reed lost.

John Smoltz
Official Photograph

An Eerie Coincidence: During the Clinton-Lewinsky episode, Monica Lewinsky lived in a Watergate apartment in Washington D.C. Her neighbor was former Senate Majority Leader Robert J. Dole (R-KS), who had run against Mr. Clinton for President in 1996.

Highest Civilian Honor: The highest honors a civilian can receive from the U.S. Government are the "Congressional Gold Medal" and the "Presidential Medal of Freedom." The Congressional Gold Medal is awarded by the U.S. Congress. The Presidential Medal of Freedom is conferred by the President.

Not Popular on College Campuses: The Prohibition Party is the third oldest existing American Political Party. It was preceded by the Democratic Party and Republicans Party. Founded in 1869, the anti-alcohol party has fielded a Presidential candidate in every Presidential election since 1872.

Historic Time: Tom Pettit was the only reporter live-on-air when Jack Ruby killed Lee Harvey Oswald.

Lee Harvey Oswald and Jack Ruby
Library of Congress

Little in Aid: Despite popular belief, the U.S. foreign aid budget is less than ½ of 1% of the annual federal budget.

Bankruptcy and Health Care: The most common reason for bankruptcy in America is the inability to pay medical bills.

Goody-Goody: The term "goody goody" was originally coined in the 1890's as a term of derision for "good government guys," or "goo-goos." These "goody-goodies" were politicians who supported government reform and an end to government graft and corruption.

Powerhouse Brothers: Bob Schieffer, the moderator of the CBS Sunday morning public affairs program, *Face The Nation,* is the brother of Tom Schieffer, who was a business partner of George W. Bush when Bush was Managing Partner and Schieffer was President of the Texas Rangers Baseball Franchise. Tom Schieffer was a supporter of Bush's political endeavors and served as Ambassador to Australia during Bush's Presidential administration.

Student Loans: About four million Americans receive student loans directly from the federal government.

Miscellaneous

Interesting Gene Pool: New Orleans Saints Quarterback Drew Breeze is the grandson of U.S. Representative Jack Hightower (D-TX 1975-1985).

Drew Breeze
Official NFL Photograph

Anti-Trust Exemptions: Major League Baseball and Insurance Companies are the only industries exempted from federal anti-trust laws.

Public Law: When legislation becomes the law of the land, it is known as "Public Law."

Bring in the Oil: The U.S. imports about twelve million barrels of oil daily.

Of Jails and Prisons: Though often used interchangeably, there is a distinction between a jail and a prison. Those sent to jail are either awaiting trial or serving a short sentence. Prison is where those convicted of a crime and sentenced to longer stays are housed. Usually, the County Sheriff's Department operates jails, whereas prisons are operated by Prison and Corrections Offices at the state level and at the Federal level by the Federal Bureau of Prisons.

Looking For Intelligence: The U.S. has 16 separate intelligence agencies, all reporting to the Director of National Intelligence.

Two-Time Barrier Breaker: In 1990, Dr. Antonia Novello became both the first Hispanic and first female U.S. Surgeon General.

Dr. Antonia Novello
Official Photograph

Not Exactly Bedtime Reading: The Patient Protection and Affordable Care Act, a.k.a. the Healthcare Reform law, was signed by President Barack Obama in 2010. The legislation is 1,880 pages long.

Dean visits all of America: During his tenure as chairman of the Democratic National Committee (2005-2009), Howard Dean visited every state and territory in the U.S. His last stop was American Samoa.

C-SPAN, A Service of America's Cable Companies: *C-SPAN* (Cable Satellite Public Affairs Network) can be reached in over 100 million homes.

New York City Mega Protest: The largest public protest in U.S. history occurred in 1982 in New York City. The protestors supported the nuclear freeze movement.

Our Friends to the North: Canada is the largest U.S. trading partner and its largest supplier of petroleum.

Miscellaneous

Civil War Draft: The U.S. Civil War was the first in which a draft was imposed. Both the South and the North drafted soldiers.

Civil War Soldiers
Library of Congress

Public Education: The U.S. has about 50 million students enrolled in over 99,000 public schools.

Quickies: *New York Times* Columnist William Safire (1973-2009) claims to have written most of his columns in about 20 minutes.

Exporting Defense: The Boeing Company, a U.S. Aerospace and defense contractor, is the largest exporter in the nation.

They Deliver for You: The U.S. Postal Service has about 3,600 retail locations in the U.S., servicing about 7 million customers a day.

No Longer Standard: The Credit Ratings Agency, "Standard and Poor's" granted the U.S. the esteemed AAA rating in 1917. They kept this rating until 2011, when they downgrading the U.S. to AA+. The Agency states they did this because of the "political brinkmanship" exhibited in the debate over raising the nations debt ceiling.

Where the Heck is that Red Phone? The emergency "red phone," depicted in many movies, was never located in the White House. Its location was in the Pentagon.

The Pentagon
Department of Defense Photograph

Why is There No Channel One? The Federal Communications Commission (FCC) confiscated Channel One in 1945 because it thought that television was using too much bandwidth. It reserved Channel One for mobile radios.

Watch for Side-Effects: The U.S. and New Zealand are the only two countries to allow direct advertising by pharmaceutical companies to the consumers.

Madam Chairman: The term "Selectman" is gender neutral.

Federal Limits: At the federal level, an individual can legally donate $2,500 to a political candidate during the primary and $2,500 during the general election campaigns.

Big Advance Over Elderly Poverty: The U.S. poverty rate for elderly Americans is 9.7%. In 1935, that number stood at over 50%.

Telecommuting Government Workers: More than 100,000 federal employees work from home.

Last Casualties: The last 40 names on the Vietnam War Memorial are the U.S. service members who died rescuing the American merchant ship, the USS *Mayaguez*. The *Khmer Rouge* of Cambodia had seized the ship and it's 39-crewmembers in international waters in 1975.

Vietnam War Memorial
Library of Congress

Why we Vote on Tuesday in November? Federal elections are held on the first Tuesday after the first Monday in November. This is not in the *U.S. Constitution*, but was established by an 1845 statute. The U.S. Congress chose Tuesday because on Sundays many Americans were in church, and Monday allowed a travel day for voters to get to their polling places. November was chosen because it was the best month for farmers to vote.

Chris Mathew's Republican Brother: Jim Mathews, the brother of *MSNBC* talk show host Chris Mathews, was the Republican nominee for Lieutenant Governor of Pennsylvania in 2006. Running with Jim Matthews was Gubernatorial candidate and NFL Hall-of-Famer Lynn Swan. The ticket lost the election, garnering just 39.6% of the vote.

Guamians at Work: About 3,600 Guamians are employed by the federal government.

Not All "Dead Heads" are Liberals: Conservative Commentator Ann Coulter is a great fan of the Grateful Dead.

The Grateful Dead
Library of Congress

Breaking Through the Glass Floor: In 1961, the Social Security eligibility age was lowered from 65 to 62 for men. The age was lowered for women in 1956.

Sure Cure for Insomnia: The Office of the Federal Register, National Archives, and Administration, publishes the *Federal Register Daily*. The document includes proposed rules and notices by federal agencies, Presidential executive orders, and Presidential documents. Any individual can subscribe to the service for $929 per year.

Fortune Spent on Lobbying: In 2009, the Pharmaceutical and Health Care Industries spent $266.8 million on lobbying. This is more than any other industry. That is $80 million more than was spent by Business Associations, which is the second highest spender.

Name that Hurricane: The U.S. Department of Commerce is responsible for naming hurricanes. Until 1978, all names were female names. They now include both male and female names.

The Man who lit a fire that Changed History: The 1963 March on Washington For Jobs and Freedom in which Martin Luther King Jr. gave his landmark *I Have a Dream* Speech was organized by Asa Philip Randolph, the President of the Negro American Labor Council.

Martin Luther King Jr. Delivering his
I Have a Dream Speech

Historic Day for GOP: The first meeting of the Republican Party occurred at The Little White Schoolhouse in Ripon, Wisconsin in 1854.

A Republic, Not a Democracy: Though many call the U.S. a Democracy, it is actually a Constitutional Republic. Rather than allowing the people to vote on every issue, the American citizenry delegates powers to the sovereign. Many of the founders viewed Democracy as anathema to the precepts of a Constitutional Republic. James Madison called Democracy: "The right of the people to choose their own tyrant." Interestingly, Thomas Jefferson called Democracy: ". . . nothing more than mob rule, where fifty-one percent of the people may take away the rights of the other forty-nine." The third Chief Justice of the United States John Marshall said: "between a balanced republic and a democracy, the difference is like that between order and chaos."

Spending Gaps: When the Federal Government stops providing essential services, many call it a "shutdown." The actual term is "spending gap." Only parts of the government actually shut down.

Satirist Mocks Democrats: Humorist Will Rodgers Sr. said: "I belong to no organized party, I am a Democrat."

Will Rodgers Sr.
Library of Congress

You Need Friends in High Places: To get into a military academy (except the U.S. Coast Guard Academy) an applicant must have a nomination from the President of the United States, the Vice President, a U.S. Senator, or a U.S. Representative.

GI: The acronym "GI" originally stood for "Galvanized Iron." Now it stands for "Government Issued."

Down With the GOP: There are 168 members of the Republican National Committee.

Oil-Rich: About 1/3 of the oil produced in the United States comes from the Gulf of Mexico.

It's a Secret: The Federal Government classifies about 16,000,000 documents annually.

Public/Private Education Dichotomy: About half of all public sector workers have a four-year college degree, compared to about thirty percent of all private-sector employees.

Diane Sawyer Enters Nixon's Arena: Diane Sawyer, now anchor of *World News with Diane Sawyer* (on *ABC*), was a press aid in the administrations of both Richard M. Nixon and Gerald R. Ford. After she left the White House, she assisted Nixon in writing his memoir *In the Arena.*

Dianne Sawyer
ABC News

It's in the Record: The United States Government Printing Office publishes *The Congressional Record* for the House and the Senate when they are in session.

Outside of the Beltway: About 85% of all federal employees do not live in the Washington D.C. area.

Don't Go Postal: Between 1829 and 1971, the Post Office Department was a Cabinet Level position and its head, the Post Master General, was a Cabinet member in the line of Presidential succession. Under the terms of the Postal Reorganization Act of 1971, the Post Office Department was changed to the United States Postal Service, and is no longer represented in the Cabinet.

Limbaugh's Bride: Katherine Rogers, the wife of conservative talk show host Rush Limbaugh, is a direct descendent of President John Adams.

Muslim Country First to Recognize U.S: In 1777, Morocco became the first country to officially recognize the U.S. as an Independent Nation.

The Evolution of the Pledge of Allegiance: Francis Bellemy, the author of *The Pledge of Allegiance*, was a Christian Socialist. *The Pledge of Allegiance* was first promulgated in the September 8, 1892 edition of the magazine *Youth's Companion.* Later that year, President Benjamin Harrison signed a proclamation requiring the Pledge to be recited in public schools on the 400th anniversary of Christopher Columbus' arrival in America. It is estimated that over 12 million American school children recited the Pledge on that day. The term: "Under God" was not added until 1954, when Congress passed and President Dwight D. Eisenhower signed legislation adding it to the Pledge on Flag Day, June 14th.

U.S. Flag

Byrd is the Word: Robert C. Byrd is the only person who served in both Houses of the West Virginia Legislature and in both Houses of the U.S. Congress.

Robert C. Byrd
West Virginia Division of Culture and History
Cecil Underwood Collection

Baltic Nation's Place in American History in 1776: In 1776, Croatia became the first nation to be officially recognized by the U.S.

Miscellaneous

Tax Hike Stuns Jersey Shore: Among the provisions in the Patient Protection and Affordability Act signed by President Barack Obama in 2010 is a 10% surcharge on all customers who use tanning beds. This inflamed Nicole Polizzi (a.k.a. Snooki of the *MTV* series *Jersey Shore*). She said she no longer tans, and said of Obama: "I feel like he did that intentionally for us."

Nicole Polizzi (a.k.a. Snooki)
Photograph Taken by Amy Nicole Waltney

Full Ginsberg: The first person to appear on all five major Sunday morning talk shows in one day was William H. Ginsburg, the first attorney for the family of Monica Lewinsky during the Clinton-Lewinsky scandal. On February 1, 1998 Ginsberg appeared on *Late Edition* on *CNN*, *Face the Nation* on *CBS*, *Fox News Sunday* on *Fox Network*, *Meet The Press on CNN*, and *This Week on ABC*. Ginsburg's appearances took their place in American folklore as the "Full Ginsburg."

Preserving America: The National Park Service, administered by the U.S. Department of Interior, includes 394 units, of which 58 are actual parks. Delaware is the only state with no units. The largest park is the 8,000,000-acre Wrangell-St. Elias National Park and Preserve located in Alaska.

Former Child Star Goes Diplomatic: Child Actress Shirley Temple, who became a household name for her role in the 1934 motion picture *Bright Eyes,* became a diplomat later in life. She served as U.S. Ambassador to Ghana under President Gerald R. Ford and as U.S. Ambassador to Czechoslovakia under President George H.W. Bush.

Shirley Temple when she was a Child Actress
Library of Congress

At Least it Looks Good on a Résumé: In Wenham, Massachusetts, the Board of Selectmen has the duty of appointing a "Lumber Surveyor and Measurer of Wood." The position carries no responsibilities and the office holder receives no remunerations.

What He Really Thinks: In 1997, then Canadian Prime Minister Jean Chrétien was caught on a live microphone telling a counterpart at the North Atlantic Treaty Organization (NATO) Expansion summit: "All this for short-term political reasons, to win elections. In fact [U.S. politicians] are selling their votes, they are selling their votes.... It's incredible. In your country or mine, all the politicians would be in prison."

The Uninformed Constituency: A 2010 poll conducted by the Marist Institute of Public Opinion found that 26% of all Americans did not know that the U.S. won independence from England.

Miscellaneous

The Boss Gets a Pardon: New York Yankees Owner George Steinbrenner (1973-2010) was convicted in 1974 of Obstruction of Justice and conspiring to make an illegal campaign contribution to Richard M. Nixon's 1972 re-election campaign. He paid a $15,000 fine. In 1989, outgoing President Ronald Reagan pardoned Mr. Steinbrenner.

George Steinbrenner
Major League Baseball

No I will not *Meet the Press*: Only three people have canceled an appearance on the national public affairs program *Meet the Press*: Prince Bandar bin Sultan bin Abdul Aziz Al Saud (Saudi Arabia Ambassador to the U.S.), Minister Louis Farrakhan (Nation of Islam Leader), and Rand Paul (2010 U.S. Senate Candidate R-KY).

The Senator's Daughter: 1940s and 1950s Actress Tallulah Bankhead was the granddaughter of U.S. Senator John Hollis Bankhead (D-AL 1907-1920) and daughter of U.S. House Speaker William B. Bankhead (D-AL 1936-1940).

Tallulah Bankhead
Library of Congress

The "Twinkie Defense:" Dan White, a former member of the San Francisco Board of Supervisors, assassinated San Francisco Mayor George Moscone and Supervisor Harvey Milk in 1979. During his murder trial, White's defense argued that his change from healthy to sugar-intensive foods led to depression. Due to this novel defense, White was only convicted of manslaughter rather than murder. This brought about the term "Twinkie Defense," which quickly entered into the American Political lexicon.

Dan White
Official Photograph

No Partisanship in the Confederacy: The Confederate State's of America did not have political parties.

The Man who took on JFK twice: Massachusetts attorney Richard Celeste was the Republican nominee against John F. Kennedy both in Kennedy's re-election bid to the U.S. House of Representatives in 1950, and in his re-election bid to the U.S. Senate in 1958. In 1950, Celeste garnered just 17.17% of the vote. In 1958, Celeste mustered just 26.23% of the vote. During both campaigns, the two never had a face-to-face encounter.

No Language Mandated: There is no official language in the U.S.

Avoiding the Draft: During the U.S. Civil War, a northern draftee had the option of paying $300 in lieu of serving in an individual battle, or he could hire someone to serve in his place.

Civil War Soldiers
Library of Congress

Origin of GOP: The phrase "Grand Old Party" (GOP) originated as a nickname for the Democratic Party. It was coined by a loyal Georgia Democrat in 1878. The term became synonymous with the Republican Party after the 1888 election, in which Republican Benjamin Harrison defeated incumbent Democratic President Grover Cleveland. The *Chicago Tribune*, sympathetic to the Republican Party, declared: "Let us be thankful that under the rule of the **Grand Old Party** ... these United States will resume the onward and upward march which the election of Grover Cleveland in 1884 partially arrested."

Dearth of Funny Money: Counterfeiting paper currency has become much more difficult in recent years. The U.S. Government estimates that approximately 1/100th of one percent of U.S. paper currency in circulation is counterfeit.

Our Share: The U.S. provides about 25% of the NATO budget.

The Cold War: The term "Cold War," describing the rivalry between the United States and the Soviet Union, was coined by financier Bernard Baruch at the unveiling of his portrait in the South Carolina House of Representatives. Baruch was a native South Carolinian. In describing the rivalry between the United States and the Soviet Union, Baruch referred to the rivalry as "The Cold War."

Bernard Baruch
Library of Congress

American Motto: E Pluribus Unum is the Latin phrase that appears on the official seal of the United States. It means: "Out of many, one." The official Motto of the country is "In God We Trust" as designated by law signed by Dwight D. Eisenhower in 1956.

Powerful Organization: The National Rifle Association (NRA) boasts over four million members.

National Rifle Association **Logo**

Franklin Prefers Turkey to Eagle: In 1784, U.S Minister to France, Benjamin Franklin, lobbied for the turkey to become the national symbol on the Presidential seal: not the American bald eagle. He said: "The bald eagle is . . . a bird of bad moral character; like those among men who live by sharping and robbing, he is generally poor and often very lousy."

Benjamin Franklin
Library of Congress

United in Name: The original name for the U.S. was "United Colonies." The Continental Congress changed the name to the United States of America in 1776.

This Is CNN: The all-news network, *CNN,* debuted in 1980. The first story they reported was President Jimmy Carter's visit to Urban League President Vernon Jordan. Jordan was in a hospital recovering from an attempt on his life. He had been shot in Fort Wayne, Indiana by serial killer Joseph Paul Franklin. Franklin was offended when he saw Jordan, an African-American man, with a white woman.

Big Bucks from the Big Boys: In 2009, lobbyists spent about $3.5 Billion to further their lobbying agendas.

Israeli Aid: Israel receives about $3 billion in foreign aid annually from the U.S. Seventy-five percent of that aid must be earmarked for purchases of military equipment made in the U.S.

The Spears Doctrine: During a 2003 interview, *CNN'S* Tucker Carlson asked pop star Britney Spears for her opinion on U.S. involvement in the Iraq War. Spears' response was: "Honestly, I think we should just trust our President in every decision he makes and should just be faithful in what happens."

Britney Spears
U.S. Navy Photograph by Chief Warrant Officer
Steve Rossman

Voter Precincts: There are about 200,000 voter precincts in the U.S.

Priority Seating: Under federal law, priority seating in public transportation must be reserved for elderly individuals and/or those with physical disabilities.

Military Footprint: U.S. troops are garrisoned in 148 countries and 11 territories. Thirteen of these nations have at least 1,000 U.S. troops. The U.S. has at least 662 military bases in 38 countries, and about 6,000 military bases in the U.S.

Big Consumer: Although the U.S. has less than 5% of the world's population, it consumes almost 25% of the world's energy resources.

Telling Time at the Pentagon: There are 4,200 clocks in the Pentagon.

Miscellaneous

Strange bedfellows: James Meredith was the first African-American student to attend the University of Mississippi. He became a pivotal figure in the Civil Rights movement, in that his enrollment effectuated civil unrest, leading President John F. Kennedy to send in military police to protect him. Later in life, Meredith became a domestic adviser to conservative U.S. Senator Jesse Helms (R-NC). Meredith also supported former Klansman David Duke in his bid to become Governor of Louisiana in 1991.

James Meredith
Library of Congress

Like Father, Unlike Daughter: Liberal Radio Talk show host Stephanie Miller is the daughter of William E. Miller, who was the Chairman of the Republican National Committee and the Republican Vice Presidential nominee in 1964.

Insider Accessibility to Information: All former CIA Directors maintain their security clearances.

The Union: Union members comprise 36% of public-sector employees and 7% of private-sector employees. In the aggregate, 12% of all U.S. workers are union members.

He's Smarter than a Sixth Grader: John H. Sununu, the former Chief of Staff to President George H.W. Bush, is a member of the elite "Mega Society" which "facilitates psychometric research" (this encompasses educational as well as psychological measurement). To gain admission, members must have scored on the one-in-a-million level on the IQ test. Only 26 people are members of this exclusive society.

John H. Sununu
Official Portrait

The Emergence of Entitlements: When Social Security was inaugurated in 1935, unemployment benefits were a part of the program.

Federal Land: The Federal Government owns about 1/3 of all land in the U.S.

Archie Bunker would call him a Meathead: Although Carroll O'Connor played the Conservative Republican Archie Bunker in the 1970s hit television series *All In the Family*, O'Conner was a liberal Democrat. He even appeared in an advertisement for U.S. Senator Edward M. Kennedy in his unsuccessful quest for the 1980 Democratic Party Presidential nomination.

Miscellaneous

Longtime Economic Overlord: William McChesney Martin Jr. was the longest serving Chairman of the Federal Reserve Board. He was nominated by President Harry S. Truman and confirmed by the U.S. Senate in 1951. An exponent of a tight money policy, Martin served for 19 years, leaving office in 1970.

William McChesney Martin Jr.
Official Photograph

A Good Problem to Have: Social Security benefits started as part of Franklin D. Roosevelt's New Deal in 1935. At the time, the retirement age was 65 and life expectancy was 63. The system was a comfort to the elderly who feared that they would outlive their money. However, few actually lived long enough to collect the benefit. Today the average life expectancy in America is 77.

The China Trade: Eighty percent of all counterfeit goods that appear at a U.S. point of entry are from China.

Gay Officials: There are more than 450 openly gay elected officials in America.

The Proper Plural Form: The plural form of Attorney General is Attorneys General, not Attorney Generals.

Castro Charitable to U.S: In 1903, shortly after the Spanish-American War, the U.S. and Cuban Governments signed an agreement wherein the U.S. can rent Guantanamo Bay forever so long as it pays Cuba the annual rent of $2,000. The current landlord, Cuban President Fidel Castro, has yet to cash a U.S. rent check.

Fidel Castro
Library of Congress

Funding U.S. Presence Along DMZ: South Korea pays $694 million annually for the garrisoning of 28,500 U.S. troops along its demilitarized zone with North Korea.

Real Money: The U.S. has a $15 trillion economy.

Uncle Sam's Economic Nerve Center: The seven-member Board of Governors of the Federal Reserve System sets the nation's monetary policy. They also superintend the twelve regional Federal Reserve Banks in the U.S. Reserve Governors are nominated by the President and confirmed by the U.S. Senate. They serve for one 14-year term. Every four years, the President nominates or renominates a Chairman and Vice Chairman of Federal Reserve. If confirmed by the U.S. Senate, they serve a four-year term.

The Donkey and the Elephant: The two major political parties in the U.S. are represented by animal mascots. The Republicans have an elephant for a mascot and the Democrats have a donkey. Both mascots, at least in their more modern form, were depicted by *Harpers Weekly* cartoonist Thomas Nast in the mid-1800s. The Democratic Donkey first entered the political sphere during the 1828 Presidential campaign. It was used to deride Democratic Presidential nominee Andrew Jackson as a "Jackass." However, Jackson manipulated the situation by emphasizing the fact that the donkey is a very principled, strong-willed animal, and as such, worthy of respect. A generation later, Nast popularized the image in a published cartoon and it became synonymous with the Democratic Party. The Republican elephant was first used by Abraham Lincoln's Presidential Campaign in 1860. The connection between the Elephant and the Republican Party was popularized by Nast in an 1874 political cartoon published in *Harpers Weekly*. Nast, a staunch Republican, supported a third term for President Ulysses S. Grant. He became disaffected with his party's moving away from its liberal principles and being frightened by Democrats who were accusing Grant of Caesarism for wanting to remain President for a third term. Although Nast drew the elephant to represent the Republican voters being scared off by the jackass dressed in lion's clothing (and not to represent the Republican Party), the elephant came to be associated with the Republican Party.

Department of Defense is Heavily Invested in Real Estate: The U.S. Department of Defense owns or leases about 75% of all federal buildings in Washington, D.C.

Before *C-SPAN:* *C-SPAN* Founder and CEO Brian Lamb was once a military social aid to President Lyndon B. Johnson. In that capacity, he accompanied the First Lady, Lady Bird Johnson, down the aisle during the wedding of the First Daughter, Lynda Bird Johnson, to U.S. Military Officer Chuck Robb.

The Wedding of Lynda Bird Johnson and Military Officer Chuck Robb
Lynden Baines Johnson Library and Museum

Jed Clampit Disses Jane Hathaway: In 1984, Nancy Kulp, who played secretary Jane Hathaway on the 1960's Television series *The Beverly Hillbillies,* was the Democratic nominee for a Congressional seat in the central Pennsylvania-based Ninth Congressional District. Buddy Ebsen, who in the same sitcom portrayed hillbilly turned millionaire Jed Clampett, endorsed Kulp's opponent, U.S. Representative Bud Shuster (R-PA). Ebsen's voice appeared in a radio commercial, asserting that he had dropped Kulp a note reading: "Hey Nancy, I love you dearly but you're too liberal for me - I've got to go with Bud Shuster." Ebsen was not a resident of the district. Shuster won the race mustering 67% of the vote.

Glossary of Political Terminology

Glossary of Political Terminology

Actual Malice: A precedent established in the Supreme Court case of *New York Times Co. v. Sullivan*, The court ruled that to establish libel against a public official, knowing falsity or reckless disregard for the truth must be proven.

Advisory Referendum: A measure that appears on the ballot which in non-binding. It is mostly used to engage popular opinion.

American Exceptionalism: Belief that America is superior to all other nations.

Anarchy: Absence of any governing authority.

Appellate Jurisdiction: The power of a Court to review lower Court decisions, and accept, modify or even overturn the decision of a lower level court.

Arkansas Project: An effort funded by newspaper publisher Richard Mellon Scaife to find damaging information on Bill Clinton.

Articles of Confederation and Perpetual Union: Written by the Continental Congress. This was the Constitution of the first thirteen colonies. This governing authority was written in 1776. Because of criticism from Federalists believing that the federal government lacked necessary power, it was eventually supplanted with the *U.S. Constitution*.

Australian Ballot: System employed in the United States in which all ballots are marked in secret.

Authoritarianism: System of government in which the state has much power over the individual.

Bicameralism: Two separate legislative chambers. At the federal level, the Congress is divided into the Senate and House of Representatives. The legislative branch in every state except Nebraska is also comprised of two chambers.

Bill of Attainder: The punishment of an individual without a trial. Article 1 Section 9 of the *U.S. Constitution* disallows this practice at the state and federal levels.

Blanket Primary: Primary in which the electorate can vote for members of different parties for different offices. For example, a voter could select a Republican candidate for Governor and a Democrat for State Senator. The leading vote-getter for each party goes on to compete in the general election.

Black Budget: Appropriations earmarked "secret" (usually military projects). They are kept hidden for national security purposes.

Blowback: A term coined by the CIA referring to the future negative unintended consequences of U.S. foreign policy, including covert operations. Many point to the Iran Hostage Crises in 1979 as being blowback by the Iranians for the U.S. support of the overthrow of Prime Minister Mohammad Mosaddeq in 1953.

Glossary of Political Terminology

Blue Dog Democrat: The modern term for a Conservative Democrat. Most come from more conservative parts of the country, including the South and the West, where the national Democratic Party is often looked upon as too liberal. The term was coined by U.S. Representative Peter Geren (D-TX 1989-1997) who said that Conservative Democrats were being choked blue by extreme Democrats and Republicans. Most Blue Dog Democrats are particularly interested in balancing the federal budget.

Boll weevils: A term referring to Conservative Democrats from the mid to late twentieth-century. A pre-curser to what is now known as a "Blue Dog Democrat."

Boondoggle: A project funded by the government with little redeeming value.

Budget Deficit: When annual government expenditures exceed annual government receipts.

Budget Surplus: When government receipts exceed government expenditures.

Bullet Vote: A voter has the option to select multiple candidates for an office, but chooses just one.

Bureaucracy: Commonly refers to the structure and regulation needed in a large organization such as a corporation or government entity to accomplish tasks.

Bush Doctrine: The U.S. will not distinguish between terrorists themselves and those who harbor the terrorists and will use force if necessary to "take out" regimes which represent a potential threat to the U.S.

Carter Doctrine: Offered in response to the Soviet Union's invasion of Afghanistan in 1980. President Jimmy Carter asserted that the U.S. would intervene militarily if necessary anywhere in the Persian Gulf to defend U.S. national interests.

Ceteris Paribus: Other things being equal.

Checks and Balances: A system in which different branches of government have oversight over the others, so none becomes omnipotent.

Clerk of the U.S. House of Representatives: The House's chief record-keeper. The Clerk is elected every two years.

Clinton Doctrine: The U.S. will intervene abroad to defend its values, including human rights.

Closed Primary: Primary election in which only members of one party are afforded the right to participate.

Cloture: Ending a filibuster. It needs the approval of 60 U.S. Senators.

CNN Effect: The belief that the images Americans see on their TV sets has a direct affect on how they view the foreign policies of their government. The term originates from the Somalia Crisis in the early-mid 1990's, when viewers saw the malnourished Somalis on TV. They then pressured their government to send troops to stop the suffering. Later, when they saw Somali's dragging a dead U.S. soldier through the streets, they demanded withdrawal.

Glossary of Political Terminology

Coattail Effect: The ability of a popular politician at the top of the ballot, such as a Governor or Senator, to bring voters to the polls who will also vote for other candidates of his/her political party further down the ballot. These other candidates could include members of the U.S. Congress, state legislators, and municipal officials.

Command Economy: System where the government rather than market forces centrally plans economic activity.

Commander-in-Chief Clause: Article 2, Section 2, Clause 1 of the *U.S. Constitution* says the President shall be: "Commander in Chief of the Army and Navy of the United States and the militia of the several states."

Common Law: The governing system based upon judicial precedence.

Common Victuallers License: A license granted by a public entity allowing one to serve alcoholic beverages.

Communism: a system of government in which the entire population owns most property, and private property is extremely limited. Ex: North Korea, Vietnam, and Cuba.

Concurrent Resolution: A measure passed by both houses of the U.S. Congress that does not have the power of law and does not need the signature of the president.

Confederation: An alliance of groups.

Congress of the Confederation or the United States in Congress Assembled: The precursor to the United State Congress. It was the governing body of the United States from March 1, 1781 to March 4, 1789.

Congressional Delegate: A non-voting representative to the U.S. House of Representatives from American Samoa, Commonwealth of the Northern Mariana Islands, Guam, the United States Virgin Islands and the District of Columbia. They are elected to two-year terms. A Congressional Delegate has all privileges afforded other members, such as speaking privileges, drafting legislation, and committee voting. However, the Delegates are not afforded the right to vote on legislation.

Congressionalist: One who believes Congress should have wide-ranging power.

Constitutional Republic: A system of government where the citizenry elect officials who must govern in a way that comports with a governing Constitution. The United States of America is an example.

Continuing Resolution: A Joint Resolution passed by Congress providing funding for government agencies at existing levels. This is a temporary measure to provide funding prior to the Congress and President working out an agreement for the full funding for the fiscal year.

Dean of the U.S. House of Representatives: Longest serving member of the House in consecutive terms. The Dean's only official duty is to swear in the Speaker of the House.

***Declaration of Independence*:** Manuscript written by Thomas Jefferson in 1776 proclaiming independence of the U.S. from Great Britain.

Democratic Leadership Council (DLC): A non-profit corporation founded in 1985 to moderate the Democratic Party and expand its voter-base to include moderate voters. Former Chairman Bill Clinton used many of the themes of the DLC in his presidential campaign in 1992. Other former chairmen include then U.S. Senator Evan Bayh (D-IN), then U.S. Senator John Breaux (D-LA), and then U.S. Senator Sam Nunn (D-GA).

Democratic Peace Theory: Belief that liberal democracies do not go to war with each other because the majority of the population will never vote to go to war or elect people who would. Accordingly, if all nations were liberal democracies, there would be no war. Many Neo-Conservatives have adopted this premise.

De-politicized Citizenry: A system where the population is not actively engaged in the political decisions of their times.

Deputy President pro tempore: Any former President or Vice President who returns to serve in the U.S. Senate is entitled to this position, which includes an increase in salary.

DINO: Democrat-In-Name-Only

Direct Democracy: System where citizens participate in drafting and voting on laws. An example is a New England style town meeting.

Down Ballot: Candidates for offices, such as U.S. Congress, the state legislature, and municipal positions, whose office is not at the top of the ballot. The top might include candidates for President, Governor, Mayor, etc.

Dual Federalism: Doctrine espoused by U.S. Supreme Court Justice Roger Taney (1777-1864) which maintained that the state and federal governments should have separate but equal powers.

Earmark: Congressionally directed spending geared toward funding specific projects or programs such as constructing a new wing at a college, building a bicycle path, or preserving an historic landmark.

Electioneering: Actively working for a political candidate or ballot initiative.

Enumerated powers: Eighteen specific powers delegated to the United States Congress from Article 1 Section 8 of the *United States Constitution*.

Executive Agreement: An accord between the President and a foreign head of government that needs a simple up or down vote by both houses of Congress to win approval.

Ex post facto Law: A law passed "after the fact." Under the *U.S. Constitution*, no American can be penalized for violating a law before it becomes the law of the land.

Fascism: Authoritarian/nationalistic political ideology. Sometimes this is the amalgamation of religious and corporate interests.

Federalism: The delineation of powers between the federal and state governments.

Federalist Papers: Eighty-five articles written by John Jay, Alexander Hamilton, and James Madison and published in *The Independent Journal* and *The New York Packet*. They advocated for the ratification of the *U.S. Constitution*.

Glossary of Political Terminology

Filibuster: In the U.S. Senate, members are permitted to speak indefinitely on a subject to avoid a vote. Only with 60 votes can the Senate vote to invoke cloture, thus ending debate on voting. Then U.S. Senator Strom Thurmond (D-SC) holds the record for the longest filibuster. He spent 24 hours and 18 minutes filibustering the Civil Rights Act of 1957. There are also non-verbal tactical procedures within filibustering to delay a vote.

Free Rider: One who receives the benefits of government policy without incurring the costs.

Free Trade: Free flow of goods and services not subject to tariffs.

Functionary: A Government Official

Gerrymandering: The manipulation of the redistricting process at the state level to benefit the majority party and/or all incumbents. The term originated to describe Massachusetts Governor Elbridge Gerry's (1810-1812) successful attempt to maximize the numerical political advantage for his Democratic-Republican Party.

Great Society: An all-encompassing term for the social programs proposed by President Lyndon B. Johnson. Legislation was enacted in areas such as Health Care, Civil Rights, and Education Reform.

Gross Domestic Product: The market value of all goods and services produced in a country, usually annually.

Gross National Product: Measures of national income and output used to estimate the welfare of an economy through totaling the value of goods and services produced in an economy.

Half-Breeds: Moderate Republicans in the latter half of the nineteenth century who favored civil service reform.

Ideologue: A person with a certain grand design or philosophical mindset of how the world should be.

Impeachment: Article Two Section 4 of the *U.S. Constitution* states that "The President, Vice President, and all other civil Officers of the United States shall be removed from Office on Impeachment for, and Conviction of, Treason, Bribery, or other High Crimes and Misdemeanors." If a majority votes in the U.S. House of Representatives for impeachment, then the articles are sent to the Senate, where a two-thirds majority is required for conviction.

Imperialism: Encroachment of an empire on territory outside its borders.

Impoundment: The refusal of a sitting president to spend funds for something that the legislature has appropriated funds for.

Incrementalism: Achieving legislative goals step-by-step by passing a series of small legislation.

Incumbent: A current holder of an office.

Inflation: The rising prices of goods and services.

Infotainment: The amalgamation of news with entertainment.

Glossary of Political Terminology

Initiative: A vehicle for the citizens to propose legislation or constitutional amendments to be placed on the ballot for an up or down vote by the electorate. Accordingly, the usual legislative process is circumvented. Twenty-four states currently have some form of the initiative option.

Injunction: A Court order requiring a person or entity to do something or to refrain from doing a certain act or behavior.

Instant Runoff Voting: A voting system where voters rank all candidates. The candidate with the fewest first place votes is dropped and the voter's second choice replaces the first choice of those who placed him/her first. This process is repeated until two candidates remain.

Invisible Hand: A term coined by the Scottish Economist Adam Smith to describe his belief that there is a natural regulator in a free-market-system.

Isolationism: Belief that a country should be averse to all relations with other nations, including commercial, cultural, and military isolation.

Joint Resolution: A measure requiring approval of both chambers of Congress before going to the president for his/her subsequent approval or disapproval.

Judicial Review: Power of the Judicial branch of government to scrutinize for constitutional permissibility, actions by the Executive and Legislative branch. If the Justices rule the actions to be unconstitutional, they become null and void.

Jungle Primary: A primary election where candidates run for office on the same ballot. If no candidate musters a majority of the vote, there is a run-off between the two top finishers. This system is used in Louisiana.

Laissez-faire: A French word translated: "to allow to do, to leave alone." The term is used to mean that the government should not regulate the economy.

Lame duck: An incumbent elected official who has lost much of his/her influence because the official's term is nearing an end and they are not seeking re-election.

Layer-Cake Federalism: A system where the federal and state governments have clearly delineated and specific functions.

LBJ Rule: In 1959, the Texas legislature approved legislation allowing a politician to run for two political offices simultaneously. This benefited Lyndon B. Johnson in 1960 as he sought both re-election to the U.S. Senate and the Presidency. After failing to secure the Democratic presidential nomination, he ran for Vice President that year. He subsequently won both the Vice Presidency and re-election to the U.S. Senate. Other Texas officials, including U.S. Senators Lloyd Benson and Phil Gramm, and U.S. Representative Ron Paul, have used the law to seek higher office while running for re-election.

Legislative Referendum: The legislature refers a measure to the voters for their up or down vote.

Glossary of Political Terminology

Letters of Marque and Reprisal: Article 1, Section 8, Clause 11 of the *U.S. Constitution* gives the President the power to "grant Letters of Marque and Reprisal, and make rules concerning captures on land and water." It allows the president to search, seize, or destroy specified assets or personal belongings of a foreign party that has committed some offense under the laws of nations.

Libertarianism: A belief that government should be a limited-purpose entity devoted to protect a person's life, liberty, and property.

Line-Item Veto: Power of the executive to reject provisions in a piece of legislation without vetoing the legislation outright. At the federal level, the Line-Item Veto Act of 1996 was nullified in *Clinton v. City of New York*, 524 U.S. 417 (1998). The U.S. Supreme Court ruled that the Act violated the Presentment Clause of the *U.S. Constitution* because it impermissibly gave the President of the United States the power to unilaterally amend or repeal parts of statutes that had been duly passed by the United States Congress. At the state level, Forty-three state Governors have this privilege.

Lobbyist: Individual, representing a cause or organization, who tries to persuade government officials to support their point of view on issues.

Local Aid: Transfer of revenue from state to municipal governments to pay for local services.

Logrolling: When two members of a legislative body agree to support each other's legislation on separate issues.

Majority and Minority Leader: In both the U.S. House of Representatives and the U.S. Senate, these elected members serve as floor leader for their respective parties. When they are not there, a designee is selected. In the House, the Majority leader is second-in-command to the Speaker of the House.

Manifest Destiny: Originally referred to the belief that the U.S. was destined to expand from the Atlantic to the Pacific Ocean. Today it has come to mean that the U.S. must increase its territory.

Mayflower Compact: A document signed by 41 Mayflower voyagers on November 11, 1620 establishing the government structure of Plymouth Colony. The signers agreed to follow the contract and: "mutually in the presence of God and one of another, Covenant and Combine ourselves together into a Civil Body Politic, for our better ordering and preservation."

Micro Governing: Governing by focusing on specific small-bore issues.

Mixed Economy: An economic system that combines forces from multiple economic structures.

Moonbat: Term of derision for a liberal.

National Debt: The accumulative amount of annual deficits.

Nanny State: A pejorative phrase for a paternalistic government.

Glossary of Political Terminology

Neo-Conservatism: Former Cold War Liberal Democrats who became disillusioned with what they viewed as the Democratic Party's dovish foreign policy. Many supported then U.S. Senator Henry "Scoop" Jackson's (D-WA) bids for the Democratic Party's nomination in 1972 and 1976. After his loss, many gradually migrated to the Republican fold and supported President Ronald Reagan. Today, they are steadfast supporters of an activist foreign policy that promotes Democracy abroad. American intellectual Irving Kristol (1920-2009) is considered by many to be the Patron Saint of this ideology.

New Democrat: A Democrat who generally strives to bring the Democratic Party to the center of the political spectrum. The term New Democrat was popularized in 1992 when the Democratic Presidential Ticket of Bill Clinton and Al Gore came from this wing of the party. Most New Democrats are business oriented and favor fiscal austerity and free trade as a vehicle for economic expansion, rather than the more liberal view that government should redistribute the nation's wealth.

Nixon Doctrine: The U.S. will provide arms to allies, but will not do the actual fighting for them.

Nomination Papers: Papers that are required to be completed when an individual wants to run for public office.

Non-Interventionism: The doctrine that dictates that a country should avoid foreign entanglements with other nations while maintaining commercial and cultural intercourse. Thomas Jefferson said the U.S. should practice: "Peace, Commerce, and honest relations with all nations, entangled alliances with none."

Nonpartisan election: An election where candidates do not run as a member of a political party. Most municipal elections fall into this category.

Off-year election: Election held in the middle of a presidential term.

Oligarchy: Rule by the wealthy few.

Open Primary: Primary election in which members of all political parties are invited to participate.

Original Jurisdiction: Power of a court to hear a case for the first time.

Paleo-Conservative: Ideological descendants of a prominent philosophy in the Republican Party between WWI and WWII. They share a non-interventionist foreign policy, support for federalism, and oppose most government intervention in the economy. Many paleo-conservatives share a populist streak, opposing what they view as attempts by power elites and multi-national corporations to exert influence. In addition, many adherents to this ideology take a hard-line stance against affirmative action and illegal immigration. Examples include President Warren G. Harding (1921-1923), U.S. Senator Robert A. Taft (R-OH 1939-1953), and political commentator Patrick J. Buchanan.

Paleo-Liberal: An ideology that couples support for muscular foreign policy, including high defense spending, with an activist domestic policy, including a munificent social safety net. This belief was conventional liberal thinking during the first half of the Cold War. U.S. Senator Henry "Scoop" Jackson (D-WA 1953-1983) was a steadfast exponent of this ideology.

Glossary of Political Terminology

Partisan Election: Election in which candidates declare party affiliation.

Partisan: One who is a steadfast advocate of the interests of his/her political party or cause.

Patron: One who finances a political cause or politician.

Phone Mark: When a legislator does not get his/her earmark placed in legislation, a call is made to a government agency demanding funding. This is kept secret from the public, and is illegal in the U.S.

Plurality: Receiving more votes than any other candidate but not a majority.

Political Football: A topic which politicians debate, but without resolution. Politicians use the issue for their political advantage.

Political Parlance: Jargon related to politics.

Politicized Citizenry: A system where the population is actively engaged in the political decisions of their times.

Popular Referendum: A measure that appears on the ballot as a result of a voter petition drive. It affords the electorate an up or down vote on legislation passed by a legislative body.

Pork barrel spending: Government funding designed to benefit a special interest rather than benefit the public interest. It is often intended to benefit a constituent, a private company, or a campaign contributor of a politician.

POTUS: President of the United States.

President of the United States: The chief executive officer of the government who is both head of state and head of government. Presidential powers are derived from Article II of *The U.S. Constitution*.

President pro tempore *emeritus*: An honorific office awarded to any former President pro tempore of the U.S. Senate. While the office has no extra powers, its holder is awarded an increase in staff and salary.

President pro tempore of the Senate: Generally the most senior member of the majority party in the Senate holds this position. This person is the second-highest-ranking official of the United States Senate and is officially the presiding officer. Usually though, he or she delegates this duty to other members. Third in line of presidential succession, the office's powers are derived from Article I, Section 3 of the *U.S. Constitution*.

President-Elect: A winner of a presidential election who has yet to assume the office.

Presidentialist: An advocate of a strong federal executive branch.

Protectionism: The restriction of goods and services from abroad in order to protect domestic industries.

Reagan Doctrine: The U.S. will provide aid to forces fighting against communism, with the grand design of rolling it back.

Reconciliation: This process allows the U.S. Senate to consider any budget legislation without a filibuster.

Glossary of Political Terminology

Republicrat: A political pejorative used to define the common interests of the Republican and Democratic parties by those who think they are two sides of the same coin and have little differences.

Resident Commissioner of Puerto Rico: Non-voting representative to the U.S, Congress from the Commonwealth of Puerto Rico. The only representative elected to a four-year term. He or she has all privileges afforded other members, such as speaking privileges, drafting legislation, and committee voting, except voting on final approval of legislation.

Rider: A provision attached to unrelated legislation. Sometimes these are provisions that may be too controversial to pass on their own.

Rider's Choice: Belief that the decision to wear a motorcycle helmet while riding a motorcycle should be decided by the biker, not the government.

RINO: Republican-In-Name-Only.

Rockefeller Republican: A moderate-liberal block of Republicans who generally favor the policies of fiscal austerity and social liberalism championed by Nelson Rockefeller who served as New York Governor from 1959-1974 and as Vice President of the United States from 1974-1977.

Root-Canal-Economics: The concomitant raising of taxes and cutting government expenditures, usually to balance the budget.

Sedition: Attempts by citizens to topple their government.

Senatorial Courtesy: When the President nominates an individual to the position of Federal District Judge, Federal Marshall, or United States Attorney, it is customary for the President to consult first with the senior U.S. Senator of that state, but only if that senior Senator is a member of the President's political Party.

Separation of Powers: Division of powers among the three branches of government.

Shadow Senator: Voters in the District of Columbia elect two residents to serve in this position. They have no office in the U.S. Senate, and have no Senatorial authority. They do receive an office in the District of Columbia, courtesy of District taxpayers. The job of the Shadow Senator is to lobby members of the U.S. Government to support greater autonomy for the District, with the ultimate goal being outright statehood.

Shadow Representative: Voters in the District of Columbia elect one resident to serve in this position. The person elected to this position has no office or authority in the U.S. House of Representatives. Their job is to lobby members of the U.S. Government for autonomy for the District, with the ultimate goal being statehood for the District.

Social Conservative: One who believes the government should enforce a moral code for its population. Most are opposed to abortion rights, gay marriage, and most support school prayer.

Socialism: A social and economic structure where property and resources are owned by the government rather than by individuals or private companies.

Glossary of Political Terminology

Speaker of the House: Serves as Presiding officer of the U.S. House of Representatives. Under the Presidential Succession Act of 1947, he or she is second in line in presidential succession. Responsibilities include: Calling the House to order, Administering the oath of office to House Members, Presiding over debate, recognizing Members to speak on the floor, and preserving order; or delegating that power to another Member of Congress, setting the legislative agenda, and leading the appointment process for the chairs of the various committees and subcommittees in the House (including conference committees which negotiate final versions of legislation).

Speaker pro tempore: Presides over the U.S. House of Representatives in the absence of the Speaker of the House.

Special Election: An election held to fill a vacancy between elections.

Spending Gap: When all but essential government services are halted because the Federal Government cannot agree on a budget.

Spoils man: A politician who supports the appointment of public officials based on partisan political considerations.

Stalwart: Republicans in the latter half of the nineteenth century who opposed civil service reform. They supported the candidacy of Ulysses S. Grant for the Republican nomination in 1880 when he sought a third term for the presidency.

Standard-bearer: A Representative of a Political party or political movement.

Stare decisis: Latin for: "to stand by things decided." This term refers to the judicial theory that previous court decisions should be precedent and not changed.

State of Nature: The "natural condition of mankind" before governments are instituted. Seventeenth Century French philosopher Thomas Hobbes maintained that all human beings are in a state of war and their lives are: "solitary, poor, nasty, brutish, and short." English philosopher John Locke believed that reason which teaches "no one ought to harm another in his life, health, liberty or possessions" is the governor in this state.

Statute: A law usually written by a legislative branch of a government.

Supply-Side Economics: An economic doctrine popularized by President Ronald Reagan and his Economic Policy Advisor, Arthur Laffer. It asserts that when marginal tax rates are decreased, economic activity increases, resulting in an increase of government revenue.

Supreme Court of the United States: The highest court in the country. Its powers are derived from Article 3 of the *U.S. Constitution.* Members are nominated by the President and confirmed by the U.S. Senate. To receive confirmation they need a majority vote. The Court is composed of eight Associate Justices and one Chief Justice. The Court serves as arbiter of the *U.S. Constitution.*

Tariffs: Taxes on trade.

Third Party: A political party not associated with the two major ones. Examples include the Green Party, the Libertarian Party, and the Prohibition Party.

Glossary of Political Terminology

Ticket Splitting: When a voter chooses candidates of different parties for different offices. For example, the voter may choose a Democrat for President and a Republican for the U.S. Senate.

Timocracy: A system of government where government participation is limited to property owners. It can also refer to a government where rulers receive their position based on the place of honor they hold in a society.

Town Meeting: A form of direct democracy in which all registered voters in a municipality are invited to attend and vote on town laws and budgets.

Transaction Costs: The cost of doing business. An example would be the commission paid to a broker to purchase bonds.

Transfer Payment: Money from a government to an individual without the obligation of the individual to pay it back.

Unfunded Liability: A liability incurred this year that does not have to be paid until sometime in the future.

Unfunded Mandate: Regulations imposed on state and municipal governments without reimbursement from the federal government.

Unicameralism: A legislative branch composed of one chamber. Nebraska is the only state that has this system.

United States Congress: The legislative branch of the United States Government. Its powers are derived from Article 2 of the *U.S. Constitution*. It is composed of the U.S. House of Representatives and the U.S. Senate. House members represent a district of a state, while senators represent the entire state. Each state has two senators and at least one representative. The representatives are apportioned based on population of the state. The smallest state in population is Wyoming, which has only 1 representative. By contrast, California, the largest state, has fifty-three representatives.

Utopia: A perfect society. The term comes from the title of a book written by English Statesman Sir Thomas More.

Veto: This term is Latin for "I forbid." It is used to refer to the rejection of a proposal by the legislative branch by a Chief Executive.

Vice President of the United States: The occupant of this office is the President and presiding officer of the U.S. Senate. Most of the time this power is delegated to the President pro tempore and to other senators from the majority party. In addition, the Vice President has the power to cast the deciding vote should the Senate vote be tied. Finally, the Vice President certifies the official count of the Electoral College during Presidential elections.

Virginia Declaration of Rights: Adopted unanimously by the Virginia Convention of Delegates on June 12, 1776, it was written by Virginia Statesman George Mason. The document affirms the Right to: "life, Liberty, and Property" and delineates restrictions on government power. Its influence is seen in the *Declaration of Independence* and in the *U.S. Constitution*.

Glossary of Political Terminology

War Powers Clause: Article 1, Section 8, Clause 11 of the *U.S. Constitution* grants Congress the power to: "Declare War."

Wedge Issue: An issue which divides supporters of a political cause, candidate, or political party. For example, both labor unions and environmentalists are traditionally part of the Democratic Party's base, yet they disagree over drilling for oil in the Arctic National Wildlife Refuge in Alaska.

Whip: A member of the congressional leadership. Both the majority and the minority party in the U.S. House of Representatives and in the U.S. Senate have one. Their paramount responsibility is to count the votes of members within their own caucus while trying to encourage members to toe the party line.

White Primary: System used in the South in the first half of the twentieth century in which non-white voters were excluded from participating in political primaries. This was ruled unconstitutional by the U.S. Supreme Court in 1944, in the case of *Smith v. Allwright*.

Wilmot Proviso: In 1846, President James K. Polk requested a $2 million appropriation to purchase land from Mexico. U.S. Representative David Wilmot (D-PA) proposed a rider to the legislation to prevent slavery in the new acquisition. It passed the U.S. House of Representatives but was tabled in the U.S. Senate. The rider finally passed in 1862. By that time, Wilmot was no longer in Congress.

Wingnut: Term of Derision for a conservative.

Winner-Take-All: The Candidate who garners the most votes wins the election.

Writ of *Certiorari:* Request of the court to review a case.

Writ of habeas corpus: Latin for "To present the body." This refers to the right of a defendant to appear before a judge and hear the charges against leveled against him/her.

Writ of *Mandamus:* A court order usually requiring a person or corporation to take some specific action.

Unitary State: A system where the Federal Government reigns supreme over the states, and where state power is only what is explicitly granted to them by the Federal Government.

***U.S. Constitution*:** The governing authority of the United States. The document was adopted on September 17, 1787 by the Constitutional Convention and Ratified on June 21, 1788. Thirty-nine Delegates signed it.

Yellow Dog Democrat: A loyal Democrat. Originally referred to an Alabama Democrat in 1928 who voted for the party's Presidential nominee Al Smith, despite their misgivings.

Yellow Journalism: When a news reporter writes his/her opinion and portrays it as a fact, without providing fair coverage of opposing points of view.

Index

A

A Connecticut Yankee at the Court of King Arthur, 98
A Pet Goat, 78
ABC, 302, 303
Abell, Chester, 9
Abercrombie, Neil, 159
Abourezk, James G., 208
Acheson, Dean, 62
Acheson, Eleanor "Eldie," 62
Ackerman, Gary, 172
Adam Putnam, 167
Adams, Abigail, 44, 45
Adams, George Washington, 7
Adams, John, 15, 16, 29, 38, 53, 58, 61, 73, 74, 89, 90, 92, 109, 240, 279, 302
Adams, John Quincy, 7, 12, 38, 44, 58, 59, 68, 73, 74, 82, 89, 92, 99, 135, 149
Adams, Louisa Catherine Johnson, 44
Adams, Samuel, 279
Aerospace, 299
Affirmative Action, 87
Agnew. Spiro, 51, 52, 58, 87, 248, 251, 266
Agricultural and Mechanical University (Texas A&M,) 289
Akaka, Daniel, 202, 203
Al Aziz, Abd, 93
Alabama, 53, 63, 120, 122, 129, 154, 157, 158, 160, 176, 205, 249, 259, 261, 270, 280, 281, 325
Alaska, 2, 110, 145, 149, 150, 200, 202, 219, 252, 280, 281, 303, 325
Albania, 31
Albright, Madeline, 62, 63
Alexander, Lamar, 264
Alger, Bruce Reynolds, 157
All In the Family, 307
All Politics is Local, 186
Allen, Oscar, 251
Altmire, Jason, 173
Ambassador to the Court of St. James (England), 38, 206
America's Cup Race, 224
American Football League, 171, 258
American Samoa, 275, 281, 315
American University, 219
Americans with Disabilities Act, 177
Amicus Curie brief, 226
Amnesty, Acid, and Abortion, 147
AMVETS, 215
Andrus, Cecil Dale, 261
Annapolis, Maryland, 173, 221
Apollo 17, 198
Apportions Bill of 1792, 2
Arafat, Yasser, 82
Arcata, California, 296
Arctic National Wildlife Refuge, 202, 325
Arends, Leslie C., 166
Argentina, 11
Ariyoshi, George, 270
Arizona, 114, 118, 120, 122, 155, 163, 211, 218, 230, 245, 257, 272
Arkansas National Guard, 9, 121, 256

Arkansas, 79, 88, 92, 96, 112, 116, 117, 119, 120, 121, 126, 148, 159, 184, 193, 209, 215, 222, 252, 254, 255, 256, 257, 260, 261, 262, 264, 265, 266, 267, 272, 273, 279, 282, 285, 313
Arlington National Cemetery, 33
Armey, Dick, 156
Army-McCarthy Hearings, 202
Arthur, Chester A., 9, 13, 16, 29, 34, 42, 86, 92, 99, 104, 108
Arthur, Ellen Lewis, 42
Articles of Confederation and Perpetual Union, 239, 241, 242, 284, 289, 313
Atkins, Chester G., 274
Atlanta Braves, 297
Atomic Bomb, 56
Austin, Richard A., 273
Australian (Secret) ballot, 280
Authorization of Use of Force, 154
Axton, Hoyt, 203

B

Baby Ruth, 40
Bachmann, Michelle, 178
Badillo, Herman, 169
Bailey, Consuelo N., 272
Baker, Howard, 218
Bald Eagle, 306
Baldwin, Chuck, 171
Baldwin, Tammy, 159
Balkans, 11
Ball, George W., 60
Baltimore Colts, 162
Bamberger, Simon, 257
Bank of America, 175
Bankhead, John Hollis, 304
Bankhead, Tallulah, 304
Bankhead, William B., 304
Barkley, Alben, 49, 50, 53, 56
Barracuda Sarah, 252
Bartlett, Roscoe, 156
Barton, Joe, 156
Baruch, Bernard, 305
Basics High School in Henderson, Nevada, 272
Battle Creek, Michigan, 195
Battle of the Alamo, 175
Bay of Pigs Invasion, 83
Bayh, Evan, 200, 316
Bedell, Berkley W., 166
Beebe, Mike, 267
Begich, Mark, 202, 219
Beirut, Lebanon, 261
Bell, Alexander Graham, 24
Bell, George T., 82
Bell, John, 125, 134
Bellemy, Francis, 302
Bender, George, 211
Bennett, Robert, 202
Bentley, Alvin M., 154
Benton, Thomas Hart, 202
Bentsen, Lloyd, 112
Berger, Victor L., 164

Index

Berkshire Hathaway Inc., 168
Berry, Marian, 167
Bevill, Tom, 158
Biden, Joseph, 195
Bill of Rights to the U.S. Constitution, 241, 242, 282, 284
bin Sultan bin Abdul Aziz Al Saud, Prince Bandar, 304
Binghamton, New York, 57
Birch, Bayh, 127
Birmingham, Alabama, 63, 280
Bishop, Timothy, 181, 195
Black, Hugo, 205
Blackbourn, Lisle, 216
Blain, James G., 130
Blease, Coleman Livingston, 210, 258
Bloody Shirt, 153
Bloomberg, Michael, 169, 294
Blumenauer, Earl 159, 167
Blyth, William Jefferson, 84
Board of Supervisors for San Francisco, California, 304
Boehner, John, 190
Boggs, Hale, 171
Boggs, Lewis, 210
Boland, Edward, 168
Booth, Newton, 256
Booze, E.G., 113
Boren, David 200, 203, 224
Boston Redskins, 176
Boston, Massachusetts, 15, 70, 73, 176, 193, 209, 253, 269, 294, 295
Boulter, Beau, 156
Boxer, Barbara, 200, 225
Boyd, Benjamin, 19
Boyda, Nancy, 176
Brady, Mathew, 23
Brandeis, Louis, 231, 233
Branstad, Terry, 267
Braun, Carol Moseley, 197
Breaux, John, 316
Breckenridge, John, 125
Breckinridge, John C., 50, 125
Breeze, Drew, 298
Brigham Wallace, Lurleen, 261
Bright Eyes, 303
Bright, Bobby, 160
Briscoe, Dolph, 252
Britt, Maurice, 273
Brooke, Edward W., 172, 199, 215
Brookline, Massachusetts, 123, 171, 283
Brooks, Mo, 170
Brown Sr., Edmund Gerald "Pat," 247, 270
Brown, Albert G., 194
Brown, Edgar Allen, 259
Brown, Jerry, 116, 123, 148
Brown, Phyllis, 71
Brown, Ron, 61
Brown, Scott, 209, 221, 274
Broyhill, Jim, 164, 223
Bruce, Blanche Kelso, 104
Brune, Elaine C., 78

Bryan, William Jennings, 62, 66, 103, 110, 128, 131, 137, 138
Buchanan, James, 16, 50, 64, 66, 82, 89, 127
Buchanan, Patrick J., 125, 320
Buck v. Bell, 229
Buffett, Howard, 168
Buffett, Warren, 168
Bullock, Bob, 267
Burdick, Jocelyn Birch, 207
Burdick, Quenton, 207
Bureau of Narcotics and Dangerous Drugs, 2
Burlison, William D., 168
Burr, Richard, 223
Burris, Roland, 197
Bush, Barbara Pierce, 46
Bush, George H.W., 4, 7, 20, 38, 58, 70, 85, 94, 95, 96, 98, 112, 116, 119, 123, 124, 125, 135, 139, 145, 146, 177, 254, 303, 307, 308
Bush, George W., 4, 7, 8, 23, 27, 29, 31, 38, 48, 55, 65, 70, 72, 78, 85, 89, 90, 93, 96, 98, 105, 112, 114, 120, 124, 125, 127, 128, 133, 139, 149, 173, 175, 177, 180, 214, 215, 218, 225, 267, 268, 269, 290, 297
Bush, Laura, 48, 175
Butler, Benjamin Franklin, 153
Butler, Nicholas, 106
Byrd Jr., Harry, 212
Byrd Sr., Harry 212
Byrd, Robert C., 63, 194, 200, 204, 206, 212, 213, 214, 219, 221, 302
Byrnes, James, 210, 259

C

Caesarism, 309
Calhoun, John C., 48, 52, 54, 58, 84
California, 26, 47, 65, 94, 107, 116, 117, 123, 125, 127, 128, 131, 135, 148, 159, 160, 165, 174, 177, 179, 190, 205, 230, 245, 247, 250, 253, 255, 256, 257, 259, 260, 266, 270, 274, 275, 279, 282, 283, 296, 324
Callaway, Howard Hollis "Bo," 164
Camacho Sablan, Kilili, 158
Cambodia, 300
Cambridge, Massachusetts, 186
Camp David, 83
Campbell, Ben Nighthorse, 206, 212
Canada, 25, 262, 298
Cannon, Joseph, 189
Cao, "Joseph" Anh, 155
Capital Rotunda, 36
Caraway, Hattie, 222
Caraway, Thaddeus H., 222
Carlson, Arne, 260
Carlson, Frank, 203
Carnahan, Russ, 155
Carswell, Harold, 193
Carter, Jimmy, 10, 11, 15, 20, 24, 30, 34, 45, 66, 70, 80, 95, 105, 107, 117, 118, 122, 126, 127, 129, 135, 142, 144, 247, 260, 263, 265, 296, 306, 314
Carter, Rosalynn, 45
Carter, Tim Lee, 166

Index

Carville, Edward, 262
Casey, William, 66
Cass, Lewis, 66
Cassidy, Eldridge, 40
Castellenos, Alex, 147
Castle Courier, 52
Castro, Fidel, 83, 308
CB Radio, vii, 47
Celeste, Richard, 304
Celler, Emanuel, 170
Cellucci, Paul, 246
Cerebral Hemorrhage, 68, 80
Chaco Territory, 11
Chad, 296
Chamberlain, Neville, 191
Chandler, Albert Benjamin "Happy," 183, 262
Channel One, 299
Charlie Wilson's War, 180
Charlottesville, Virginia, 69
Chase Samuel P., 232
Chelsea Morning, 39
Cheney, Dick 39, 56, 58, 87, 123, 139
Chicago Cubs, 13
Chicago Tribune, 124, 305
Chicago, Illinois, 25, 29, 90, 109, 123, 124, 150, 166,
    170, 172, 208, 226, 249, 294, 305
Chief Justice of the United States, 30, 34, 229, 231,
    233, 235, 260, 301
Chiles, Lawton, 206
China, 23, 34, 240, 291, 292, 308
Cholera, 36
Chrétien, Jean, 303
Christian Coalition, 297
Christie, Chris, 248
Christmas, 1, 27, 37, 90
Chu, Judy, 163
Church, Frank, 127, 209, 215
Ciciline, David N., 295
Civil Rights Act of 1957, 205, 317
Civil Service Reform, 86, 222
Civil War, 8, 39, 67, 71, 111, 194, 290, 292, 299, 305
Clausen, A.W., 175
Clay, Henry, 127, 263
Clements, William P., 252
Cleveland Browns, 162
Cleveland, Grover, 1, 5, 24, 29, 33, 40, 42, 43, 47, 71,
    72, 76, 88, 103, 110, 129, 130, 145, 149, 305
Cleveland, Ruth, 40, 46
Clevenger, Raymond, 167
Clinton v. City of New York, 319
Clinton, Bill, 6, 10, 26, 27, 28, 33, 40, 41, 58, 61, 69,
    72, 79, 82, 84, 88, 96, 97, 116, 117, 118, 119, 122,
    124, 126, 135, 139, 145, 147, 148, 164, 170, 184,
    215, 235, 252, 254, 256, 257, 260, 262, 264, 265,
    267, 284, 297, 313, 316, 320
Clinton, Chelsea, 39
Clinton, George, 55, 57, 58
Clinton, Hillary, vii, 41, 44, 62, 104, 217, 225, 256
Clinton, Roger Sr., 40, 84
CNN, 149, 296, 303, 306, 314
Coburn, Tom, 197
Coca-Cola, 258

Cocaine, 93
Cochran, Thad, 203
Cold War, 305, 320
Collector of Customs, 222
Collins, Cardiss, 166
Collins, George W., 166
Collins, Martha Layne, 249
Collins, Susan, 218
Colson, Charles, 82, 296
Columbia Trust Bank, 38,
Columbus, Christopher, 302
Combast, Larry, 156
Condit, Gary, 182
Confederate States of America, 38, 46, 62, 290
Congress of the Confederation, 239, 315
Congressional Bike Caucus, 167
Conkling, Roscoe, 86, 108, 222
Connally, John, 51, 117
Connecticut, 98, 123, 173, 201, 242, 259, 268, 273,
    290
Continental Congress, 306
Constitutional Convention, 90, 240, 241, 242, 284,
    325
Consumer Fireworks, 283
Continental Congress, 240, 289, 313
Cool J., LL, 270
Coolidge Sr., Calvin, 37
Coolidge, Calvin, 14, 16, 19, 21, 23, 30, 31, 37, 57,
    70, 76, 105, 108, 119, 231
Cornell, Robert, 171
Cosmopolitan Magazine, 71
Cox, Channing, 14
Craig, William, 71
Cramer, William C., 164
Crisis of Confidence Speech, 80
Critique of the Gotha Program, 242
Crocket, Davy, 175
Cross, Doris, 65
C-SPAN, 183, 298, 309
Cuba, 17, 31, 308, 315
Culp, Nancy, 309
Culver, Chet, 267
Cummings, Edward Estlin, 18
Curley, James M., 295
Curtis, Charles, 53, 206
Cushing, William, 234
Custer, Armstrong, 89
Custis Lee, Mary Anna Randolph, 39
Czechoslovakia, 303

D

Daddario, Emilio, 173
Dailey American Advertiser, 75
Daley, Richard M., 294
Daley, Richard, J., 150
Dallas, Texas, 31, 157
Dana, Charles Anderson 130
Darr, A., Mark, 273
Daschle, Tom, 196, 211, 216
Daugherty, Harry M., 37
Davis, Artur, 161, 164

Index

Davis, Clifford, 154
Davis, Henry G., 103
Davis, Jefferson (U.S. Senator (D-AR,) 193
Davis, Jefferson, (President of Confederate States of
    America), 38, 46, 62, 289
Davis, John W., 119, 133
Davis, Loyal, 46
Davis, Nancy, 32
Dawes, Charles G., 51, 57
Dayton, Jonathan, 239
De Priest, Oscar Stanton, 172
Dean, Howard, 273, 298
Debs, Eugene V., 104, 107
Decatur, Illinois, 103
Declaration of Independence, 69, 81, 239, 240, 241,
    242, 281, 315
Delaware, 130, 239, 241, 248, 281, 283, 303
Delay, Tom, 156, 179
DeMint, Jim, 217
Democratic National Committee, 61, 86, 136, 298
Democratic National Convention, 27, 33, 130, 134,
    140, 141, 145, 150, 215
Dent, Grant Julia, 46
Detroit Lions, 85
Dewey, George, 131
Dewey, Thomas E., 106, 124, 126,
Dickenson, Charles, 8
Dickey, Jay, 159
Dickinson, John, 239, 241
Dicks, Norm, 157
Diddy P., 270
Dills, Ralph C., 274
Dingell John Sr., 167
Dingell, John Jr., 161, 167
DioGuardi, Joe, 160
Dionne, E.J., 147
Diphtheria, 40
District of Columbia, 36, 104, 113, 180, 183, 315, 322
Dixon, Illinois, 85
Djou, Charles, 166
Doggett, Lloyd, 160
Dole, Robert J., 10, 124, 125, 136, 150, 195, 196, 212,
    297,299
Dolly, 43, 45
Domenici, Pete, 196
Douglas, Frederick, 139
Douglas, Jim, 250
Douglas, Paul, 120
Douglas, Stephen A., 18, 125
Doxey, Wall, 207
Draper, Eric, 26, 27, 31, 48, 72, 96, 114, 128
Dreams of My Fathers, 90
Drinan, Robert, 171
Driscoll, John T., 273
Dukakis, Michael, 123, 126, 248, 253, 269, 275
Duke, David, 307
Durbin, Dick, 120, 122

E

Eagan, Mary, 168
Eagle Scouts, 1

Eagleton, Thomas, 51, 147
Earmarks, 200, 293
Eastland, James, 220
Easy Rider, 203
Eaton, John Henry, 192
Ebsen, Buddy, 309
Edwards, Chet, 155
Edwards, Edwin, 263
Edwards, Elaine, 263
Edwards, John, 53, 204, 212, 223
Ehrlich, Robert, 261, 271
Eighteenth Amendment to the U.S. Constitution, 41,
    282, 284
Eisenhower, Dwight D., 9, 12, 22, 27, 28, 30, 33, 56,
    58, 62, 83, 85, 94, 95, 96, 98, 106, 107, 110, 125,
    137, 138, 143, 216, 249, 284, 293, 302, 305
Eisenhower, Mamie, 44
Electoral College, vi, 111, 117, 118, 121, 125, 129,
    130, 135, 137, 140, 141, 149, 188, 291, 324
Ellington, Noble, 275
Ellison, Keith, 155
Emancipation Proclamation, 98
Emil Varney Collection, 12
Emma E. Booker Elementary School, 78
Engelmann, Siegfried, 78
En-Lai, Chou, 23
Equal Justice Under the Law, 234
Equal Rights Amendment, 170
Erdeich, Benjamin, 160
Erickson, Edward, 262
Eshoo, Anna Georges, 156
Evans, Billy, 21
Evans, John, 258
Evanston, Illinois, 247
Everett, Edwin, 19
Executive Order 11905, 93

F

Fabus, Orval, 254, 258
Face The Nation, 297
Fairbanks, Charles, 54, 103
Faircloth, Lauch, 223
Faithless Elector, 291
Fala, 130
Fall, Albert B., 213
Fallin, Mary, 159
Falwell, Jerry, 95, 210
Farley, James, 86, 130
Farnum, Billie, 167
Farrakhan, Louis, 304
Fattman, Ryan, 294
Federal Bureau of Prisons, 298
Federal Communications Commission, 299
Federal Election Commission, 114
Federal Register Daily, 299, 300
Federal Reserve Board, 308
Federal-Agent-At-Large, 2
Feingold, Russell, 63, 192, 209
Felton, Rebecca Ann, 194
Fenway Park, 193
Ferguson, Miriam A., 248

Index

Fillmore, Millard, 17, 26, 27, 34, 42, 60, 71, 75, 84, 111, 132, 184
Financial Disclosure Forms, 157
First President of the United States in Congress Assembled, 289
Fitzgerald, John "Honey Fitz," 193
Fitzgerald, John F., 38, 203
Five O' Clock Club, 181
Flag Day, 302
Fletcher, Arthur Allan, 124
Florida, 8, 104, 164, 175, 176, 179, 182, 206, 279, 280
Foley, Tom, 187, 188, 190
Folsom, Frances, 43, 46, 47
Folsom, Oscar, 43
Fono, 275, 281
Ford Motor Company, 6, 157
Ford Sr., Gerald Rudolf, 97
Ford, Betty, 45, 47, 123
Ford, Gerald R., 10, 19, 21, 28, 34, 45, 47, 51, 65, 70, 71, 74, 76, 78, 79, 85, 87, 90, 92, 93, 97, 98, 107, 116, 117, 123, 125, 128, 135, 136, 150, 168, 224, 263, 302, 303
Ford's Theater, 6
Forester, Cecil Scott, 11
Former Presidents Act of 1958, 67
Foss, Joe, 256
Foster, Vincent, 69
Foster, William Z., 127
Founding Fathers, 84, 242
Fox Network, 303
Fox News Sunday, 303
Frank, Barney, 171, 274, 275
Frankin, Al, 215
Franking Privileges, 225
Franklin D. Roosevelt Memorial, 130
Franklin D. Roosevelt Memorial, 130
Franklin, Benjamin, 153, 240, 306
Franklin, Joseph Paul, 306
Freemont, John C., 127
Freemont, Ohio,
Freudenthal, Dave, 271
Frist, Bill, 216, 222
Frost, Martin, 160
Fulbright, J. William, 91, 198
Full Ginsburg, 303
Fuller, Melville, 233

G

Gabrieli, Chris, 180, 283
Gallop Poll, 296
Galvanized Iron, 301
Garagiola, Joe 116
Gardner, Dorothy, 97
Garfield, James, 1, 25, 32, 43, 66, 68, 80, 86, 93, 108, 118, 141, 184, 222
Garn, Jack, 203
Garner, John Nance, 49, 56, 58, 61, 86
Gates, Wallace Madge, 30
Geithner, Timothy, 63
General Electric, 293
Gentleman's Quarterly, 7

George, Walter, 194
Georgia, 107, 117, 144, 148, 164, 171, 188, 194, 204, 210, 215, 246, 247, 251, 255, 262, 264, 265, 282, 297, 305
Geren, Peter 314
Gerry, Elbridge, 49, 52, 55, 241, 242, 317
Gettysburg Address, 34
Gibbons, Jim, 270
Gifford, Frank, 88
Gilbert and Sullivan, 235
Gingrich, Newt, 104, 188, 189, 190, 191
Ginsberg, Ruth Bader, 235
Ginsburg, William H., 303
Giradi, Joe, 62
Girl Scouts of America, 46, 47
Giuliani, Rudolph, 180
God Almighty, viii, 220
Goldman Sachs Group Inc., 106
Goldwater, Barry, 82, 104, 107, 108, 111, 120, 134, 138, 150, 210
Good Luck Margarine, 47
Goode, Virgil, 170
Goodlate, Bob, 159
Goody Goody, 297
Gore, Al, 52, 53, 54, 55, 58, 135, 140, 148, 149, 183, 320
Gore, Albert, Sr., 205
Gossett, Charles, 262
Gouverneur, Samuel L., 39
Graham, Lindsey, 212, 218
Graham, William Alexander, 53
Gramm, Phil, 124, 155, 181, 204, 208, 215, 318
Gramm-Latta Omnibus Reconciliation Bill, 181
Grand Old Party, 305
Grand Rapids, Michigan, 168
Grant, Julia, 4
Granger, Kay, 172
Grant, Ulysses S., 4, 7, 9, 10, 13, 38, 46, 66, 68, 88, 91, 98, 129, 309, 323
Grasso, Ella, 268
Grateful Dead, 300
Gravel, Mike, 197
Graves, Bibb, 205, 259
Graves, Sam, 155
Great Brittan, 281
Greeley, Horace, 129
Green Bay Packers, 85, 216
Gregg, Judd, 199, 218
Gremlins, 203
Griffith Stadium, 21
Griffith, Parker, 160, 161, 170
Grucci, Felix, 181
Gruening, Ernest, 197, 217
Guam, 180, 269, 274, 315
Guild, Curtis, Jr., 260

H

Haddock, Granny "D," 199
Hadley, Elizabeth Jane Rucker, 49
Hagelin, John, 138
Hail To the Chief, 76

Index

Hale, John P., 116
Haleyville City Hall, 158
Haleyville, Alabama, 158
Hall, David, 271
Hall, Linda, 196
Hall, Ralph, 170, 176
Halleck Charles A., 74, 187
Halleck, Charles 293
Halliburton, 58, 139
Hamilton, Alexander, 316
Hamlin, Hannibal, Jr., 55
Hammerschmidt, John Paul, 79
Hammons, John Tyler 294
Hanabusa, Colleen, 182
Hance, Kent, 173, 177
Hancock, John, 279
Hancock, Winfield S., 141
Hannon, Mary Josephine "Josie," 32, 38
Hanson, John, Jr., 289
Hanukah, 23
Happy Warrior, 142
Haralson, Jeremiah, 153
Harding, Florence, 18
Harding, Warren G., 4, 18, 28, 34, 37, 80, 84, 105,
    107, 108, 113, 135, 149, 213, 320
Harkin, Tom, 63
Harman, Jane, 180
Harpers Weekly, 309
Harrison, Benjamin, 6, 14, 26, 21, 31, 36, 37, 72, 80,
    92, 103, 129, 149, 302, 305
Harrison, William Henry, 15, 30, 35, 58, 60, 74, 78,
    80, 92, 93, 113, 121, 143, 146
Hart, Melissa, 175
Hartmann, Robert T., 85
Harvard University Business School, 31, 173
Harvard University, 11, 53, 54, 73, 216
Harvey Oswald, Lee, 297
Hass, Phillip, 7
Hastert, J. Dennis, 187, 188
Hatch, Frank, 270, 274
Hatch, Orrin, 196
Hatfield, Mark, 208
Hathaway, Jane, 309
Hathaway, William, 51
Hawaii, 2, 104, 110, 112, 122, 150, 159, 166, 182,
    194, 200, 201, 202, 203, 249, 268, 270, 282
Hay, John, 3
Hayden, Carl, 155
Hayes, Rutherford B., 11, 24, 25, 28, 48, 64, 75, 84,
    105, 117, 137, 140, 149, 153, 290
Hayes, Webb, 84
Hayworth, J.D., 163
Healey, Kerry, 272, 283
Hechler, Ken, 176
Hecht, Chic, 214
Heflin, James Thomas, 218
Heinz, John, 213
Helms, Jesse, 117, 307
Helmsley, Leona, 200
Henderson, Charles B., 204
Henderson, David B., 185
Hendricks, Thomas A., 247

Henry L. Bellmon, 248
Henry Lee, Richard, 240
Her, 17
Hernandez, Marion, 179
Herter, Christian, 62
Hickey, John, 262
Highland Park, Texas., 139
Hightower, Jack, 298
Him, 17
Hiroshima, Japan, 56, 187
Hitler, Adolph, 191
Hobbes, Thomas, 323
Holing Jr., Adolph A., 37
Holmes, Wendell Oliver, 229, 230
Holton Jr., Abner Linwood, 265
Holtzman, Elizabeth, 170
Holy Bible, 6, 26, 32, 75
Honolulu, Hawaii, 166
Hoover, Herbert, 22, 23, 30, 32, 42, 65, 67, 79, 89, 91,
    108, 131, 134
Hoover, Irwin H. 98
Hoover, Lou, 42, 47
Hope, Arkansas, 252
Hornblower, Horatio, 11
Horner, Tom, 260
House Agricultural Committee, 156
House Clerk, 174
House Committee on Appropriations, 169
House Committee on Armed Services, 169, 178
House Committee on Banking and Currency, 169
House Committee on Rules, and the Committee on
    Standards of Official Conduct, 160
House Committee on the Budget, 169
House Committee on Financial Services, 169
House Committee on Transportation and
    Infrastructure, 174
House Committee on Transportation and
    Infrastructure, 169
House Committee on Ways and Means, 160, 169, 175,
    179
House Energy and Commerce Committee, 156
House Permanent Select Committee on Intelligence,
    156
House Permanent Select Committee on Intelligence,
    156, 160
Houston, Sam, 247
Hruska, Roman, 193
Hubschman, Harold, 283
Huckabee, Mike, 252, 255, 257, 266, 273
Huddleston, Walter, 118
Huffington Post, 28
Huggins, A.P., 153
Hughes, Sara, T., 31
Hull, Blair, 203
Hull, Jane, 120
Humphrey, Hubert, 11, 52, 111, 122, 126, 129, 130,
    136, 140, 142, 145, 224
Hunt, Guy, 249
Huntsman, Jon Jr., 253
Huntsville, Arkansas, 256
Hussein, Saddam, 296
Hutchinson, Kay Bailey, 202, 226

Index

Hutchinson, Tim, 199, 209
Hyde Park, New York, 43

I

I Have a Dream Speech, 301
Idaho, 171, 209, 215, 245, 246, 261, 269, 284, 285
Illinois, 33, 34, 35, 62, 109, 110, 111, 122, 140, 164, 166, 170, 172, 184, 189, 192, 197, 203, 204, 208, 210, 223, 247
Impavid, 145
In God We Trust, 305
In the Arena, 302
Independence, Missouri, 78, 144,
Indiana, 31, 129, 133, 143, 149, 199, 200, 218, 246, 247, 306
Ingersoll, Robert F., 140
Inouye, Daniel, 194, 195, 200, 201, 202, 203
Iolanthe, 235
Iraq War, 154, 306
Israel, 306

J

Jackson, Andrew, 1, 8, 16, 22, 24, 29, 36, 52, 58, 69, 71, 74, 79, 84, 89, 149, 206, 309
Jackson, Curtis, a.k.a. "50 Cent," 7
Jackson, Henry "Scoop," 320
Jackson, Jesse, 121, 173
Jackson, Mississippi, 89
Jackson, Rachel, 23. 26
Jagt, Guy Vander, 167
Japan, 174, 187
Jay, John, 316
Jefferson City, Missouri, 89
Jefferson, Thomas, 1, 5, 17, 33, 58, 69, 73, 74, 77, 81, 82, 89, 90, 109, 136, 155, 240, 301, 315, 320
Jefferson, William, 7, 72, 84, 160, 176
Jenkins, Louis Elwood "Woody," 198
Jenkins, Lynne, 176
Jersey Shore, 303
Jesus Christ, 1
Jindal, Bobby, 268
Johnson City, Texas, 41
Johnson, Andrew, 28, 30, 34, 50, 67, 68, 70, 71, 77, 92, 99, 218
Johnson, B., Lyndon, 14, 17, 20, 28, 30, 31, 41, 64, 66, 74, 76, 77, 78, 80, 81, 82, 87, 90, 92, 94, 95, 96, 97, 99, 107, 108, 111, 120, 134, 171, 205, 209, 217, 224, 284, 293, 296, 309, 317, 318
Johnson, Eastman, 11
Johnson, Gary, 264
Johnson, John Neely, 250, 259
Johnson, Lady Bird, 44, 309
Johnson, Lynda Bird, 309
Johnson, Richard M., 50, 54, 59, 121
Johnson, Sam E. Sr., 41
Johnson, Tim, 211
Jones, Ben, 171
Jones, Stephanie Tubbs, 225
Jones, Steve, 200
Jones, Tommy Lee, 53

Jordan, Barbara, 141, 182
Jordan, Vernon, 306
Judicial Review, 229, 318

K

Kagan, Elana, 218, 235
Kahn, Florence, 162
Kanjorski, Paul, 174
Kansas, 96, 124, 141, 176, 196, 208, 218, 245, 262
Kaptur, Marcy, 158
Kariotis, George, 269
Kasich, John, 175, 182, 267
Kassebaum, Nancy, 195, 218
Keep the Ball Rolling, 146
Kefauver, Estes, 112, 120, 205
Kelley, Frank J., 273
Kennedy Jr., Joseph, 130
Kennedy Sr., Joseph, 38, 130
Kennedy, Edward M., 42, 118, 142, 193, 196, 198, 200, 205, 216, 218, 220, 221, 260, 307
Kennedy, Jacquelyn Bouvier, 45
Kennedy, John B., 273
Kennedy, John F., 6, 8, 10, 12, 17, 25, 28, 32, 33, 38, 42, 45, 60, 73, 74, 76, 80, 81, 83, 87, 98, 110, 115, 132, 138, 140, 145, 165, 192, 196, 216, 218, 219, 224, 293, 296, 304, 307, 308
Kennedy, John Francis, 203, 273
Kennedy, John M., 273
Kennedy, Patrick J., 275
Kennedy, Robert F., 98, 103, 202, 203
Kentucky Colonel, 284
Kentucky, 54, 123, 148, 195, 249, 281, 284, 285
Kerry, John F., 215, 224
Kerry, John, 112, 114, 120, 195, 213, 214, 221
Kerry, Teresa Heinz, 213
Key West, Florida, 206
Khmer Rouge, 300
Kid Gloves Harrison, 6
Kim, Chang-jun "Jay," 165
Kimberly-Clark Corporation, 183
Kinderhook, New York, 6, 69
King George lll, 242
King Jr., Leslie Lynch, 97
King Richard lll of England, 22
King Sr., Leslie Lynch, 97
King, Angus, 115
King, Ed (Governor of Massachusetts,) 126, 260, 265, 270, 274
King, Ed (Mayor of Mount Pleasant, Iowa,) 295
King, Edward F. (Candidate for Massachusetts Governor,) 265
King, William Rufus, 53, 57, 59
Kline, John, 161
Knowland, William, 204
Kohl, Herbert, 192
Korbel, Joseg, 63
Kristol, Irving, 320
Ku Klux Klan, 153
Kucinich, Dennis, 177
Kuwait, 254
Kyle, John, 122

Index

L

La Follette Robert M., Sr., 119, 233
Lafayette, Prentiss Walker, 167
Laffer, Arthur, 323
LaHood, Ray, 62
Lakien, John, 216
Lamb, Brian, 309
Landon, Alfred, 61, 111, 134, 141, 148, 150
Landrieu, Mary, 198, 202
Langevin, James, 177
LaRouche, Lyndon, 105, 118, 121
Late Edition, 303
Latin, 6, 42, 221, 305, 323, 324, 325
Laurens, Henry, 289
Lawrence, Richard, 22
Laxalt, Paul, 117, 214
Lazio, Rick, 225
Leahy, Patrick, 196, 207
Leary, Georgia, 247
Lee, Anna Randolph Custis, 39
Lee, Barbara, 154
Lee, Robert E., 39
Leif Ericson Day, 96
Lend-Lease Act, 93
Levin, Charles Lewis, 162
Lewinsky, Monica 10, 303
Liberia, 92
Lieberman, Joseph, 201, 212
Lincoln, Abraham, 2, 3, 6, 10, 13, 18, 19, 43, 50, 55, 63, 71, 72, 74, 79, 80, 89, 98, 125, 292, 309
Lincoln, Blanche, 201, 213, 267
Lincoln, Evelyn, 3, 76
Lincoln, Mary Todd, 3
Lincoln, Nebraska, 89
Lincoln, Robert Todd, 43
Line-Item-Veto, 246, 290
Lingle, Linda, 249, 268
Lions Club, 247
Lippman, Walter, 209
Literary Digest, 111
Little Rock Central High School, 9
Little Rock, Arkansas, 9, 92, 121, 256
Little, John Sebastian, 252
Locke, John, 323
Lockwood, Belva Ann Bennett, 232
Lodge Jr., Henry Cabot, 81
Lodge Sr., Henry Cabot, 213
London, England, 44
Long, Huey, 83, 251
Long, Russell B., 171
Longworth, Nicholas, 40, 119, 133, 189
Lord Chancellor, 235
Los Angeles Times, 32
Los Angeles, California, 18, 150, 270
Louisiana, 120, 155, 166, 176, 197, 198, 202, 251, 253, 263, 268, 275, 284, 307, 318
Love Story, 53
Lucas, Frank, 162
Luckett, Edith, 46
Lugar, Richard, 199, 218
Lukas, Scott, 216

Lukens, Donald "Buz," 190
Lurton, Horace, 229
Luther King Jr., Martin, 176, 301
Lynn, Massachusetts, 260

M

MacArthur, Douglas, 138, 175
Mackie, John, 167
Maddox, Lester, 117, 255, 262
Madison, Dolly, 43, 45
Madison, James, 3, 5, 25, 26, 32, 55, 57, 58, 74, 82, 89, 156, 229, 301, 316
Mahoning County, Ohio 154
Maine, 51, 109, 115, 143, 218, 233, 272, 285
Major League Baseball All-Star Game, 8
Major League Baseball, 8, 116, 183, 191, 234, 298, 304
Malaria, 5
Malaysia, 30
Mammoth Oil Company, 213
Manassas, Virginia. 111
Manhattan Project, 56
Manhattan, New York, 56, 65
Mansfield, Neely Matthew, 219
Marblehead, Massachusetts, 13
Marbury v. Madison, 229
March on Washington For Jobs and Freedom, 301
Marcy, William, 206
Marine 1, 76
Marion Court College, 76
Marist Institute of Public Opinion, 303
Markell, Jack, 248
Markey, Edward, 165
Marshall, Jim, 180
Marshall, John, 1, 229, 301
Marshall, Thomas Riley, 48, 58, 132
Martin, Joe, 186, 187
Martin, William McChesney, 308
Martinez, Susana, 268
Marx, Karl, 242
Maryland, 111, 173, 181, 201, 241, 246, 251, 261, 266, 271, 280
Mason, George, 241, 242, 324
Mason, Stevens T., 254
Massachusetts Bay Colony, 282
Massachusetts House of Representatives, 253, 274
Massachusetts State House, 279
Massachusetts State Senate, 253
Massachusetts Treasurer and Receiver-General, 273
Massachusetts, 13, 44, 62, 68, 70, 71, 76, 88, 104, 109, 115, 123, 125, 126, 147, 166, 171, 172, 173, 180, 185, 186, 192, 193, 195, 199, 203, 205, 216, 218, 220, 221, 231, 233, 242, 245, 246, 249, 250, 251, 252, 253, 258, 260, 264, 265, 266, 269, 270, 271, 272, 273, 274, 275, 279, 280, 282, 283, 284, 285, 294, 295, 303, 304, 317
Matheson, Allen, ii
Mathews, Chris, 300
Mathews, Jim, 300
Mattingly, Mack, 210
Mauro, Gary, 267

Index

Maury Maverick, 153
Maverick, Samuel, 153
Maybank, Burton, 259
Mayflower Compact. 253
Mays Willie, 63
McAdoo, William Gibbs Jr., 65
McAuliffe, Terry, 126, 127
McBride, Herschel, 294
McCain, John, 106, 108, 110, 111, 112, 113, 114, 120,
    121, 122, 124, 125, 127, 128, 135, 145, 148, 149,
    211, 218, 221
McCall, Carl, 270
McCarthy, Eugene, 48, 103
McCarthy, Joe, 81, 202, 217
McCarthyism, 217
McClellan, Scott, 4
McConnell, Mitch, 118, 195
McCormack, John, 186
McCrae, Tom, 267
McDonald v. Chicago, 226
McGovern, George, 111, 117, 125, 129, 141, 147,
    157, 211
McGovern, Jim, 157
McKellar, Kenneth, 205
McKinley, William, 35, 43, 64, 73, 80, 98, 110, 131,
    137, 184, 189
McLaughlin, John, 207
McMahon, E., Michael, 178
McNamara, Robert, 64
Mechem, Edwin, 262
Medicaid, 292
Medicare, 78, 175, 291, 292
Meet the Press, 212, 303, 304
Mega Society, 307
Merchants Exchange Building, 232
Meredith, James, 307
Merrill, Denise, 273
Mexican-American War, 68, 240
Mexico, 58, 174, 196, 263, 268, 301, 325
Michigan, 74, 76, 87, 124, 135, 157, 167, 168, 179,
    195, 254, 273
Middlesex County, Massachusetts, 220
Mihos, Christy, 283
Milk, Harvey, 304
Miller, Joe, 222
Miller, Stephanie, 307
Miller, William E., 107, 307
Miller, Zell, 214, 215, 251
Mills, Ada, 117
Milton, Massachusetts, 123
Milwaukee Bucks, 199
Milwaukee, Wisconsin, 133, 199
Minimum Wage, 283, 293
Minnesota State Fair, 86
Minnesota, 86, 104, 106, 113, 114, 138, 142, 169, 210,
    251, 253, 260, 261, 262, 264, 265, 268, 273, 280,
    285
Minnesota Republican Central Committee, 260
Minnick, Walter, 171
Mississippi River, 3

Mississippi, 3, 38, 111, 116, 122, 129, 134, 148, 153,
    164, 167, 170, 185, 194, 197, 203, 248, 282, 284,
    307
Missouri, 51, 73, 75, 78, 89, 106, 107, 144, 155, 169,
    181, 260
Mitchell, John, 63
Mohamed, Ali, 172
Mondale, Walter, 55, 57, 113, 136, 143, 273
Mongolia, 29
Monroe, Hestor Maria, 3, 39
Monroe, James, 3, 21, 26, 39, 59, 69, 74, 82, 89, 92,
    132, 135, 140, 156,
Montgomery, Alabama 176
Moore, Nancy, 217
Moran Sr., James, 176
Moran, Jr., James, 176
Morella, Connie, 154, 181
Morocco, 302
Morris, Dick, 154
Morris, Gouverneur, 241
Morse, Wayne, 217, 219, 220
Morton, Levi, 49, 108
Moscone, George, 304
Mount Everest, 264
Mount Pleasant City Hall, 295
Mount Pleasant, Iowa, 295
Mount Vernon, 90
MSNBC, 300
Mueller, 103
Mugwamp, 86
Muhlenberg, Frederick, 185
Mulford Act, 255
Mundt, Karl, 192
Murkowski, Lisa, 202, 222
Murtha, John, 162, 163
Muskogee, Oklahoma, 294
My American Cousin, 43, 79
Myers, Michael, 177

N

Nader, Ralph, 129, 139, 296
Nadler, Jerrold, 154
Nagasaki, Japan, 56
NASA, 198
Nast, Thomas, 309
National Archives, 2, 52, 70, 94, 134, 139, 241, 299,
    300, 308
National Debt, 292, 293, 319
National Football League, 162, 171, 258
National Governors Association (NGA), 256
National Hockey League, 251
National Menorah, 4
National Park Service, 24, 39, 303
National Rifle Association, 68, 98, 305
National Women's Hall of Fame, 45
Naval Observatory, 55
Nebraska, 72, 133, 168, 208, 218, 226, 233, 280, 313,
    324
Nelson, Ben, 218
Nelson, Gaylord, 51
Nepal, 264

Index

Nethercutt, George, 187
Nevada, 107, 117, 204, 214, 220, 233, 246, 270, 272, 280, 281, 283
New Deal, 98, 134, 308
New England, 110, 134, 207, 316
New Hampshire, 93, 116, 124, 135, 138, 146, 147, 150, 199, 218, 233, 239, 245, 246, 272, 279, 280, 281, 285
New Jersey, 109, 131, 165, 169, 239, 245, 248, 283, 284, 285
New Mexico, 196, 263, 264, 268
New Orleans, Louisiana, 155, 166, 171, 298
New Times Magazine, 211
New York City, New York, 3, 14, 46, 109, 180, 217, 232, 294, 298
New York Magazine, 7
New York Mets, 269
New York Sun, 130
New York Times Co. v. Sullivan, 313
New York Tribune, 129
New York Yankees, 62, 230, 304
New York, 7, 19, 29, 41, 42, 43, 45, 46, 62, 73, 86, 104, 109, 115, 126, 129, 130, 131, 133, 134, 142, 145, 159, 160, 169, 170, 172, 178, 180, 181, 183, 188, 192, 203, 217, 222, 230, 231, 232, 241, 246, 247, 253, 260, 269, 270, 271, 279, 283, 294, 298, 299, 304, 313, 316, 319, 322
New Zealand, 299
Newlands, Francis, 233
Newmax Media, 69
Newsweek Magazine, 180
Nicolay, John G., 3
Nigh, George, 250
Nixon, Richard M., 2, 10, 12, 20, 23, 24, 26, 27, 28, 30, 31, 51, 56, 58, 65, 82, 87, 88, 92, 94, 98, 99, 100, 106, 110, 117, 122, 125, 126, 128, 130, 132, 138, 140, 141, 144, 145, 147, 148, 159, 169, 193, 207, 224, 230, 247, 265, 266, 270, 296, 302, 304
Nobel Peace Prize, 34
Noble Foundation, 14
No-Fault Automobile Insurance Legislation, 275
Nolan, Mae Ella, 163
Nolo Contender, 51, 52, 87
None Of The Above, viii, 142
Norris, George, 233
North Atlantic Treaty Organization (NATO), 303, 305
North Carolina, 76, 117, 132, 223, 246, 256, 279, 285
North Carolina Constitution, 279, 297
North Dakota, 207, 261, 279, 285
North Hampton, Massachusetts, 70
North Korea, 308, 315
Northern Marianna Islands, 158
Novak, Robert, 147
Novello, Antonia, 298
Nuclear Football, 161
Nuclear Freeze Movement, 298
Nunn, Sam, 202, 316
Nye, Gerald, 213

O

O'Brien, Conan, 171

O'Callaghan, Mike, 272
O'Connor, Carroll, 307
O'Daniel, Wilbert Lee, 224
O'Malley, Martin, 261
O'Neil Jr., Thomas P. "Tip," 186
O'Neill, James Edward "Tip," 191
Oak Ridge Cemetery, 19
Obama, Barack, 8, 9, 16, 18, 28, 34, 39, 70, 72, 88, 90, 91, 95, 99, 106, 109, 111, 112, 113, 114, 115, 116, 120, 121, 122, 124, 131, 133, 134, 135, 145, 146, 148, 164, 184, 192, 197, 203, 204, 206, 208, 211, 221, 223, 235, 260, 290, 295, 296, 298, 303
Oberstar, James, 169
O'Connor, Sandra Day, 210, 230, 232
Odell Jr., Benjamin Barker, 73
Odessa, Texas, 177
Ohio, 40, 60, 64, 75, 80, 84, 105, 107, 109, 113, 114, 133, 140, 143, 153, 175, 190, 225, 281, 284, 295
Oklahoma, 107, 110, 112, 120, 121, 159, 162, 182, 200, 245, 246, 248, 250, 271, 275, 294
Old Tippecanoe, 143
Olver, John, 159
Olson, Pete, 176
Olympic Games, 27
Oregon Bottle Bill, 281
Oregon, 103, 198, 201, 272, 281, 282, 283, 285
Original Jurisdiction, 232, 320
Out Of Many, One, 305
Oval Office, 22, 95, 290

P

Pacheco, Romualdo, 256
Packwood, Robert, 201
Palestinian Liberation Organization (PLO,) 82
Palin, Sarah, 39, 124, 149, 252
Palmer, Alice, 9
Palmer, John M., 110
Palo Alto, California, 47
Panama Canal Zone, 122
Paraguay, vii, 11
Parker, Alton B., 103
Parkinson, Mark, 262
Parnell, Harvey, 222, 272
Parnell, Pat, 158
Parnell, Sean, 158
Pastore, John O., 207
Pataki, George, 270
Patient Protection and Affordability Act, 161, 178, 303
Patrick, Deval, 260, 271, 295
Paul, Rand, 304
Paul, Ron, 171, 318
Pavlick, Richard. 8
Pawlenty, Tim, 114
Payne, Donald, 165
Peanut One, 105
Pelosi, Nancy, 160, 163, 187, 188, 190, 191
Pendleton Civil Service Reform Act, 86
Pennsylvania, 110, 114, 162, 163, 170, 175, 181, 185, 239, 240, 241, 242, 285, 300, 309
Pensacola, Florida, 206

Index

Pentagon, 297, 306
People's Day, 255
Peoria Notre Dame High School, 62
Pepper, Claude, 192
Pepsi-Cola, 258
Perdue, Beverly, 256
Perdue, Sonny, 264
Perot, H., Ross, 115, 122, 126, 139, 144, 145
Perpich, Rudolph Sr., 264
Perry, Rick, 4, 148, 249
Persian Gulf War, 154
Peters, Andrew J., 15
Pettit, Tom, 297
Pew Research Center, 162
Philadelphia Athletics, 1
Philadelphia, Pennsylvania, 1, 145, 240, 241, 242
Philip, Asa, 301
Philips Academy in Andover, Massachusetts, 8, 32, 123
Pierce, Franklin, 11, 26, 29, 32, 46, 53, 57, 59, 62, 77, 93, 109, 116
Pinchback, Pinckney Benton Stewart, 263
Pitman, Benjamin, 13
Pittsburgh Steelers, 162
Pittsfield, Massachusetts, 71
Plains, Georgia, 30
Platt, Thomas C., 73
Plymouth Colony, Massachusetts, 319
Poff, Richard, 164
Polis, Jared, 182
Polizzi, Nicole, a.k.a. Snooki, 303
Polk, James K., 23, 28, 36, 64, 85, 127, 184, 325
Polk, Sarah, 36
Pope John Paul 11, 296
Pope John Paul II, 171, 296
Pope Paul VI, 14
Pope Pius XI, 113
Pothier, Aram J., 262
Potomac River, 12
POTUS, 99, 321
Powers, Abigail, 42
Presentment Clause of the U.S. Constitution, 319
President Pro Tempore, 29, 189
Presley, Elvis, 2
Primary Seatbelt Laws, 280
Profile in Courage Award, 165
Providence College, 275
Providence, Rhode Island, 295
Proximire, William, 207
Pryor, Mark, 199, 209
Puerto Rico, 95, 154, 170, 180, 233, 272, 285, 322
Pyle, Gladys, 131
Pythagorean Theorem, 184

Q

Quakers, 30
Quayle, Dan, 52, 179, 232
Quincy Daily Journal, 132
Quincy, Illinois, 132
Quinn, William, 249
Qur'an, 155

R

Racketeer Influenced and Corrupt Organizations Act (RICO,) 154
Rampton, Calvin, 248
Randolph, Edmond, 242
Randolph, Edmund, 241
Randolph, Philip, 301
Rankin, Jeannette, 174
Rayburn, Sam, 186, 284
Reagan, Nancy, 46, 256
Reagan, Ronald, 2, 24, 27, 30, 32, 36, 46, 58, 70, 76, 80, 85, 94, 95, 98, 113, 115, 117, 118, 125, 128, 135, 142, 143, 148, 156, 175, 177, 181, 190, 191, 210, 235, 247, 253, 255, 256, 304, 320, 323
Reconstruction, 120, 157, 164, 197, 248, 249, 253, 265, 273, 275
Red Cross, 3
Red Phone, 299
Reed Thomas Bracket, 137, 185, 189
Reed, Ralph, 297
Reese, Jim, 177
Register of the Federal Treasury, 104
Rehnquist, William, 235
Reid, Harry, 214, 220, 272
Reno, Janet, 59
Representational Allowances, 177
Republican National Convention, 109, 128, 135, 140, 167, 215
Resident Commissioner of Puerto Rico, 170, 322
Resolute Desk, 290
Revels, Hiram, 194
Rhode Island, 218, 233, 245, 246, 281, 282, 284, 295
Rhode Island House of Representatives, 275
Rice, Angelina, 63
Rice, Condoleezza, 63
Richard F. Knelps, 256
Richard Gephardt, 157
Richards, Ann, 248, 269
Richards, Keith, 255
Richardson, Bill, 263
Richardson, Elliot, 65
Richmond, Cedrick, 166
Richmond, Virginia, 73
Ripon, Wisconsin, 301
Robb, Chuck, 309
Robbins, Kenneth Seymour, 46
Roberts, Albert H., 284
Roberts, John, 231
Robertson, Pat. 146
Robertson, William H., 222
Robinson, Joseph T., 193
Rock River, 85
Rockefeller, Nelson, 56, 104, 322
Rockefeller, Winthrop Paul, 273
Rockwell County, Texas, 176
Rocky Mountains, 188
Rodgers, Will Sr., 301
Roe v. Wade, 77
Rogers, Mike, U.S. Representative (R-AL,) 157
Rogers, Mike, U.S. Representative (R-MI,) 157, 181
Rolling Stones, 255

Index

Roman Republic, 241
Romania, 24
Romney Mitt, 110, 216, 246, 251, 252, 253, 264, 271
Romney, Milton, 249
Romney, Willard "Mitt," 249
Rooney, Tom, 176
Roosevelt, Alice, 40, 133
Roosevelt, Eleanor 37, 44, 45, 47, 143
Roosevelt, Franklin D., 17, 27, 35, 37, 41, 43, 44, 47,
    56, 58, 61, 70, 73, 77, 80, 83, 86, 93, 94, 98, 111,
    126, 130, 131, 133, 134, 142, 143, 148, 168, 174,
    308
Roosevelt, Sarah Ann Delano, 41, 43
Roosevelt, Theodore, 3, 13, 20, 25, 35, 36, 39, 40, 54,
    60, 71, 73, 83, 86, 89, 98, 103, 109, 133, 134, 211,
    271, 290
Rosellini, Albert, 250
Ross, Ben C., 246
Ross, Mike, 159, 184, 226
Ross, Nellie, 262
Ross, Richard J., 274
Rovagg, Karl, 142
Rowan and Martin's Laugh In, 126
Ruby, Jack, 297
Ruddy, Christopher, S., 69
Rule of 80, 234
Rush, Bobby, 184
Russell, Donald, 262
Russell, Richard, 82, 209
Ruth, Babe, 94, 230, 308

S

Safire, William, 299
Sailor Boy, 89
Salem, Massachusetts, 13
Sali, Bill, 171
Salinger, Pierre, 17
San Diego, California, 295
San Francisco, California, 162, 188, 190, 257, 294,
    304
San Marcos, Texas, 81
Sanders, Bernie, 63, 194
Sandoval, Brian, 270
Santa Anna, Antonio Lopez de, 202
Sarasota County, Florida, 78
Sarbanes, Paul, 201
Saudi Arabia, 93, 304
Saund, Dalip Singh, 179
Sawyer, Diane, 302
Schembechler, Bo, 76
Schenectady, NY, 180
Schieffer, Bob, 297
Schieffer, Tom, 297
Schmitt, Harrison, 198
Schrank, John, 133
Schroeder, Patricia, 181
Schweiker, Richard, 128
Scott Lord Dimmick, Mary, 37
Scott, Tim, 182
Scott, William Lloyd, 211
Scott, Winfield, 53

Scottsdale, Arizona, 230
Sears, Bobby Lee, 262
Sebelious, Kathleen, 262
Second Continental Congress, 239
Secretary of the U.S. Senate, 226
Segal, Erich, 53
Selected Incorporation Doctrine, 226
Selectman, 42, 274, 294, 299
Selma, Alabama, 176
Senate Agriculture, Nutrition, and Forestry
    Committee, 213
Senate Committee on Appropriations, 194, 214
Seneca Falls, New York, 45
Seneca, South Carolina, 212
Sensenbrenner, James, 183
Sergeant-at-Arms of the U.S. House of
    Representatives, 226
Sergeant-at-Arms of the U.S. Senate, 207
Serrano, Jose, 172
Sestak, Joe, 184
Seven Dwarfs, 231
Shallas, Jacob, 239
Shamansky, Robert Norton, 175
Sheppard, Morris, 224
Sherman, John, 60, 64
Sherman, Roger, 242
Shields, James, 210
Shivercrats, 125
Shivers, Allan, 125, 269
Shuster, Bud, 309
Siegelman, Don, 254
Silent Majority Speech, 28
Singapore, 256
Situation Room, 290
Skelton, Ike, 169, 178
Smallpox, 20
Smathers, George, 192
Smith, Adam, 318
Smith, Albert, 160
Smith, Gordon, 201
Smith. Al, 113, 133, 134, 142, 325
Smoltz, John, 297
Snelling, Richard A., 273
Snowe, Olympia, 218
Soccer Mom, 147
Social Security Administration, 77
Social Security, 77, 292, 300, 307, 308
Sock it to Me, 126
Sorento, Barry, 72
Sotomayor, Sonia, 234
Souder, Mark, 226
Souter, David, 233
South Carolina, 52, 148, 149, 169, 182, 195, 210, 212,
    217, 218, 222, 223, 258, 259, 285, 305
South Dakota, 125, 208, 211, 216, 246, 256, 258, 279,
    280
South Korea, 308
Souza, Pete, 8, 14, 23, 32, 33, 72, 88, 90, 93 109, 115,
    121, 122, 123, 128 131, 146, 204, 208, 211
Soviet Union, 305, 314
Space Shuttle "Discovery.", 203
Spanish-American War, 240, 258, 308

Index

Speakers Journal, 188
Spears, Britney, 306
Special Election, 181, 210, 221, 222, 259, 323
Specter, Arlen, 196
Spoils System, 206
Spratt, John, 169
Springer, Jerry, 295
Springsteen, Bruce, 248
St. Albans School, 54
Stalwart, 86, 323
Standard and Poor's, 299
Stanford University, 91
Stanford, Terry, 223
Staples Center, 33
Stark, Peter, 159
Stassen, Harold E., 106
State of the Union Address, 66, 75, 99, 232
State University of Buffalo, 75
Statute of Virginia for Religious Freedom, 69
Stein, Sam, 8
Steinbrenner, George, 304
Stenholm, Charlie, 170
Steppenwolf, 203
Stern, Howard, 247
Stevens, John Paul, 230
Stevens, Ted, 200, 219
Stevenson I, Adlai E., 57
Stevenson, Adlai, 106, 107, 111, 112, 120, 125, 143
Stipe, Gene, 275
Strauss, Solomon Oscar, 60
Strayhorn, Carole Keeton, 19
Streptococcal Throat Infection, 20
Strickland, Ted, 267
Suffolk University, 294
Sununu, John H., 307
Supreme Court of Puerto Rico, 233
Sutton, Massachusetts, 294
Swann, Lynn, 300
Swift, Jane, 246, 253, 258
Symington, Fife, 257
Symington, Stuart, 126, 140
Symms, Steve, 215

T

Taekwondo, 154
Taft, Alphonso, 38
Taft, Robert A., 138, 320
Taft, William Howard, 4, 11, 21, 22, 30, 33, 34, 38, 54, 85, 98, 106, 109, 123, 133, 229
Taney, Roger, 316
Tansworth, New Hampshire, 42
Taylor, Alfred, 267
Taylor, Charles S. 202
Taylor, Gene, 154, 160, 164, 170, 178, 180
Taylor, George Edwin, 132
Taylor, Robert, 267
Taylor, Sarah Knox, 38
Taylor, Zachary, 2, 27, 30, 38, 43, 60, 71, 78, 132
Team Reform, 253
Temple, Shirley, 303

Tennessee, ix, 55, 67, 68, 107, 112, 120, 163, 179, 205, 218, 247, 264, 267, 272, 280, 284
Tester, John, 226
Texarkana, Texas, 126
Texas Declaration of Idependence, 202
Texas Rangers Baseball Team, 90
Texas Southern University Tigers, 28
Texas State Teachers College, 81, 94
Texas Tech, 173
Texas, 8, 11, 19, 81, 86, 90, 94, 97, 106, 108, 112, 117, 120, 122, 125, 126, 135, 139, 148, 153, 155, 156, 157, 162, 170, 172, 173, 175, 176, 177, 181, 182, 202, 205, 245, 247, 248, 249, 252, 267, 268, 269, 280, 281, 282, 284, 289, 297, 318
Thanksgiving, 95, 241
The Alamo, 202
The Audacity of Hope, 90
The Babe Ruth Story, 94, 308
The Beverly Hillbillies, 309
The Boeing Company, 299
The Confederate State's of America, 304
The Conference Handshake, 233
The Constitution of the State of New Hampshire, 280
The General Grant National Memorial a.k.a. Grant's Tomb, 4
The Governor and the Dishwasher, 262
The Guinness Book World Records, 263
The Life and Times of Jesus of Nazareth, 1
The Little White Schoolhouse, 301
The Malaise Speech, 80
The Mary Tyler Moore Show, 45
The McLaughlin Group, 207
The Montana Constitution, 283
The Negro American Labor Council, 301
The Ordeal of Woodrow Wilson, 33
The Patient Protection and Affordable Care, 298
The Pledge of Allegiance, 302
The Plumed Knight, 140
The Presidential Medal of Freedom, 297
The Pusher, 203
The Ramones, 272
The Second Circuit Court of Appeals, 234
The Square Deal, 54
The Stockholm International Peace Research Institute, 291
The University of Notre Dame, 70
The Victors, 76
The Washington Post, 2
This Week, 303
Thomas, Clarence, 232, 235
Thompson, William Colridge .294
Thune, John, 216, 220
Thurmond, Strom, 145, 195, 205, 217, 222, 223, 259, 317
Tierney, John, 159
Tilden, Samuel, 117, 149
Tillotson, Neil, 138
Time Magazine, 103, 120, 147, 149, 189, 192, 224, 253, 269, 296
Tip & Ty, 143
Tippecanoe and Tyler Too, 143
Tippecanoe River, 143

Index

To Tell The Truth, 250
Todd, Paul, 167
Tompkins, Daniel D., 48, 51, 58, 132, 246
Townley, A.C., 285
Traficant, James, 154
Treen, David C., 253
Trinity Church of Christ, 90
Truman, Anderson Shipp
Truman, Bess, 15, 45, 46, 78
Truman, Harry S., 4, 7, 15, 20, 30, 36, 47, 45, 46, 49, 53, 56, 67, 71, 73, 74, 75, 78, 85, 90, 91, 94, 95, 99, 100, 112, 124, 126, 136, 140, 144, 145, 206, 221, 235, 308
Tsongas, Paul, 147, 274
Tuberculosis, 5, 57, 59
Tuck, Dick, 274
Tucker, Jim "Guy," 255, 261
Tunney, John V., 205
Twain, Mark, 98
Twinkie Defense, 304
Tyler, John, 9, 14, 37, 40, 41, 58, 60, 67, 143, 294

U

U.S Minister to France, 306
U.S. Capitol Rotunda, 225
U.S. Circuit of Appeals for the Fourth Circuit, 58
U.S. Coast Guard Academy, 301
U.S. Congress, v, 7, 31, 86, 87, 96, 97, 136, 137, 144, 1, 154, 155, 156, 159, 160, 161, 162, 163, 164, 165, 167, 169, 171, 172, 174, 175, 176, 177, 178, 179, 181, 182, 184, 186, 197, 206, 207, 219, 221, 225, 226, 239, 240, 246, 282, 291, 292, 297, 300, 302, 315, 316
U.S. Constitution, 32, 41, 53, 77, 80, 99, 121, 136, 137, 139, 160, 162, 163, 170, 185, 192, 193, 225, 229, 239, 240, 241, 242, 282, 284, 292, 293. 300, 313, 315, 316, 317, 319, 321, 323, 324, 325
U.S. Dollar, 296, 307
U.S. House Judiciary Committee, 159
U.S. Navy, 41, 61, 76, 134, 184, 205, 221, 268, 306
U.S. Postal Service, 292, 304
U.S. Secret Service Agency, 10
U.S. Senate Committee on Foreign Relations, 198
U.S. Senate Judiciary Committee, 231
U.S. Supreme Court, 10, 14, 15, 77, 164, 193, 205, 210, 218, 224, 229, 230, 231, 232, 233, 234, 235, 240, 292, 316, 319, 325
U.S.A. Patriot Act, 209, 296
Udall, Mark, 159
Under God, 302
Underwood, Cecil 250, 263, 302
UNICEF, 47
Unified Budgeting, 292
Union Carbide Corporation, 84
Union College, 180
Unitarian Atheist, 159
United Kingdom, 119, 290
United Nations Convention on the Prevention and Punishment of the Crime of Genocide Treaty,, 207
United States Census, 2
United Colonies, 306

United States Holocaust Memorial Museum, 196
United States Military Academy, 7, 96
United States Naval Academy, 221
Unity College, 95
Unity, Maine, 95
University of Arkansas Razorbacks, 28
University of Denver, 63
University of Michigan, 76, 85
University of Minnesota, 251
University of Pennsylvania, 253
University of Virginia, 69
Unsinkable II, 172
Unsinkable, 172
Up From Slavery, 25
Urban League, 306
USS Mayaguez, 300
USS Quincy, 93
Utah, 104, 106, 108, 110, 111, 122, 245, 248, 257, 282, 284, 285

V

Van Buren, Hannah, 44
Van Buren, Martin, 4, 6, 23, 33, 44, 69, 71, 74, 82, 89, 95, 119, 121, 144, 206
Van Hollen, Chris. 181
Vandenberg, Arthur, 91
Vandiver, William Duncan, 181
Vaughan, Harry H., 78
Ventura, Jesse, 138, 253, 265
Vermont, 37, 72, 106, 112, 115, 146, 194, 196, 245, 246, 272, 273, 282, 283
Veterans Administration, 63
Vietnam, 48, 52, 60, 64, 74, 142, 162, 166, 179, 209, 300, 315
Vietnam War, 48, 64, 142, 179, 209, 300
Vietnam War Memorial, 300
Vilsack, Tom, 295
Vinson, Carl, 161, 202
Vinson, Fred M., 235
Virginia Declaration of Rights, 324
Virginia, 5, 12, 39, 40, 41, 52, 69, 73, 90, 93, 97, 103, 105, 107, 109, 111, 120, 121, 133, 135, 156, 164, 170, 189, 200, 204, 205, 206, 208, 211, 212, 214, 219, 221, 233, 240, 242, 245, 246, 250, 263, 265, 272, 282, 284, 285, 302, 324
Vitter, David I., 97, 217
Volpe, John, 250

W

Waldie, Jerome, 159
Waldorf Astoria Hotel, 14
Wallace, George C., 122, 270
Wallace, Henry A., 61
Wallace, Madge Gates, 15
Walsh, David I., 193
War of 1812, 49, 240, 246
Warren, Charles B., 51
Warren, Earl, 260, 266
Washburn University, 124
Washington Redskins, 162, 176

Index

Washington Senators, 1
Washington Times, 56
Washington, Booker T., 25
Washington, D.C., 6, 10, 65, 67, 92, 130, 161, 172, 177, 219, 241, 253, 297, 309
Washington, George, vii, 5, 6, 22, 28, 32, 35, 39, 45, 58, 71, 74, 75, 90, 92, 94, 96, 99, 118, 135, 140, 198, 289
Wasilla High School Basketball team, 252
Watergate, 5, 10, 63, 85, 125, 168, 169, 265, 296, 297
Waters, Maxine, 162
Watson, Thomas E., 194
Watts, J.C., 182
Weaver, Robert C., 64
Webster, Daniel, 60, 61
Weicker Jr., Lowell, 201, 259
Weld, William F., 246, 266
Wellesley College, vii, 44, 62
Wellesley, Massachusetts, 44
West Branch, Iowa, 3
West Coast University, 91
West Virginia, 135, 200, 214, 263
West, Allen B., 182
White House Christmas Tree, 21
White House Easter Egg Roll, 32
White House, vi, vii, viii, 1, 3, 4, 5, 6, 7, 8, 9, 11, 12, 14, 16, 17, 18, 19, 21, 23, 27, 31, 32, 33, 36, 37, 39, 42, 43, 45, 46, 47, 48, 55, 56, 58, 69, 72, 78, 80, 82, 83, 84, 88, 89, 90, 91, 92, 93, 95, 96, 97, 98, 104, 105, 106, 109, 113, 114, 115, 116, 121, 122, 123, 127, 128, 131, 139, 146, 148, 161, 184, 204, 208, 211, 256, 290, 291, 296, 299, 302
White, Dan, 304
White, Frank, 79, 126
Whitten, James L., 161
Whittier, Sumner G., 63
Wicker, Roger, 197
Wilder, John Shelton, 272
Williams, Sidney, 162
Williamstown, Massachusetts, 253
Willkie, Wendell, 131, 134, 149
Wills, J. Anthony, 27
Wilmot, David, 325
Wilson, Charles, 180
Wilson, Edith B., 46
Wilson, Eleanor, 65,
Wilson, Henry, 12
Wilson, Pete, 295
Wilson, Woodrow, 3, 15, 26, 30, 33, 58, 65, 66, 76, 109, 131, 132, 133, 143, 213, 233
Winthrop Rockefeller (charitable) Organization., 267
Wirt, William, 59, 115, 146
Wisconsin, 51, 89, 119, 132, 164, 183, 192, 210, 233, 245, 257, 258, 285, 301
Wizard, 253
Wold, John S., 170, 180
Wollman, Henry L., 256
Wollman, Roger L., 256
Woodhull, Victoria, 104, 139
Woods, Rosemary, 10
World News with Diane Sawyer, 302
World Trade Center, 78

World War I, 30, 52, 66, 174, 240, 320
World War II, 30, 110, 187, 320
Worley, David, 188
Wrangell-St. Elias National Park, 303
Wright, Jeremiah, 90
Wright, Jim, 172
Wrigley Field, 230
Wyden, Ronald, 198, 201
Wyman, Jane, 12
Wyoming, 112, 139, 165, 170, 198, 226, 246, 262, 271, 272, 280, 283, 324

Y

Yale University Law School, 85
Yale University Library, 94, 308
Yale University, 4, 17, 89, 94, 173, 215, 308
Yankee Doodle, 13
Yankee Stadium, 14
Young, C.W. Bill, 173
Young, Don, 158
Young, Solomon, 7
Youth's Companion, 302

Z

Zogby International, 231

Copies of this book may be obtained from the website:

www.politi-geek.com

or from:

The Harvard Book Store
Cambridge, Massachusetts
(617) 661-1515
www.harvard.com

or from:

www.Amazon.com

Made in the USA
Charleston, SC
14 December 2011